Jesus' Tomb in India
The Debate on His Death and Resurrection

THE NEAR EAST - c. 100 A.D.
YUZ ASAF'S PROBABLE JOURNEY
TO SRINAGAR ⟶

ROMAN EMPIRE

ARMENIA

CASPIAN SEA

Antioch

Nisibis

Damascus

Jerusalem

Euphrates

Tigris R.

R.

Ctesiphon

Charax

Persis

PARTHIAN EMPIRE

Kashan

Bactra

Jalalabad

Ghazni

Srinagar

Mari (Murree)

Taxila

Indus R.

Mathura

KUSHAN EMPIRE

Persian Gulf

Tropic of Cancer

A R A B I A

R E D   S E A

40°

60°

80°

40°

20°

0   100 200   400   600   800   1000 MI.

0   200   600   1000 KM.

Jesus' Tomb in India
The Debate on His Death and Resurrection

By
Paul C. Pappas

ASIAN HUMANITIES PRESS
Berkeley, California

ASIAN HUMANITIES PRESS

Asian Humanities Press offers to the specialist and the general reader alike, the best in new translations of major works as well as significant original contributions, to enhance our understanding of Asian literature, religions, cultures and philosophies.

Library of Congress Cataloging-in-Publication Data

Pappas, Paul Constantine.
  Jesus' tomb in India: the debate on his death and Resurrection/
by Paul C. Pappas.
      p.   cm.
  Includes bibliographical references and index.
  ISBN 0-89581-946-5
    1. Jesus Christ—Crucifixion. 2. Jesus Christ—Resurrection.
3. Christianity—Origin. 4. Jesus Christ—Biography—Apocryphal and
legendary literature. 5. Jammu and Kashmir (India) in Ahmadiyya.
6. Ahmadiyya—Doctrines. 7. Holy Shroud. 8. Holy Light of
Jerusalem. 9. Jammu and Kashmir (India)—Religion. 10. Jerusalem—
Religion. I. Title.
BT450.P36 1991
232.9'7—dc20   91-19080
                                                                  CIP

Printed in the United States of America

In memory of my father
Rev. Constantine D. Pappas

To my mother,
Evangeline

Contents

Preface

The figure of Jesus has been mysterious and highly controversial through the years, primarily because Jesus has been proclaimed by most of his followers as the Son of God and divine in nature. However, Jesus of the New Testament and of the Christian tradition is a complex figure because he is the product of a Judaeo-Greek-Eastern milieu and of a synthesis of many past ideologies or religious views. Inconsistencies that scholars have discovered in the details of the New Testament writings and later insertions that were made in the gospels have given rise to many controversies, especially over Jesus' death and resurrection. Great suspicion has existed up to the present about Jesus' aim or role in Palestine, and countless books have been written debating whether Jesus the Messiah, the Davidic King, was a political or a religious leader and whether or not he really died on the cross. The absence of a body in the empty tomb has given rise to many questions and answers. The prevailing Jewish view is that Jesus' disciples simply moved the body and hid it elsewhere. But if Jesus was indeed seen alive after his crucifixion, a question remains about his newly adopted land. Where did he go to live and die undetected? The answer given in one of the gospels, that Jesus ascended to heaven, is not taken seriously by most scholars. Although devout Christians generally accept Jesus' ascension, the issue remains controversial among biblical scholars. Interestingly, the Muslims, who deny Jesus' divinity and resurrection, accept his ascension to heaven. The general Muslim view appears to be that Jesus did not die while on the cross, but was taken up by God directly to heaven. But whether or not Jesus actually died on the cross is rather difficult for the Muslims to answer, primarily because the Koran is rather vague and subject to interpretation.

One Muslim sect, however, the Ahmadiyya, asserts that Jesus did not die on the cross, but was brought down alive and restored to health by his friends. The founder of the Islamic Ahmadiyya movement, Hazrat Mizrat Ghulam Ahmad, and his followers, the Ahmadis, have defended the thesis that Rozabal, the Tomb of Yuz Asaf, in Srinagar, India, is really the tomb of Jesus. They have produced both literary and archaeological evidence to prove that Yuz Asaf was Jesus Christ, who, after his crucifixion, went to live and die in Kashmir, in northern India; and they are confident that they have found Jesus' final resting place.

This work critically reviews the Ahmadi thesis and seeks to assess the facts on which they base their contention. Unfortunately, the tomb of Yuz Asaf has not yet been scientifically examined to the present, and although a few publications have appeared in Asia and Europe, nothing has been published in America to arouse the interest of the public and especially of archaeologists and anthropologists who may want to search out the facts. Such an examination by scientists would be fascinating because it is possible that Yuz Asaf's grave does date from the time of Jesus. Possibly a comparative study could be made of the occupant's physical remains, if any, and the image depicted on the Shroud of Turin. Through correspondence with the Director of Tourism of the state of Kashmir, this author has discovered that the grave of Yuz Asaf appears to be ancient and could date back to the first century.

The Greek Orthodox Christians, however, insist that they have the genuine empty tomb of Jesus in Jerusalem, and that every year Jesus' divinity and holy resurrection are verified by the miracle of the Holy Light. Thus far, no scientific study has been conducted of this great miracle of Orthodox Christianity and very little is known about it in the West. With the exception of a few works in Greek, nothing specifically has been published in this country on the miracle of the Holy Light. However, this author has been assured by his Beatitude, Diodorus, the Greek Orthodox patriarch of Jerusalem, through his chief secretary, Bishop Timothy of Porphyroupolis, that this significant miracle indeed does take place once every year. There is a great need, therefore, to arouse the Western world's interest in this wondrous miracle and, if possible, to examine it scientifically. At least scientists could determine whether or not there is a natural explanation for this great event.

I would like to express my gratitude to Theohari (Harry) Papadopoulos, graduate of West Virginia Institute of Technology and now candidate for the Ph.D. in chemical engineering at Stevens Institute of Technology (Hoboken, New Jersey), for his help and enthusiastic encouragement as I wrote this book. I am most grateful to his Beatitude, Patriarch Diodorus of Jerusalem and Bishop Timothy, as well as to Rev. Stanley S. Harakas of the Greek Orthodox Holy Cross Seminary (Boston) for their prompt help in this endeavor. I extend my deep appreciation to Patricia A. Butenis, Consul at the American Embassy in New Delhi, to the Director of Tourism of the state of Kashmir, to Adam Smith, my former student, and to George Allen, a fellow church member. In addition, I wish to thank for their assistance Drs. Lynda Ann Ewen and Mostafa Shaaban, and the Faculty Research Committee of West Virginia Institute of Technology. Last, but not least, I would like to thank my wife Pamela for her support and patience in this arduous task.

1. The Complex and Mysterious Christian Origins

The Jewish Sects and the Development of Christian Concepts

The life of Jesus has been as mysterious as his origin and Christian mysteries such as the tomb of Jesus in Srinagar, India, the Shroud of Turin, and the Holy Light or Fire of the Resurrection in Jerusalem continue to perplex us. But they also lure us on to find the true Jesus and to discover the facts about his life based on sound scholarship and scientific evidence. Only in the twentieth century has the general public become aware of scholarly disputes over the origins of Christianity and over the genuineness of the crucifixion and resurrection which might have been merely a clever plot. Since the discovery of the Dead Sea Scrolls in 1947 at ancient Qumran, it has become evident that Jesus was a product of his socio-religious environment and that his teachings were not much different from those of Jewish Messianic sects during his life which proclaimed the imminent coming of the Messiah.

Jewish Messianic sects rose during the second century before Christ, while the Jews were struggling to liberate themselves from an oppressive Greek rule. Following Alexander the Great's death, Palestine was administered until 200 B.C. by the Greek ruler of Egypt, Ptolemy, and his heirs. Palestine then came under the control of the Seleucid kingdom which had taken over a great part of Alexander's Asian conquests, including Syria and Babylon. Greco-Hebrew relations were good at first. The Jewish synagogues where the sacred texts were studied with chants and recitations appeared to the Greeks to be philosophical schools much like their own rather than religious centers. Gradually, as the Greeks discovered that Judaism was a religion and a national cult with its center in the Temple of Solomon in Jerusalem, opposition in the form of gossip and violence appeared first in Alexandria, Egypt and then in other cities. The Jews were above all accused of worshiping a golden ass' head in the Temple of Solomon and offering human sacrifice. Such antisemitic display was caused in part by a religious antagonism between polytheism and monotheism, but also by Jewish missionary zeal in proselytizing to the Gentiles. In addition, privileges formerly conferred

1

by the Greek rulers on the Jews, cultural differences, and Jewish social insularity contributed to the rise of antisemitism.[1] This antisemitism reached its nadir in the second century before Christ when the Seleucid monarch Antiochus Epiphanes IV decided to force the Jews to become pagan Greeks. Ordered to worship the Greek gods, the Jews earnestly turned to their religion, seeking help from their God, Yahweh (Jehovah). Apocalyptic writings appeared revealing the future; in the Hebrew Old Testament these are attributed to Daniel. Jewish sects arose, calling upon their people to prepare themselves for the imminent coming of the Messiah; and after a few years of intensive fighting led by Judas Meccabeus and his brothers, the Jews successfully rebelled against the Greeks, recovering Jerusalem in 164 B.C. and liberating themselves in 142 B.C. In order to populate the Holy Land with God's people, they forced all non-Jews within liberated Palestine to adopt their Jewish religion; and they were determined to prepare the Jews and the world around them for the coming of the Messianic Age, when idolatry would be eradicated and the nations of the earth would worship the only God, Jehovah. The most effective of these Jewish sects in converting the masses to their Messianic movement was that of the Pharisees. The Pharisees desired to bring Israel back to God in righteousness and to be God's instruments in bringing salvation to the whole world. Therefore, they interpreted the Torah or the written law to assure the sanctification of every aspect of Jewish life and adhered more strictly to the letter of the law than to its spirit (for which Jesus attacked them). To spread God's salvation, they used extensive propaganda to convert the Gentiles to their Messianic aspirations and their belief in a free will limited by God's predestined purpose.[2] They also believed in the immortality of the soul, the resurrection of the dead, and the observance of the ancient traditions, especially the laws of purity, priestly tithing and the Sabbath. Following Rome's destruction of the Temple of Solomon in Jerusalem in 70 A.D., the Pharisees perpetuated Judaism through the rabbinical schools and the expansion of the Mishnah and Talmud (collections of orally transmitted decisions or rules through centuries of Pharisaic and rabbinic leadership), thus serving the needs of the times.

The Sadducees, a small priestly and wealthy minority, controlled the office of the high priest and the profits of the Temple of Solomon as descendants of Solomon's high priest, Zadok. They had a monopoly over Temple activities and appointments of dignitaries and functionaries. They took politics more seriously than religion; and therefore, unlike the Pharisees, they had been willing to cooperate with their Greek rulers and later on with the Romans to preserve their wealth and privilege. Although they believed in strict adherence to the Torah, they rejected the idea of an immortal soul and of the resurrection of the dead. Neither did they believe in the imminent coming of the Messiah or in predestination. When the Temple of Solomon was destroyed during the revolt of 66-70 A.D., the Sadducee officials ceased to exist.

The strictest of these sects, the most mystical and most radical in ideology, was that of the Essenes. The Essenes (the holy ones, the saints) had beliefs and practices so similar to the early Christians that for a long time they were mistakenly identified as an early Christian sect. It is now generally accepted that the Essenes were Christianity's precursors. Although historians have been aware of the Essenes for a long time through the first century A.D. writings of Philo of Alexandria, a Jewish theologian, Pliny the Elder, a Roman naturalist, and Flavius Josephus, a famous Jewish historian, the discovery of the Dead Sea Scrolls of the Qumran community, probably the largest of the Essenic congregations, enhanced our knowledge of the Essenes and of the mysterious origins of Christianity unrecorded by early Christians.

The Scrolls reveal that the Essenes were the product of a religious milieu extending beyond the borders of Palestine. Founded by the Teacher of Righteousness, a shadowy figure who apparently suffered martyrdom late in the second century B.C., the Essenes proclaimed a new covenant with God, and like the Pharisees and other sects that arose later on, looked forward to the coming of the Messiah as prophesied by the latter prophets of the Old Testament. They evidently borrowed ideas not only from the Greek Pythagoreans and pagan mystery schools, but also from eastern cults and from the Zoroastrians of Persia (founded by the Persian prophet Zoroaster [Zarathustra] of the sixth century B.C.). The Zoroastrians believed in the struggle between the forces of the good god of light and the forces of the evil god of darkness. They held that eventually good will triumph over evil and there will be a judgment day when the good god will judge all souls on the basis of their recorded deeds in the Book of Judgment. Essenic writings from Qumran, such as the *Book of the Order* (or *Manual of Discipline*) and the *Zadokite Document*, reveal that the Essenes had an order of hierarchy of priests called the "sons of Zadok," whom the prophet Ezekiel designated in his vision of the restored Temple as the only legitimate priests. Thus, both Essenes and Sadducees claimed Zadok, the high priest of Solomon, as their forerunner. However, the Essenes held the Temple in Jerusalem as unclean and the priests (Sadducees) as corrupt. They eagerly awaited, therefore, the fulfillment of Ezekiel's prophecy, when a new temple would be erected by God and the proper sacrificial cult of priests restored. According to the Qumran text, *The War of the Sons of Light and the Sons of Darkness*, the Essenes regarded themselves as members of God's army, the sons of light, the chosen or the elect, ready to drive out from the earth the sons of darkness of the evil god Belial. This would be accomplished through an elaborate war plan for Armageddon, when the Messiah would appear at the end of the present era to establish himself as lord of the earth.[3]

The Essenes had an organization and ritual practices similar to those of the early Christians. Their communities had overseers or bishops as well as three priests and twelve good laymen to assist the priests, resembling the Christian presbyters (priests) and deacons (assistants). Prospective members received permission to join the community after a two year probation followed by a ceremony during which the individual swore to obey all the sect rules and not to reveal any of its secrets to outsiders. They worshipped God, whom they identified with light at early dawn. Early Christians also identified God and Jesus with the sun light and worshipped them at early dawn and at sunset, a practice that is still retained in the Eastern Orthodox and Catholic churches during matins and vespers. The Essenes purified themselves by bathing in water every day at eleven o'clock in the morning, and they ate a common meal at noon, a practice also popular among early Christians. Also, like the early Christians, they lived in communities throughout Palestine in urban and rural areas, following a strict monastic life of purity and prayer. They surrendered their wealth into a common fund and received the goods of their community according to their needs. Because of the historian Josephus, the Essenic cult was believed to have been primarily a male celibate cult, with the exception of one community that did accept marriage strictly for propagation. However, the Dead Sea Scrolls have revealed that the Essenes had rules that specifically applied to married members and their children. At Qumran, they unearthed the graves of women and children. Anyway, there is no mention of celibacy in any Essenic document.[4]

Essenic beliefs were also similar to those proclaimed by the New Testament of the Christians. Jesus and his followers believed that the end of the known world was near and that the appearance of God's kingdom was impending. These similarities in belief make it all the more difficult to discover how much of Jesus' message was Essenic and how much original. The early Christians referred to themselves as children of light (as did the Essenes), and although they accepted Jesus as the Messiah, they were still waiting for the Messianic Kingdom to come through Jesus' second coming. The New Testament contains ideas found in Essenic writings, especially in the *Testaments of the Twelve Patriarchs*, used by early Christians but not incorporated into the New Testament, and in the *Didache* (also called *The Teachings of the Twelve Apostles*) and *The Shepherd of Hermas*. These Essenic texts contain the same moral ideals, such as, to hate no one, and to be upright and humble, as preached by Jesus in the gospels. So closely do Essenic beliefs resemble those of the Christians that biblical scholars suspect that, if Jesus was not an Essene, he must have been well read in their writings. But Jesus must also have been well versed in Pharisaic thought, including, perhaps, that of the famous rabbi, Hillel, Jesus' contemporary.[5]

Many Essenic concepts were not the monopoly of the Essenes, but paralleled the Apocrypha and Pseudepigrapha of the Old Testament—in other words, the non-canonical Jewish scriptures circulating between 200 B.C. and 100 A.D. and also earlier strata of the Talmud. Many of these ideas were to be found in other ancient Jewish sects as well, including the Samaritans and also the Mandaeans of Iraq and Iran, who had their origins in Palestine and in the writings of the ancient Greek philosophers, especially the Stoics (popular in the Roman-Oriental world from the first century B.C. until the third century A.D.).[6]

By the time the Romans conquered Palestine under Pompey in 60 B.C., there were numerous Jewish sects, many of which resembled the Essenes and, therefore, one another. Some of these were the Samaritans, Rechabites, Nazareans, Galileans, Daily Baptists, and Marbutheau (Aramaic for Baptists). The Samaritans of northern Palestine, the land of the former kingdom of Israel (920-720 B.C.), opposed the beliefs of the Judaean Jews in the south, the land of the former kingdom of Judaea (920-586 B.C.). They refused to accept the Temple of Solomon in Jerusalem as the center of their religion and they predated the Essenes in origin. According to Epiphanius' *Panarion*, a voluminous fourth century A.D. work against heresies that mentions the early Jewish sects, the Essenes might have evolved from the Samaritans and also, perhaps, from the Rechabites, who believed in living in tents and not owning property or drinking wine. The Jewish writer Philo mentions the Therapeutae of Alexandria, composed of scholarly monastics resembling the Essenes whom later on the

Church Fathers mistook for Christians, but whose literature has perished.

In the first century A.D., there also sprang up an extreme violent sect of Jews called the Zealots. The Zealots, whom Josephus also called Sicarii (one who murders with a *sica* or dagger) and Brigands, were founded by a teacher called Judas the Galilean assisted by a Pharisee named Saddok (Zadok). They were men rigidly faithful to their God and his laws. They were also violent fanatics determined to purify the land of Yahweh from foreign influence and pagan contamination and thus initiate the coming of the Messiah, the Son of David. Led by Judas, they rebelled in 6 A.D. against the oppressive rule of the Romans and their puppet, King Herod Antipus, the ruler of Galilee (4 B.C. to 39 A.D.). Judas was quickly defeated and executed, and later on, as a prudent course of action, Herod Antipus also killed John the Baptist, even though his message of repentance and righteousness, as a preparation for the coming of the Messiah, was not violent. Nevertheless, the revolt against Roman rule and its supporters continued, led by the sons of Judas. Two of them, Jacob and Simon, were killed by the Roman procurator in 46-48 A.D., while another son, Menahem, was a leader in the early days of the revolt of 66 A.D.

Violence had become the accepted order not only for the Zealots but for all Jewish sects that yearned to purify the land and to establish the Messianic Kingdom with the coming of the Messiah. Even the Essenes, it seems, were willing to employ violence. A forge for making weapons was found at Qumran, and the debris excavated there revealed arrowheads and weapons that, evidently, the Essenes used to fight the Romans. It is suspected that all these Jewish sects, including the Sons of Zadok or Zaddikim (Zadokites), the Sons of Light, the Sons of Truth, the Men of Melchizedek, the Ebionites (the Poor), the Hassidim (the Essenes) and the Nazareans are of the same movement—not different groups, but different appellations or metaphors for the same group. They were all Messianic, violent, and oriented toward the dynastic legitimacy of the high priesthood. The high priest of both King David and Solomon was called Zadok, either as a personal name or as an official title. He was regularly referred to as the Priest Messiah who would come, and he was traditionally accepted as the advisor and collaborator of the future lay Messiah, the anointed one, the rightful king, or the Davidic Messiah, meaning simply an earthly king of David's line appointed by God to rule just as David and Solomon and every Jewish king of the House of David had been.

The whole movement might have begun during the Maccabean rule (142-63 B.C.), when the legitimacy of the high priesthood (of Zadok or of the Zadok or even Zaddik) was revived and the high priest was referred to as "a zealot for the law." The Zealots obtained this name for being "zealous for the law," a term which applied to all defenders of traditional values, including early Judaic or Nazorean Christians. The term Sadducee might have been a corrupt form of Zadok or Zaddik. However, after the Roman conquest of Palestine, some of the Sadducee priests evidently aligned with the Roman appointed King Herod the Great (37-4 B.C.), retaining their Temple privileges, while the rest of the priests, who acquired the name Essenes, denounced such collaboration with an illegitimate king, remaining true to the Davidic Messiah principle. The Essenes were probably not passive mystics but violent apocalyptics, and evidently more religiously oriented than the more politically minded Zealots. Interestingly, Judas of Galilee who founded the Zealots, was a zealot of the law. It is suspected that the Nazoreans or early Christians in Jerusalem might have been a part, perhaps the central committee, of this general violent movement to reestablish the old Judaic monarchy from David's heir, that is, Jesus, and to usher in the genuine priesthood. The Pharisees, on the other hand, were divided, many of them, including rabbi Hillel, aligning with the Sadducees.[7]

Led by dissident priests (the Essenes), Palestine was seething with Jewish rebellions and Messianic leaders. Jesus was not the only Messiah. In 35 or 36 A.D., the probable year of Jesus' crucifixion, a Samaritan Messiah led an uprising that was ruthlessly crushed, and such unsuccessful uprisings also took place in the fifties when another Messiah appeared, supposedly from Egypt, and tried to take Jerusalem. Thadeus, a prophet who aroused the masses after Jesus' crucifixion, and who had summoned his followers to watch him cross the Jordan river dry shod, was also led to his execution. Eventually, the Zealot compaign of terror against the Romans and their supporters culminated in an all out war against Rome, the Zealot War of 66-70 A.D. During this war, first Menahem and then Simon bar Giora declared themselves messianic kings. The results were disastrous for all Jews. After the Jewish factions turned against each other in Jerusalem, the Zealots and their supporters were ruthlessly defeated, Jerusalem and the Temple of Solomon were completely destroyed, and a band of Essenes or Zealots or Sicarii led by Eleazar, a descendant of Judas of Galilee, held out at Fort Masada, south of Jerusalem, only to commit mass suicide in 73 A.D. The Romans,

under the emperor Hadrian, built in 130 A.D. a new city called Aelia
Capitolina at the site of Jerusalem with a temple to Jupiter on the place
where Jehovah's temple had once stood. But the Jews were not finished.
In 132 A.D., Simon bar Kozibah rebelled against Rome and was pro-
claimed by the Rabbi Akiba as "Bar Kochba" (son of a star, the star of
Jacob—Num. 24:17), or, in other words, the Messiah. Simon and his
followers were defeated. Aelia Capitolina was rebuilt; the temple of
Jupiter was re-erected, and no Jew was allowed to enter this city.
Eventually, Jews could enter the city once a year to weep at the spot
where Jehovah's temple had once stood.[8]

Greek Ideas and their Influence on Christianity

The origins of early Christian ideas and beliefs about Jesus and
his mission are to be found not only in a synthesis of Jewish and
Eastern beliefs during the first century A.D., but also in a more complex
and elaborate synthesis of Greek ideas. This makes the quest for the
historical Jesus even more mysterious and difficult, as Jesus' message
and person are colored with Greek notions and concepts. With the
Greek conquest of the Judaic world, many Jews were influenced by
the superior Hellenistic culture of the ancient Greeks and from then
on were divided into the Hellenized (Greek speaking) Jews and the
Aramaic (Semitic speaking) Jews. Because of a large number of Hellenized Jews in Alexandria, not only were the Jews of this city compelled
to produce a Greek translation of the Old Testament (*Septuagint*) in
250 B.C., but their greatest thinker, Philo (25 B.C. to 50 A.D.), sought
to reconcile Jewish religious ideas with Greek philosophy, which
indicates that fundamental Greek ideas are also to be found in the
first five books of the Old Testament, thought to have been written
by Moses. Many Jews, however, were not able to accept both Moses
and Greek philosophy, and thus gave up all loyalty to Jews and Judaism
to become Greek; among these was Philo's own nephew. However,
Philo's emphasis on the logos philsophy of the Greeks, which maintained
that God creates through his word or reason, his attempt to bring the
logos into relationship with the Old Testament, and his use of the
Greek allegorical method to interpret this religious text made an impact
on Christian scholars and influenced the Church Fathers (certain bishops)
in the development of Christian theology.

Christianity is to a great extent a product of Greek thought.
Following Philo's example, the Christian leaders began to use Greek

philosophy, especially that of Plato and Aristotle in order to explain, clarify, and defend the Bible. They also sought to satisfy in general the questions and criticisms of the pagans, newly converted intellectuals, and heretics. However, these attempts only produced a Jesus who was more Greek than Jewish in his thinking. The early Church bishops, many of whom had studied at the pagan philosophical schools of Athens, incorporated Greek concepts into Christian theology and assimilated Greek distinctions, terms and ideas into a formidable intellectual defense of Christian doctrines. Plato's rational defense of the existence of another mental world governed by ultimate reason (God) and his concept of an immortal (tripartite and in essence uncompounded) soul, which gives life to and controls the body but which is always seeking to find the ultimate, was used by such Christian theologians as Gregory of Nyssa (fourth century), St. Anthony the Great (fourth and fifth centuries), Hesychios of Jerusalem (fifth century) and John of Damascus (eighth century). Aristotle's ten categories or most simple modes of being (especially substance [essence] and relation) aided such theologians as Gregory of Nyssa, Gregory Nazianzen, Basil the Great, John of Climacos, John of Damascus, and others to divide existence rationally into two fundamental substances, material and spiritual. Aristotle's rational defense of purpose as revealed by the material world, which is deliberately striving towards an ultimate goal through an order of hierarchical forms of earthly creatures, his concept that virtue is a mean between excess and deficiency, and his distinction between voluntary (deliberate) and involuntary (unintentional) acts were also used by the Church bishops and theologians to explain Christian truths and the Church's position on various issues.[9]

Both Plato and Aristotle had emphasized reason in trying to understand nature and the universe and had defended their hypotheses or conclusions on a rational basis. It is because of this appeal to reason that the Church Fathers used their ideas. But man's struggle to acquire accurate knowledge, to separate the facts from myths on the basis of reason and logic and sound sensory proof, and to liberate inquiry from sophistry and the controls of authority has been formidable. Even Plato, when he could not realistically explain a concept, would invent a story in the form of an allegory that often had little to do with reality. Heraclitus of Ephesus and Pythagoras, who came before Plato, and many others did the same.

By the third century before Christ, the Greeks had become disillusioned. Many of them had lost their earlier faith in reason and in their ability to acquire universal knowledge as a means of resolving all natural and social problems and creating a society conducive to happiness. In the midst of wars and social unrest and a general moral deterioration, two important Greek philosophies arose in the third century B.C., Epicureanism and Stoicism. Both professed that man must seek to find happiness from within by developing rationally a proper mental attitude towards life's vicissitudes. Epicureanism, which accepted the ancient atomic theory, emphasized the pain-pleasure principle in ethics, the cultivation of moderate pleasures, and above all the acquisition of happiness through contemplation. Stoicism, however, which was far more popular than Epicureanism, professed the importance of acquiring knowledge through reason and peace of mind (*ataraxia*) through an attitude of indifference to pain and pleasure. It aimed at self-sufficiency and emphasized the importance of fulfilling one's earthly duty in a predestined world ruled by God's universal laws. On that basis, it upheld the brotherhood of all men who function in accordance to God's laws, proclaimed a world governance for all and denounced slavery as evil (making them the first philosophers to do so). Unlike the Epicureans, the Stoics also generally believed in an immortal soul and in a pantheistic God who was the mind and soul of the universe, permeating the universe with his creative power. Thus, the world process of creation was a revelation of God's reason or the logos.[10]

Stoicism, made a greater impact on the pagans, Jews, and Christians than did atheistic, atomic Epicureanism. It had a humanizing effect on Roman law and Roman officials. Christian theologians like John Climacos and John of Damascus used such Stoic terms as, "preconceptions" or "desires" and "passionlessness" or "peace of mind" (tranquility) to talk about getting rid of evil desires coming from the devil and finding oneself passionlessness or in a state of purity, which enables one to see the divine light. Christians in general found the Stoic message of brotherhood and submission to God's predestined laws acceptable. The Stoic usage of the allegorical method became popular among Hellenized Jews and Christians.[11]

Unfortunately, beginning with the first Stoics, Hellenistic philosophy was permeated with allegories. Allegories may be interesting but not factual. They may be used to explain away contradictions between experience and idealism, but they are not rational. And, when they are literally taken as true, the mind has reverted to primitivism and fanaticism, a child like intellect, making sound inquiry difficult. For the Stoic Sallustius, the whole material world was only a great myth, "a thing whose value lies not in itself but in the spiritual meaning which it hides and reveals." For Cleanthes, the universe was in the beginning "a mystic pageant, in which the immortal stars were the dancers and the sun the priestly torch-bearer."[12]

Philosophy was rapidly evolving into symbolism and mysticism. The general trend was away from the material world toward the inward world of the soul and the acquisition of salvation. The true savior of men was not he who protected them from natural catastrophes, but he who saved their souls through his mystical knowledge of the divine. Such a man was deified as the "image of God" or the "son of God," making him God. The Greek thinkers of the classical period (fifth century B.C.) had insisted on moderation in religion, maintaining that there were essential differences between man and God. But eventually, not only pseudo-philosophers and religious teachers who claimed to have the power of knowledge (gnosis), but also Hellenistic rulers, who had the power of sovereignty, gave themselves such titles as "God's manifestion," "benefactor" and, the most common, "saviour." Some of the learned saw mystical secrets in language itself, because the universal spirit communicated with man through various cryptic or sacred words, which could be found in Greek as well as in the Babylonian and Egyptian languages, once their hidden meaning was understood. By reflecting on these mystical words, a philosopher could come to know the mysterious messages, the divine enigma.

Astrology was introduced to the Hellenistic world and soon infected it like a plague. The Epicureans remained immune, but not the Stoics, who, with a few exceptions, succumbed to it. Many of the Stoics had already accepted a belief in the deity of the stars and planets, in the pervading forethought of the divine mind, and in the sympathy of all creation, whereby all of its parts are affected by the suffering of one. Astrology presented a beautiful illustration of this sympathy in its explanation of the effect that movement and positions of the stars and planets had on human affairs. The seven planets played a terrifying role in the soul's effort to find God and freedom by escaping from the sport of fate caused by the planets and chance caused by the moon. (The Essenes were also influenced by astrology and by the esoteric studies in general, including numerology, which subsequently coalesced into the Cabala.)

The last pagan Greek philosophical school to appear in the third century A.D. was Neoplatonism. Founded by Plotinus, it emphasized mystical meditation to find God rather than Plato's rational, mathematical contemplation of geometric forms. For the Neoplatonists, the shortest, most direct route to God and knowledge was the path of meditation and not that of reason. Although a few Greeks in Alexandria and elsewhere adhered to mathematical reasoning and science and made some notable contributions in mathematics, physics, medicine, and technology, and although a few skeptics and cynics were still to be found, the majority of Greek thinkers became religious and superstitious. Having visions of heaven and God while in ecstasy was just as popular with the pagans, including the Neoplatonists, as it was with the Christians. According to Plotinus' pupil Porphyry, Plotinus was mystically united with God four times within five years. In any case, Christian thinkers were influenced by Neoplatonist concepts of a thinking God from whom emanates mental energy as light coming from the sun that forms and sustains the universe, of the division of the universe into an upper invisible world of souls and a lower visible world of earthly creatures, and of a hierarchical order of beings leading to God. Even though they rejected the Neoplatonic notion of pantheism, that is, that the world is related to God in essence as emanated divine energy, Christian theologians used the terms energy and emanation in their attempts to explain creation and the universe. Christian theologians, such as Justin Martin, Clement of Alexandria, Origin, and others, sought to preserve Greek philosophy and to understand and defend on a rational basis the existence of an immortal, omnipotent, omniscient, perfect and purposeful God who had nonetheless created an imperfect world. However, eventually, after a long and even violent intellectual struggle that gave rise to many heresies during the Middle Ages, Christian theologians also generally concluded, as the ancient Greeks had, that we cannot prove or understand God by reason, but must rely on feeling, faith and mysticism. And we must trust divine revelation on the basis of the word of infallible authority, the Church.[13]

Pagan Cults and their Impact on Christianity

Christianity was a synthesis not only of Greek ideas but also of Greek ritual practices and beliefs present in the pagan or Oriental cults. These religious cults had begun to come to Greece from the East and Egypt by the seventh century B.C. Promising their members salvation, union with a god (such as Dionysus, the god of wine), and immortality through a formal ritual, they became popular and spread throughout the Roman Empire. They were noted for their concepts of virgin birth, redemption, and resurrection, and for such deities as Adonis, Tamuz, Osiris, Sol Invictus, and Mithras. The Sol Invictus cult from Syria and the Zoroastrian cult of Mithras from Persia were sun cults that had become popular among the Roman soldiers, and their beliefs and rituals were borrowed to some degree by Christianity. This was especially the case with the cult of Mithras which accepted the immortality of the soul, dualism, the triumph of good over evil, judgement day, and the resurrection of the dead. Mithras, the sun-god, was born of a virgin in a cave on December 25, and worshipped on Sunday, the day of the conquering sun. He was a savior-god who rivaled Jesus in popularity. He died and was resurrected in order to become a messenger god, an intermediary between man and the good god of light, and the leader of the forces of righteousness against the dark forces of the god of evil.

Eventually, Jesus replaced Mithras in this capacity. Philosophically, the Persian dualism of Mithras was not as attractive to the Greeks as monotheism. Jesus was transformed into a Judao-Greek sun-god of a new cult. By a decree in 321 A.D., Constantine the Great, the first Christian Roman emperor, declared Sunday a day of worship, not Saturday or the Sabbath of the early Christians and Jews. In addition, those converted to Christianity did not want to part completely with their cult beliefs and practices; and there was also the need to popularize Christianity, to make it more attractive to the masses, and thus to enable it to compete successfully with the pagan religions, which it certainly did. Therefore, the Christians retained some of these beliefs and rituals, the mysteries, but transformed them into Christian sacraments which offer the divine grace of salvation. The followers of Mithras, who had an eucharistic meal, believed that they were saved by the blood of the bull slain by Mithras to give life to the earth, the Christians by the blood of the lamb, symbolizing Jesus. Christmas Day, originally celebrated on January 6, was changed to the popular day of December 25, the winter solstice. Generally speaking, Christianity owes to the mystery cults "the notions of secrecy, of symbolism, of mystical brotherhood, of sacramental grace and above all, of the three stages in the spiritual life: ascetic purification, illumination and epopleia (vision of the deity leading to blessedness)."[14]

The Essenic Early Christians

Christianity evolved, evidently, from a Jewish sect called the Nazareans. The pre-Christian Nazareans were probably an Essenic group whom Epihanius identified with the Daily Baptists. Its members later became the early Christians called the Nazoreans, Nazirites, or Nazarenes, who retained their Judaic beliefs and practices and obscurely evolved into the Ebionites (the Poor), a sect found in the Middle East that rejected Jesus' virgin birth and divinity. Jesus was referred to as Jesus of Nazareth or the Nazoreos. But since there was no village of Nazareth, he was, perhaps, called this in reference to his membership in the Nazorean sect. Jesus' brother, James the Righteous (Jacob the Just), who became the head of the Christians or Nazoreans in Jerusalem, was, according to the *Memoirs* of Hegisipus, an Essene sectarian who abstained from meat and alcoholic drinks. His New Testament epistle, which contains Essenic ideas, testifies to this. He was stoned to death in 62 A.D. in Jerusalem as leader of the Christians by orders of the high priest, Ananas, during a weak period of Roman rule, when the Roman procurator had died and not yet been replaced. Another brother of Jesus, Judas or Jude, quotes in his New Testament epistle from Essenic sectarian texts, the *Book of Enoch* and the *Testament of Moses*, revealing the strong influence of Essenism on early Christians. The present Nazoreans or Mandaeans of the Lower Euphrates river in Iraq were once Palestine followers of John the Baptist and non-Christians. They accepted John the Baptist, another Essene sectarian and Jesus' cousin, as their Messiah, and their writings reject Jesus as a false Messiah, probably because he ate and drank with sinners. In these writings, Jesus attempts to be baptized by John and is turned down as a deceiver, but John finally yields because of a message that he receives.[15]

Jesus Remains Mysterious in the Early Christian Writings

Jesus remains mysterious even in the early Christian writings, including the New Testament. Greek-Eastern beliefs made their impact on the New Testament books, including the gospels, just as they had on the writings of the Essenes. This influence makes it difficult to know accurately what Jesus actually said, how he thought, and what he did. Jesus' message is colored with non-Judaic ideas. No one kept notes for an accurate biography of Jesus. Jesus himself did not write anything, and the gospels, which were produced long after Jesus was gone, were not written by any of his disciples, with the exception, perhaps, of the gospel of St. John, the last to be written.

Other factors make it difficult to discover the real Jesus and to know him as an historical figure. The early Christian communities, which at first used only the Jewish Old Testament, underwent considerable development before the production of the New Testament. In other words, the New Testament did not produce the Church, but the Church produced the New Testament in order to provide for its changing needs during its development. Because they thought that Jesus' second coming was impending, early Christians were not much concerned with writing biographies or a history of the movement. Nor did they feel a need for a permanent organization. They merely had an oral tradition and an eschatological catechesis based on the Old Testament, in which was prophesied not only Jesus' Messianic mission and details as to the time and place of his birth, manner of his death, and his resurrection, but also predictions of his glorious reappearance to judge the world. In addition, they had some writings about Jesus' message, including Paul's letters containing sermons, memoirs, rituals, but also an eschatological catechesis on Jesus' second coming.[16]

Gradually, starting about 65 to 70 A.D. (long after Jesus' passion in 36 A.D.), the Christians produced catechetical or didactic material for the indoctrination of believers; these eventually grew in volume. It was to satisfy the need for indoctrination materials that the greater part of the New Testament was produced, with the exception of Revelation and Letter to the Hebrews. The gospels and the Acts sought to satisfy the catechetical needs of a movement that was still Messianic but rapidly becoming a temporal, lasting institution with beliefs, rituals and personnel. Those converted desired that the events be explained to them for they had not experienced them and even perhaps had come from a different environment from that in which the events had occurred. Although the Christians of the New Testament sought accuracy, they insisted also on relevance. They sought to give approved answers to questions concerning Jesus and to explain his mission and what he taught. There were also questions about his crucifixion, which took place so quickly, along with his burial and mysterious resurrection, and about the activities of his disciples, who were performing miracles. Since the gospels were explanations rather than accurate biographies or histories, their narratives are often at variance. But these differences are small when compared with the wider religious literature prevalent at that time among different Christian sects, before the selection of the present gospels and the writings of the New Testament in general by the Church Fathers.[17]

Jesus as Conceived by the Gnostic Christians

The image of Jesus the man is greatly distorted and made more difficult to discover by the writings of the Gnostic sects. During the second and third centuries A.D., the Church Fathers selected the four gospels because they were canonical, that is, part of the list or canon of approved books. The several gospels that were rejected were called apocryphal or bastard because they did not agree with the teachings of the Church and the accepted gospels. They belonged to minority sects that kept them secret so that they alone might have the mysterious revelations of what Jesus had really meant in his sermons. The Church Fathers of the second and third centuries A.D. denounced these works as heretical and sought to destroy them, but many of them were buried in the sands of Egypt, where they were discovered in modern times. In winter 1886-87, French archaeologists digging in Christian graves at Akhmim in Upper Egypt found a parchment containing the *Gospel of Peter*, the *Apocalypse of Peter* and the Jewish Christian *Book of Enoch*. Another such discovery occurred when papyri were found at Oxyrhyncus, Egypt, with records mostly fragments, of the sayings of Jesus. But the most important discovery was made in 1945 in upper Egypt near the village of Nag Hammadi. There, two brothers working in the area unearthed a jar containing the now famous Nag Hammadi texts, which consist of several gnostic works, acts, apocalypses, and gospels, including the *Gospel of Thomas, Gospel of Truth, Gospel of Philip, Gospel of the Egyptians*, and others. Some of these writings are Essenic and Jewish rather than Christian. Collectively, these diverse Gnostic texts range from secret gospels, poems, and semi-philosophical descriptions of the origin of the universe, to myths, magic and instructions or mystical practices. Many of the acts and gospels bear the names of Jesus' disciples for credibility, and, generally speaking, they contain, like the *Gospel of Thomas*, the sayings of Jesus, which merely proclaim the beliefs of individual Gnostic sects. They are not biographical and lack historical reliability. Although scholars knew something about Gnosticism through the Church Fathers' polemics, the discovery of these texts has enhanced their knowledge of Gnostic beliefs.

The Gnostic Jesus was the product of an ideological synthesis. Gnosticism, which comes from the Greek word gnosis (knowledge), is a modern term used to describe the strange variety of sects which arose late in the first century A.D. in Syria and Egypt spreading out eventually into the Graeco-Roman world. Generally, the Gnostics (Knowers) believed in a redeemer Son of the Supreme God, who came to earth from heaven to save man from the demonic powers of darkness that are keeping man imprisoned in this world. The Son was born of a virgin and took on a human form so that the demons would not know of his conception or recognize him. He came not to save from sin, but to give knowledge (which is itself salvation) to all those who are the elect of God and, therefore, capable of acquiring it. Part of this knowledge consists of sacred passwords that one will need at death to pass through the circles of the planetary system and through a series of heavens to find the redeemer Son and his father, the Supreme God. The idea of a savior god who comes to earth and returns to heaven was nothing new. It was present in the mystery cults which also emphasized secrecy in their mysteries that united the individual with the saviour god. It appears, therefore, that the Gnostics existed before Christian times, but eventually many of these groups incorporated Jesus in their beliefs along with Greek, Jewish, and Oriental ideas of dualism, and Jesus became their redeemer, the Son of the Supreme God. He was not physically real, not God incarnate, but God who had manifested himself in the form of a human being. His physical body was merely appearance and, therefore, so was his suffering, death, and resurrection. Such ideas were not eradicated by the Church, and they reappeared and were similarly expressed again in the sixth century in Egypt as the heresy called Monophysitism.

The Gnostic texts, which take up the history of Gnosticism about where the Dead Sea Scrolls terminate the history of the Essenes, reveal the Christianization of Gnosticism through an ideological synthesis, a gradual process. The first gnostic, mentioned in the book of Acts and attacked by the second century Church Fathers Justin and Irenaeus, was not a Christian. He was Simon Magus (the Magician) of Samaria, whose followers believed that he had come from heaven to save them by giving them knowledge. The same was held to be true of Simon's master and competitor, the Samaritan Dositheus, and of Simon's disciple Menander, who lived and taught in Antioch in the early second century. All three men claimed to be divine Messiahs and were worshipped as such by their followers. For the Simonians, knowledge was personified in Helena, Simon's female companion, a prostitute from Tyre. Although these Gnostics were not Christians, eventually many Gnostic sects became Christian, identifying their redeemer god with Jesus. Gradually, even some Jews, evidently Essenes, who had been waiting for the Messiah's first coming, and some Christians, who had been waiting for his second coming, became disillusioned, gave up waiting, and agreed with the Christian Gnostics that most of the disciples of Christ had misunderstood him. Jesus was not speaking of an earthly kingdom to come in the future but of a heavenly kingdom that each individual will find when he dies. The *Gospel of Thomas* rejected the idea that the Kingdom of God was an actual event soon to appear in history, as the Church and its selected gospels maintained. The Kingdom was only an internal transformation of one's self through the acquisition of the gnosis. The Gnostic knew that he was a spiritual being who had fallen from heaven into an illusory human existence, which he would transcend in order to return to the true reality of his spiritual origin. He alone had the secret and mysterious knowledge (gnosis) given by Jesus to a few of his disciples after his resurrection. A Gnostic who received the divine light or knowledge from Christ became himself a Christ. He recovered his divine nature.

The Gnostics, evidently, did not distinguish the human from the divine. Valentius, a Gnostic, maintained that humanity itself reveals the divine life, but he thought that he adhered to the beliefs of St. Paul and St. Luke, and the fact is that many of the Gnostic concepts are to be found in the canonical gospels. But the Gnostics went beyond the limits of canonical tenets by maintaining that man is not different from God except in the loss of knowledge. The *Gospel of Thomas* even accepted pantheism, the belief that everything is God. The Naasenes, who used this gospel, believed that stones were animate beings.

The Gnostics rejected the concept of sin upheld by the established Church, insisting, like the *Gospel of Truth*, that ignorance alone brings suffering in life, making it like a terrible nightmare—a Platonic idea. Those who lack the gnosis, they maintained, are living in stupor as though they lack sleep or are drunk. Terror, pain, and confusion, which caused the material universe and the human body, are located in the body, which must be brought under control by enlightenment. St. Paul's teaching that Jesus' body carried all the sins of mankind and was destroyed so that Jesus might triumph over evil and the power of darkness for all humanity was an alien notion. The gnostic, who sought to recover his divine nature through the gnosis in solitude, spurned materialism and bodily desires pretty much like the Christian monks in the Egyptian desert, but he also rejected prayer, fasting, and almsgiving emphasized by Judaism and early Christianity. He had no obligations towards his fellow men, only to himself. Although the radical Gnostics rejected family, sex, business, and politics as illusions, some of them, like the Valentinians, married, had children, and worked. However, like the devout Buddhists, they regarded such activities as of secondary importance to the solitary mystical path of gnosis attained only by the few spiritual-intellectual elite. The Gnostic emphasis was on individualism. Each human being had the ability to discover his divine human self or the light within him. He did not need the authority of the Church, its clergy, sacraments, creed and New Testament canon in order to gain salvation.[18]

Not all the Gnostic sects were Christian. Some of the Nag Hammadi texts are more philosophical and Neoplatonic than Christian or Jewish. Plotinus, the leader of Neoplatonism, mentions the Gnostics as members of his school, but his polemics indicate that he turned against them. In his *Life of Plotinus*, Porphyry, his pupil, wrote that Plotinus in his treatise "Against the Gnostics" attacked such sectarians, who had produced revelations by Zoroaster and Zostrianos, Nicotheus, Allogenes and Messos, and others, and who alleged that Plato had not entered the sanctum of intelligible reality. The Nag Hammadi library contains texts titled *Zostrianos* and *Allogenes*, refuted by the Neoplatonists, and such texts as the *Trimorphic Protennoia* and *Mersanes*, which are rather similar in philosophic leaning. When Plotinus attacked Gnostic magic chants addressed to the higher powers, he might have had in mind such hymnic texts as the *Three Steles of Seth*.

Some of the Nag Hammadi texts are Hermetic, developed from Egyptian lore, and were already known to scholars before the Nag Hammadi discovery. They recite dialogues of initiation between the gods Hermes Trismegistos (Thoth in Egyptian) and his son Tat, and fuse together Platonic, Stoic, and Neopythagorean ideas with Eastern religious concepts. Whether the Hermetic texts are Gnostic or not is subject to interpretation and depends on how one defines Gnosticism. A few texts, such as the *Sentences of Sextus*, are not Gnostic. But generally, the Hermetic religion, which had no sacraments, held beliefs similar to those of the Gnostics. Hermetic literature, which appeared about the same time as the gospels and the Gnostic texts, depicts the god Hermes as mind (nous) and his son Tat as the word (logos). The members had a duty to preach the gnosis received from their god and to subdue their earthly nature so that they might liberate their spiritual nature. However, in almost all of the Hermetic liturgies, a mediator was needed to explain to each god seeker and proselyte the deeper hidden truth of life known only to the grand master in Alexandria, Egypt (or, for other similar sects in Babylon or Jerusalem).

The Gnostics, who were rather ecumenical in their religious ideas, were ready to receive comparable views from all philosophies and religions. If Seth (the third child of Adam and Eve) who received his gnosis from Adam, could be identified with Jesus by the Sethian Gnostics, the Gnostics could also produce Christianizing syncretisms of Hermes and Zoroaster. Gnosticism was not so much an alternate form of Christianity as it was a radical response to an evil world, an attempt to escape from it through an inner mystical transcendence. It was a wide movement that emerged within Christianity, Judaism, Neoplatonism, the mystery religions, and the like, and it was noted for its one common stance, escapism from reality. Christian monasticism, which emphasized withdrawal from the world into the wilderness as a hermit (erematic) or into a monastery as a monk (cenobic) to find communal utopia, resembled to some degree the Gnostic ideal. It is not surprising that the Nag Hammadi texts were discovered within sight of the Basilica of Saint Pachomius, the founder of Christian monasticism. The texts themselves were probably produced in a Pachomian monastery.[19]

Jesus in the New Testament Remains a Mystery

Although the Gnostic Jesus was a revelation from God, unearthly and rather mystical, the Jesus proclaimed by the canonical writings of the New Testament was quite real, with an earthly existence and a physical body. He lived, taught, died, and rose from the dead in Palestine during the first century A.D., and therefore, he was an historical figure. That Jesus was a real person is certain because even pagan Roman writers such as Tacitus (60-120 A.D.), Pliny (62-113 A.D.), and Suetonias (75-160 A.D.) mention him as a teacher and miracle worker who lived and died in Palestine in the first century A.D.[20]

Although the writers of the gospels were concerned with relevance and what the facts meant for their faith, they also sought reliable information based on an oral and a written tradition, a collection of the words and deeds of Jesus from witnesses. Luke tells us that many had undertaken to compile accounts of events based on the traditions handed down "by those who were eyewitnesses from the beginning and became ministers of the word" (Luke 1:2). Thus, Luke indicates that literature existed prior to the writing of the gospels. However, he also points out that he has examined the whole course of events in detail in order to write a correct narrative with authentic knowledge of what transpired (Luke 1:3-4). (According to tradition, not accepted by many scholars, Luke wrote his gospel based on the words of Paul and Mark and on the preaching of Peter.) St. Paul emphasized the importance of genuine happenings as part of the tradition. "If Christ was not raised, our proclamation is in vain and our faith is in vain, and we are found to be bearing false witness against God" (1 Corinthians 15:14-15). And the First Epistle of John begins with the words: "That which was from the beginning, which we heard, which we beheld with our eyes, which we saw and hands handled . . . we beheld and we testify."

Obviously, these early Christians could not divorce faith and fact; theology had to be based on historical events. Any mythical notion in a Platonic or Gnostic sense was denied. The author of 2 Peter (1:16-17) states: "It was not by following cleverly devised myths that we made known to you the power and presence of our Lord Jesus Christ and his coming; we saw him with our own eyes . . . ," and then we heard the voice from heaven on the sacred mountain proclaiming him His beloved Son. St. Paul was very careful to indicate which commandments came from Jesus and which advice from Paul himself. In setting rules on marriage and divorce, he points out that, according to Jesus, married couples are not to divorce (1 Corinthians 7:10-11). However, on problems arising out of mixed marriages, he makes it clear that it is he who is solving them and "not the Lord" (7:12). And, in dealing with the lives of unmarried individuals, he states that he does not have a command from the Lord, but gives "judgement as a man mercifully permitted by the Lord to be trustworthy" (7:25). There can be no doubt that for St. Paul the authority of the words of Jesus were binding upon him and upon his congregation.[21]

However, in spite of the emphasis on accuracy and historical reliability, Jesus remains mysterious. The numerous discrepancies in the gospels and in the New Testament writings in general cast doubt on their authenticity and make it difficult to unravel the real Jesus. Because they were concerned with theological relevance, each evangelist had his own church community in mind and its related problems. He was, therefore, selective in his choice of sources taken from wide and extensive material. Relevance was also applied in the selection of all the New Testament writings. In his *History of the Church* (p. 108), Eusebius writes that, although Peter's first epistle was accepted as genuine, his second was considered to be uncanonical, but many "have thought it valuable and have honored it with a place among the other Scriptures." The same applies to the Epistle to the Hebrews, Eusebius continues, which the Roman church did not accept as the work of Paul, and doubt was also expressed concerning the Apocalypse. Because the synoptic gospels of Mark, Luke, and Matthew were written during the latter part of the first century A.D., they are in partial agreement and their outlines of Jesus' ministry are generally the same. But their variance in their details and their accounts of Jesus' personality, which are even more pronounced when compared with the gospel of John written somewhat later, are so numerous that one wonders if they were at all concerned with accuracy.[22]

Most scholars agree that Mark wrote the first gospel. His gospel, therefore, contains an attitude of imminent expectation of Jesus' second coming. It is possible that Mark was St. Peter's son and, perhaps, an eyewitness who wrote his gospel, perhaps, from Rome. His gospel was written around 70 A.D., during or after the Zealot rebellion against Rome. Therefore, he seeks to exonerate the Christians from any responsibility in the uprising and from any hatred toward the Romans by blaming the Jews for Jesus' crucifixion. Pilate is reluctant to condemn Jesus, and at the cross, the Roman centurion concedes that Jesus is the Son of God. Mark also seems to be trying to separate the Christians from the Jews as much as possible. Jesus attacks the Scribes and Pharisees and appears not to be bound by Jewish teachings. Jewish political Messianism is repudiated. Not only is there no Davidic genealogy to be found in Mark's gospel, but Jesus himself ridicules the Davidic descent of the Messiah as illogical (12:35-37) and manifests a compromising non-rebellious attitude toward the Romans when asked about the payment of tribute to Caesar. Mark does proclaim Jesus as the Messiah and the Son of Man (final judge of all mankind) who voluntarily died for man's salvation. The Jewish opposition to Jesus totally failed. By willingly giving himself for the ransom of many with his crucifixion and by triumphing over death with his resurrection, a prelude to the Messianic Kingdom soon to come, Jesus fulfilled his earthly mission and set the stage for the defeat of Satan and the forces of evil.[23]

Although Mark wrote his gospel in Greek, evidently, from Italy, Matthew wrote his in Aramaic, perhaps, from Egypt and Luke in Greek, probably, from Greece. Both of them wrote their gospels later than Mark and both used Mark's gospel generally retaining his outline of

Jesus' ministry. All three of them used a collection of sayings and of deeds of Jesus referred to as Q (quelle, meaning source), which were a part of the written tradition. Nearly all of Mark's gospel is found in Matthew and over half of it in Luke. There is a striking similarity of words in all three gospels, especially in Greek. But both Matthew and Luke often modify Mark's version of events. Unlike Mark, Matthew expresses a Judaic rather than a western view. He emphasizes Jesus' restricted mission to the Jews and his obedience to the Mosaic law, which Jesus expanded into a new law. In a series of parables, Luke (Chapters 15 and 16) emphasizes God's free grace and forgiveness and extends Jesus' mission to the gentiles. Matthew seeks to reveal that Jesus fulfilled the Old Testament prophecies concerning the Messiah, and in this endeavor he does not hesitate to introduce a series of events that evidently did not take place, such as the killing of the children by King Herod and the journey of the child Jesus to Egypt. Both Matthew and Luke mention Jesus' virgin birth, Matthew to reveal again that a prophecy had been fulfilled, Luke to show that Jesus was more than a man. But neither Mark nor John mentions such an extraordinary event. The fact is that the myth of a virgin birth was popular and widespread in ancient times, because it affirmed the supernatural character of famous leaders. Virginal conceptions, angelic appearances, wondrous births or temptations of the devil were all characteristic in stories of great men and founders of religions, including Buddha of India, Zarathustra of Persia, Confucius of China, and Muhammad of Arabia, not to mention famous Greeks and Romans who were conceived by the gods.

Many other differences exist between Mathew and Luke. Matthew attempts to demonstrate that Jesus was the Davidic Messiah. He produces a genealogy of three divisions based on fourteen generations from Abraham to David and from David to the Babylonian Captivity, and another fourteen generations from the Babylonian Captivity to Jesus (Matthew, 1:1-17). The number fourteen was regarded as mystical because it came from an old Hebrew abbreviation of the name David to DVD, which in alphabetic mathematical symbols is equivalent to the number 14. Matthew evidently made the order to fit this significant number. Therefore, although his first division of fourteen names of men is identical with that of the Old Testament, his second division is not consistent and contains many discrepancies. Luke, who also produced a genealogy of Jesus starting with God and Adam, contradicts Matthew. Luke's genealogy from Abraham to Adam contains the

additional name of Admin for a total of fifteen names (3:23-38). After
David, the names are different except for the names Shealtiel and
Zerubbabel. Even though Jesus was the son of God and Mary, both men
trace the descent of Jesus from David through Joseph, Mary's husband,
and not Mary; but the two cannot even agree on Joseph's father. In
Matthew's genealogy, Joseph's father is Jacob, but in Luke's, he is Heli.
According to Luke, the number of generations between David and
Jesus is forty-three; according to Matthew twenty-eight. The total
number of generations from Abraham to Jesus for Luke is fifty-seven,
for Matthew only forty-one. The Old Testament genealogies reveal
that these two New Testament genealogies were made up or arranged
to underline one's royal or priestly status (as in the Pantateuch and the
Chronicler, which present the closest parallels to Matthew's genealogy)
or the character qualities of one's famous ancestors. They were not
written to reveal one's biological tree. Christian writers, including
Eusebius, have tried in various ways to defend these contradictory
genealogies, maintaining that some of the names were those of adopted
rather than actual fathers or that one of the gospels traces its genealogy
from Mary's line; but scholars consider their explanations to be weak
and debatable. Whether Jesus was the son of David, therefore, is not
clear. In any case, neither the gospel of Mark nor that of John contains
any genealogies. Differences between Matthew and Luke are also to
be found in their Sermon on the Mount (Matthew 5:3-10; Luke 6:20-26),
the Our Father (Matthew 6:9-13; Luke 11:2-4), the healing of the
centurion's servant (Matthew 8:5-13; Luke 7:1-10), and the important
words on the institution of the Eucharist (Matthew 26:26-28; Luke
22:19-20). Matthew does not record the rigorous ascetic sayings of
Jesus, but Luke does, indicating that it will be almost impossible for
the rich and greedy to enter God's kingdom.[24]

Differences also exist between Luke and Mark on Jesus' personality.
Although Luke is more faithful to his source than Matthew, he changes
the language of Mark's account, omits what he considers unsuitable,
and uses stories that he thinks more appropriate. Luke often changes
or rejects stories that revealed Jesus acting improperly because of
anger. Therefore, he alters Mark's narration of Jesus' violent cleansing
of the Temple in Jerusalem. In Luke, no force is used. Nor does Luke
permit Jesus to exclaim, as Mark does, that he will destroy the Temple.
Jesus could not be depicted as being provocative toward his fellow
countrymen to whom he gave the opportunity to receive him (even
though they rejected him). Luke does not portray any rage on the part

of the Messiah, whom he seeks to depict as calm, in control of himself, and confident in the execution of his mission. But Luke's Messiah is not devoid of emotion. Therefore, in Luke one finds Jesus weeping for Jerusalem's tragic fate, and in Luke alone Jesus is identified with the suffering servant, because for Luke suffering is essential for redemption.[25]

Still greater differences are to be found when the synoptic gospels are compared with the gospel of John, which was written around 95-100 A.D., or perhaps even later. The synoptic gospels reveal that Jesus' ministry was at first concentrated in Galilee, but in John, Jesus goes back and forth from Galilee to Jerusalem. In the synoptics, the cleansing of the Temple from the merchants occurs toward the end of Jesus' ministry; in John, near the beginning. The synoptic gospels tell of Jesus healing those possessed by demons, of repentance and forgiveness of sins, of prayer, fasting and charity; but these accounts are not to be found in John. However, they are found in writings of the first century A.D. that reveal the popular Judaism of that period. In John, Jesus is revealed as God on earth, in control of his destiny, strong, awesome, and determined. Only in John does one find the story of Jesus raising his friend Lazarus from the dead, and it is most curious that such a great miracle was not recorded in the synoptic gospels. (Jesus was not alone in this. The old Testament prophet Elijah performed the same kind of miracle, raising a dead man to life.) But John's gospel also differs in the form and content of the sayings of Jesus. Instead of the synoptic parables and short, pointed sayings, John presents extended discourses by Jesus on his relation to the Father and on his disciples' relation to both the Father and the Son. Jesus' message in the synoptics centers on God's kingdom; in John, it centers on Jesus himself. Although John's emphasis and tone are rather different, he tells us in his narration of Christ's crucifixion that "he who beheld has born witness, and his testimony is true, and he knows that he speaks truly, so that you also may believe" (19:35). John's testimony appears to be true, but it also has a theological emphasis and a significance which results in faith. The gospel of John was very controversial even among early Christian writers, but as Clement and Origen of Alexandria explained, John produced an allegorical work conveying the esoteric and spiritual meaning of Jesus, while the synoptics provided a literal and historical account of Christ's work.[26]

Inconsistencies, primarily in the details, are also to be found in the Acts of the Apostles written, perhaps, by Luke, Paul's companion in his later years. Paul's miraculous conversion is described three times in the Acts, once in the third person and twice in the first person. In the first passage (9:3-7), after being blinded by the heavenly light and hearing Jesus speak, "the men who were traveling with him stood speechless. They heard the voice but could see no one." In the second passage (22:9), St. Paul states: "my companions saw the light, but did not hear the voice that spoke to me." And, in the third version (26:14), Paul says that he and his companions all fell to the ground and that he, Paul, heard a voice in Hebrew. The variance is even greater in the words attributed to Jesus, who miraculously speaks to Paul on the road to Damascus. In the first version (9:6), after identifying himself, Jesus tells Paul to "get up and go into the city, and you will be told what you have to do." In the second reference (22:10), the instructions are almost the same. He is to go to Damascus. But in the third passage (26:16-18), Paul is not commanded to go to Damascus. After identifying himself, Jesus tells Paul: "I have appeared to you for a purpose: to appoint you my servant and witness, to testify both what you have seen and to what you shall yet see of me. I will rescue you from this people and from the Gentiles to whom I am sending you. I send you to open their eyes and turn them from darkness to light, from the dominion of Satan to God, so that, by trust in me, they may obtain forgiveness of sins, and a place with those whom God has made his own." Obviously, these differences are the result of editing that had taken place in the past.

Discrepancies also exist between the Acts and Paul's epistles concerning Paul's miraculous conversion and Paul's activities in and out of Damascus. Although three times in Acts Paul did not see Jesus but heard him, in Corinthian I (9:1), Paul asks in confirmation: "Did I not see Jesus our Lord?" Thus he accentuates the fact that he had seen Jesus. In his epistle to the Galatians (1:11-12), which most scholars accept as authentic, actually written by Paul himself, Paul indicates that he had a spiritual conversion, a revelation. "I must make it clear to you, my friends, that the gospel you heard me preach is no human invention. I did not take it over from any man; no man taught it to me; I received it through a revelation of Jesus Christ." The same point is hinted at again in Galations (1:15-16): "But then in his good pleasure God, who had set me apart from birth and called me through his grace, chose to reveal his Son to me and through me, in order that I might proclaim him among the Gentiles." In the Acts (9:28-29; 26:19-20), Paul flees from Damascus, goes to Jerusalem, and preaches throughout

Judaea. In Galatians (1:17-24; 2:1-5), Paul writes that he went from Damascus to Arabia, returned, and then went to Jerusalem where he met Cephas (Peter) and James, the Lord's brother. "Next," he continues, "I went to the regions of Syria and Cilicia, and remained unknown by sight to Christ's congregation in Judaea." Thus, according to Galatians, Paul did not preach in Jerusalem or in Judaea, as stated in Acts. Although both Paul and Luke and the other evangelists in general desired to be accurate, binding themselves to the authority of witnesses and the words of Jesus, mistakes obviously were made either by the authors themselves or through the years by scribes who copied these texts. The texts were also edited by the omission or addition of words, which changed the meaning of some passages. It is suspected that Acts was written by several individuals and that Luke might have written the first quarter of this work, even though tradition has attributed it to him. But these contradictions in the details of the New Testament writings have given rise to skepticism among scholars concerning the accuracy of their presentation of the words and deeds of Jesus. Do they really tell us who Jesus was and what took place, it is asked, or is Jesus to a great extent the product of good myths conceived to persuade and convince the public of his divinity and mission? [27]

Understanding Jesus and who he actually was is made even more difficult by St. Paul's conception of Jesus as the Redeemer Messiah, which appears in Paul's doctrines on sin and salvation. Although Paul accepted the Judaic view that man sins against God by transgressing against His laws, he did not accept the Jewish notion that sins could be removed by good works. For the Jews, God forgives one who genuinely repents, and one could balance future sins with good works to come out ahead in the end. But for Paul, justification for salvation can be based only on faith, apart from works (Romans 3:28). He rejected adherence to the Law, displayed in formal and superficial customs such as circumcision, and defended abiding by the law discreetly and in spirit as one who, although uncircumcised, has totally surrendered himself to God's will, and has thus peformed an act in the truest sense (Romans 2:17-29). Paul also upheld the Gnostic view that the god of this world is Satan (II Cor. 4:4), who controls man through his flesh, and only the intervention of Jesus can save mankind. In his epistles (but also in Mark's gospel [3:27]), we find the idea that Jesus came to the world to defeat Satan (Gal. 1:4; Rom. 8:3; I Cor. 15:24-28) and to save mankind from Satan's bondage, from sin (Rom. 4:25; I Cor. 15:3).

On the cross, Paul tells us, God's love for man was revealed, the sins of all mankind represented in the flesh of Jesus were destroyed, and through the glorious resurrection of his body, a body that can by mystically shared by those redeemed, Jesus triumphed over the powers of evil forever for all humanity (I Cor. 15:54). To find salvation, in the sense that one comes to know that he has been saved, one must surrender himself to God's grace as manifested in Jesus and, through baptism and faith, unite himself with the risen body of Christ the savior to become in Jesus a new creation (Rom. 6:3-11, 14; I Cor. 6:14; IICor. 4:14; Phil. 3:10; Gal. 2:20). Although Paul did not exclude love and morality as essential for gaining eternal life, his emphasis on salvation by faith— a faith bestowed on the select by God's grace since creation (Rom. 4:3-25; Gal. 1:15-16), whereby one submits to, lives for, and unites with Christ to escape death—transformed the Judaic notion of an earthly Messiah into a mystery cult concept of the Redeemer. Christ became like any of the mythical pagan gods, Dionysus, Adonis, or Tamuz, through whom their followers gained eternal life in a mystical union provided by their mysteries or rituals.[28]

The teachings of St. Paul became controversial among the early Christians. II Peter (probably written in the second century) indicates that Paul's letters are inspiring, "though they contain some obscure passages, which the ignorant and unstable misinterpret to their own ruin, as they do other scriptures" (3:16). James, the Lord's brother and the respected leader of the Jewish Christians in Jerusalem, refuted Paul's emphasis on faith without works. In his New Testament epistle, James asserts that faith without works cannot save. It is barren and dead. Even the devils have faith like that and believe in God, James writes, but "they merely tremble" (2:14-18). Although the Church eventually upheld Paul's mystical theology of Christ the Redeemer and his refutation of the Jewish religious practices, it sided with James in accepting that both faith and the deeds of a free will seeking God's grace are necessary for eternal salvation. However, Paul's rejection of the Jewish tradition with its emphasis on obedience to the Law through formal rituals was unacceptable to the Jewish Christians of Jerusalem (the Nazoreans or the later Ebionites), who remained committed to traditional Jewish beliefs and practices. Although after the Jerusalem conference of the apostles with Paul, James and the Nazoreans were willing to allow uncircumcised Gentile Christians to forego the Jewish tradition and the Mosaic law, they and even Peter refused to celebrate the Lord's Supper and to eat with them, which angered Paul.

Neither did the Nazoreans accept Paul's concept of salvation through a mystical union with Jesus, the Redeemer God, or his doctrine of justification by faith predestined by God. They maintained that Christ was not born of a virgin, but at his baptism was filled with the Holy Spirit and became the Son of God. They accepted Christ as of God, but not as God in essence. He was filled with God's Spirit while on earth as man, and thus retained two natures. The Nazoreans evidently considered Paul to be their enemy. They refuted Paul's contention that his gospel was true and equal to that of the Apostles because it was given to him by a revelation from Christ, and evidently they also rejected the popular Church's contention that its doctrines were true because their formulation was guided by the Holy Spirit. True doctrines, the Nazoreans maintained, were to be based on Holy Scripture and the Judaic tradition. This Jerusalem Church, led by the family of Jesus (martyred James was succeeded by Symeon, son of Clopas and Jesus' cousin, who was also martyred under Roman Emperor Trajan for being a member of the royal house of Judah), was looked upon as the leader of Christianity, but the impending Zealot rebellion of 66 A.D. forced the Jerusalem Christians to flee to Pella across the Jordan River and subsequently to lose the leadership.[29]

The complex roots and evolution of Christianity have made it very difficult for scholars to unravel the mystery of Jesus' earthly existence. The Essenic origin of Christian ideology, its synthesis with Greek and Oriental mystery cult ideas and rituals proclaiming mythical redeemers which appeared on earth to save mankind, and the denial of Christ's humanity by the Gnostics have raised doubts among scholars concerning the true Jesus. The discrepancies discovered in the New Testament writings have added to this skepticism about the accuracy of their facts and the ability of their authors to be truthful. The New Testament proclaims Jesus as God incarnate, who came to save mankind from sin, who died and was resurrected, but who will return to establish his Kingdom on earth. Because Jesus was a real person in history, doubts would have existed concerning his divinity and, therefore, the sincerity of the New Testament writers. The fact is that for the Jews, the Davidic Messiah was to appear only once in order to establish and to rule God's Kingdom throughout this earth. Jesus, however, was depicted as similar to the pagan mythical gods, going to heaven to rule from there with his Father until his second coming. Jesus, the awaited Davidic Messiah of the Jews who was to be of God, but still human, became almost identical with the redeeming resurrected gods worshipped by the pagans. The discrepancies in the details of the New Testament writings and their revelation of a Messiah more pagan than Jewish in concept added to the mystery surrounding Jesus. But the greatest doubts and debates among scholars have risen over the New Testament discrepancies concerning the death and resurrection of Jesus and his bodily ascension to heaven.

2. The Debate Over Christ's Death and Resurrection

The Inexplicable Crucifixion

The central theme of the four gospels is the story of the crucifixion, burial, and resurrection of Jesus. These events constitute the foundations of Christianity. Without the crucifixion, Jesus could not have died for man's salvation as a redeemer, and without the resurrection he could not have been accepted as the Son of God and of the same substance as the Father. As St. Paul declared (I Cor. 15:14), "if Christ was not raised, then our gospel is null and void, and so is your faith." The gospels generally agree that Jesus was crucified, that he died on the cross, and that he was buried and resurrected. However, they raise more questions than they answer because of the many discrepancies that biblical scholars have found in their details.

Numerous scholars have appeared since the eighteenth century explaining why Jesus was crucified, whether or not he died on the cross, and whether there was a genuine resurrection. In the eighteenth century, Herman Samuel Reimarus of Hamburg, Germany, maintained that Jesus was merely a revolutionary who failed and whose body was removed from the tomb by his disciples, who then proclaimed his resurrection. Both nineteenth- and twentieth-century scholars, such as David Friedrick Strauss, Christian Herman Weisse, and Bruno Bauer, have emphasized Jesus' humanity and moral teachings and have maintained that Jesus was primarily a teacher who thought of himself as the Son of Man rather than the Son of God. However, Albert Schweitzer in his *Quest for the Historical Jesus* argued that even in the synoptic gospels Jesus thought of himself as the Messiah, the Son of God, and believed that the Kingdom of God was about to appear during the lifetime of his listeners. Jesus was convinced that he would return in glory on the clouds of heaven with the angelic host in order to bring the end of this world and of human history.[1] Thus, for Schweitzer, Jesus was a real figure, but was primarily concerned with eschatology and its fulfillment. Generally, Schweitzer and many other reputable scholars, including Jewish scholars Joseph Klausner, S. G. F. Brandon and Hugh

Schonfield, agree that Jesus was a historical figure who was condemned and crucified around 36 A.D. by the orders of Pontius Pilate, Roman prefect of Palestine from about 26 to 36 A.D. However, they dismiss the gospel miracles as myths, question the gospel version of his crucifixion and regard the story of the resurrection as the product of psychological manifestations or revelations experienced by the disciples and St. Paul.

Albert Schweitzer maintains that Jesus deliberately brought about his own death. He asserts that Jesus eventually realized that, as the Messiah, he could bring about God's Kingdom only with his own suffering and death. He had been expecting the Kingdom to make its appearance as a result of his preaching and healing and casting out of demons. When he sent his disciples out to do the same, they were successful in fighting evil spirits and defeating Satan, but God's Kingdom did not appear. After rethinking his position, Schweitzer writes, Jesus evidently decided that his efforts had not been enough and that something more drastic was required. In Isaiah, he discovered what God had determined for him as the Messiah. Upon informing his disciples of his God-given role as the Messiah, which was one of suffering and death and instructing them to keep this a secret, he marched on with them to Jerusalem. The Jerusalem masses held him as the Messiah, with shouts of hosanna in anticipation of the Kingdom soon to be established. But the Pharisees and the Scribes, who were not aware of the imminent coming of God's Kingdom, turned against him. They had no real evidence to convict and kill him until Judas betrayed him.[2]

The role of Judas the Iskariot and the words of Jesus on the cross, "My God, my God, why hast thou forsaken me?" (Mark 15:34; Matt. 27:46), perplexed Schweitzer. Why should God utter these words to God? He concluded that Judas, who was one of Jesus' most trusted disciples in charge of the treasury, relied on Judas to effect his betrayal and crucifixion. Jesus was convinced that, once he was on the cross, God with his angelic host would bring him down from the cross still alive, reveal him as the Messiah to all, and give him full authority and power to usher in God's Kingdom. For this reason, Schweitzer says, we find in the gospel of John (13:27) Jesus telling Judas, "Do quickly what you have to do." Jesus was determined to be crucified, and thus he sent Judas to betray the secret that he was the Messiah. He was crucified, but only to discover while dying in agony that he had been wrong. He was not the Messiah. He would die, and God did not care. Observing his beloved teacher dead on the cross, Judas realized that all had been in vain. The pain became unbearable and he hanged himself. Schweitzer rejected the story of the resurrection and ascension as popular legends not essential to Jesus' mission. For Schweitzer, Jesus' teachings and works are sufficient to place him above all men in stature.

Joseph Klausner, however, says that, once in Jerusalem, Jesus did not know that his death was imminent. He knew that he had enemies, especially among the Sadducees and Pharisees, and therefore he had notions of impending death, but that is all. Judas had become convinced that Jesus was not the Messiah. Unlike the Messiah, Jesus was afraid of his enemies, whom he had been evading or seeking to escape. He had also contradicted himself by teaching observance of the religious Law to the letter, in every detail, while also permitting the consumption of forbidden foods, and showing disrespect toward the Sabbath observance and the washing of hands. Not only were his teachings and actions contradictory, but in Jerusalem, where he was to subdue the Pharisees and destroy the Romans, Jesus merely made nightly escapes to Bethany and revealed vain arrogance and contempt for the old traditions. For these reasons, states Klausner, and not for the thirty pieces of silver mentioned in Matthew (from a passage which he took from Zachariah [11:12-13]), Judas betrayed Jesus. He found Jesus lacking as a Messiah, weak and incapable of any organized action that could succeed. Judas therefore, says Klausner, let the high priest or the local Jewish authorities know where Jesus was to be found after the Passover meal, and Judas personally went to the Garden of Gethsemane on the Mount of Olives to make sure that Jesus alone would be arrested and not any of his disciples. According to Klausner, only a few of the supplementary details in the gospels concerning the night at Gethsemane and what was said by Jesus during his arrest can be accepted as true. The fact is that the gospels are not in agreement on the details.[3]

Jesus was found guilty of blasphemy by the High Priest, writes Klausner, because when asked, he admitted to being the Messiah, the Son of Man, who according to all the synoptic gospels will be "sitting at the right hand of Power and coming with the clouds of heaven" (Mark 14:62; Matt. 26:64; Luke 27:70). According to Jewish Law, the blasphemer or false prophet, the beguiler and seducer, was to be stoned to death and hanged with ropes from a cross. But to have blasphemed, Jesus would have had to pronounce the word Jehovah or, in Hebrew, Yahweh, the name of God. Jesus did not. Therefore, he committed no blasphemy only a political crime, by posing as the Messiah. The

Sanhedrin, which was composed mostly of Sadducees, was not able to pass the death sentence on him. Because it was the eve of the Passover and the eve of the Sabbath, as John's gospel states, and still day (not during the Passover, which falls on the eve of the Sabbath in the evening, as the synoptic gospels write),the Sanhedrin quickly turned Jesus over to Pilate for having assumed the role of Messiah or King of the Jews. By turning him over while there was still daylight, they hoped to escape the seven-day delay that would be caused by the Passover feast and to avoid any political outbreaks from the Galilean Zealots who had arrived in Jerusalem in large numbers. The Jewish leaders thought of Jesus as a rebel without any special spiritual nature, and they wanted him executed to save the masses from Pilate's cruel vengeance, which would have come in case of any disturbance. Although the gospels seek to clear Pilate of Jesus' death by pointing out that he even sought to release him but failed, and then washed his hands of the whole matter, Philo and Josephus, the Jewish historians reveal him as a ruthless man who did not hesitate to provoke and kill Jews, especially one who dared to call himself the Messiah. Once Jesus was turned over to Pilate, says Klausner, no Jew took part in Jesus' trial and crucifixion. It was all done by Pilate, that man of blood.[4]

Jesus, writes Klausner, was crucified for political reasons, not for his religious views. Pilate killed him as "King-Messiah," which for non-Jews meant "King of the Jews." It is for this reason that on the cross-beam above, the Romans placed an inscription: "The King of the Jews" (Mark), "This is Jesus, King of the Jews" (Matthew), "This is the King of the Jews" (Luke) and "Jesus of Nazareth, King of the Jews" (John). According to Matthew (27:46) and Mark (15:34), Jesus died on the cross after exclaiming (a verse from Psalm [22:2]): "My God, my God, why hast thou forsaken me?" Such words, which are at variance with Christian beliefs concerning the divine nature of Jesus and his predestined passion, says Klausner, must have been uttered by Jesus; otherwise, the Church would not have allowed them in print. John does not record these words because they were inconsistent with his presentation of Jesus as the divine Logos, while Luke substitutes the more suitable words (23:46), "Father, into thy hands I commend my spirit." But Jesus, who was imbued with the spirit of the Scriptures through his extensive knowledge of them, began (at his baptism) and ended his career by quoting the Scriptures, even while he was dying in agony on the cross.[5]

Klausner dismisses the story of the resurrection as the product of the disciples' spiritual vision, similar to St. Paul's. The fact is that Joseph of Arimathaea, a member of the Jerusalem Sanhedrin, after obtaining permission from Pilate, buried Jesus in his private tomb hewn in a rock and sealed it with a heavy stone. As requested by Joseph of Arimathaea, Jesus' bones were not broken, but the Roman centurion confirmed his death piercing Jesus' side with his lance as ordered by Pilate. Klausner presents the hypothesis that Joseph of Arimathaea secretly removed Jesus' body at the close of the Sabbath. Because Joseph was, according to the gospels, one of Jesus' disciples looking for God's Kingdom, there was some measure of truth to the report spread by the Jews that Jesus' disciples stole his body. But for the most part, the report was merely the malicious invention of enemies unable to explain the declared miracle. The truth is that there was no resurrection except as a revelation. Paul compares his own spiritual vision of Jesus to that of Peter and James and the other Apostles and many more at Galilee (I Cor. 15:5-8). Since the Acts (9:3; 26:19) and Galatians (1:16) indicate that Paul's vision was not of flesh and blood, Klausner writes, but a vision "born of the light," "an heavenly vision" in which God "had revealed in me his Son," the other Apostles' visions could only have been spiritual, a divine revelation, and not physical.[6]

S. G. F. Brandon agrees with Klausner that Jesus was crucified for political reasons. Although the synoptic gospels, especially that of Mark, attempt to indicate that Jesus was condemned by the Jews for religious reasons, blasphemy and false prophecy, nevertheless, it appears that the Sanhedrin had other reasons. The Jewish high priests, Annas and especially Caiaphas, feared that the masses had already accepted Jesus as the Messiah, the King of the Jews from David's line, and might cause violent disturbances against the Romans, which would in turn generate a violent retaliation from Pilate. Thus, according to the gospel of John (18:14), Caiaphas counseled the Jews that it would be expedient to have one man die for many. He was undoubtedly worried, says Brandon, because during Jesus' entry to Jerusalem, the masses were calling him King of Israel or the Messiah, the Son of David. Obviously, for the masses, Jesus was the King who would liberate Palestine from the Romans in order to establish his Messianic Kingdom. But Caiaphas must have become even more alarmed when Jesus, with the help of others, violently attacked the money-changers at the Temple of Solomon. It was probably a short disturbance, but it must have alarmed the Sanhedrin because the Zealots also caused a violent disturbance nearby. It is reasonable to assume, writes Brandon, that these two simultaneous attacks were connected. The Romans were able to put down the Zealot disturbance and to arrest some participants, including Barabbas. The Jewish council was not able to arrest Jesus until Judas told them where to find him. Jesus' intentions in the garden of Gethsemane the night before his crucifixion are not known, but resistance was offered, says Brandon, and it was probably of greater intensity and magnitude than the gospels tell us. Judas had probably warned the Sanhedrin that an armed resistance was likely. Jesus was crucified between two thieves, a common name for Zealots, writes Brandon, which suggests that Pilate and the Sanhedrin connected Jesus with the Zealot activities in Jerusalem.[7]

Brandon indicates that Jesus might have been sympathetic toward the Zealots, a violent sect of nationalists, who desired to overthrow the Romans by force of arms and thus to initiate the coming of the Messiah. Jesus' disciple Simon was a Zealot, as mentioned in Luke (6:15), but Mark (3:18), not to antagonize the Romans, tries to disguise this by using the word Canaanean rather than Zealot in reference to Simon. Judas the Iskariot was also a Zealot; the Greek work Iskariot was probably in reference to the Sicarii, another name for the Zealots. Although the gospels testify to Jesus' message of love and peace, writes Brandon, they also indicate a tendency toward violence on the part of Jesus' disciples. According to Luke (22:36,38), Jesus told his disciples to sell their clothes and to arm themselves, and they answered that they had two swords with them; to which Jesus replied, "It is enough." Jesus named James and John, the sons of Zebedee, "Boanergess, Sons of Thunder" (Mark 3:17; Luke 9:54), probably because they were prone to violence; and to Peter, he gave the title "Barjona" (Matt. 16:17), which means outlaw or rebel. In the Garden of Gethsemane, Jesus' disciples carried swords. Jesus had to be taken by stealth, and one of his disciples cut off the ear of the high priest's servant (Matt. 26:51-54; Mark 14:47; Luke 22:49-51). John, writing his gospel somewhat later (18:10), identified this sword-wielding disciple as Simon Peter. All these are not indications of an organization whose members were pacific and altruistic, but quite the contrary. Jesus, Bandon says, must have been sympathetic toward the Zealots because their goals were the same, the establishment of the Messianic Kingdom. In any case, the gospels' silence concerning the Zealots as well as the Essenes might have been an indication of Christian acquiescence to common views.

That the gospels contain no such explicit indication, Brandon asserts, was probably because Jesus was crucified and the Zealot revolution resulted in failure and persecution. Therefore, the evangelists and Christians in general, out of fear, could only blame the Jews for Jesus' crucifixion and absolve the Romans. At the same time, they denounced violence to mislead the Romans. Thus, writes Brandon, Mark attempts to reveal that Pilate held Christ to be innocent, but was forced to have him executed by the Jewish leaders. Matthew (Matt. 27:25) goes even further by blaming the Jewish people for Jesus' condemnation who accept full responsibility when they shout to Pilot: "His blood be on us and on our children." In addition, Matthew, who evidently represented the Alexandrian Jewish Christians, reveals Christ as a complete pacifist. Not only does he stop the armed action of his disciple in Gethsemane on his behalf, but pronounces the famous phrase (Matt. 26:52-54), "all who take the sword will perish by the sword." Matthew seeks to repudiate Zealot violence, says Brandon, and even earlier in his gospel, in the Beatitudes, Jesus emphasizes, "the poor in spirit," the "meek" and the "peacemakers," and commands all to love their enemies (Matt. 5:3, 5, 43-44).[8]

Hugh Schonfield, in his *Passover Plot*, holds that Jesus deliberately brought about his own death. Jesus set out to fulfill the Old Testament prophesies concerning the Messiah's rejection, betrayal, torture and crucifixion. He spoke at first in parables, because he did not want to be arrested for claiming to be the Messiah. He carefully plotted every step of his ministry, says Schonfield; and, according to John's gospel, several months before the Passover, he secretly went to Jerusalem. There, Jesus prepared the stage for the events soon to follow just before the Passover. He disclosed his design to no one, not even to Peter. He enlisted the help of Lazarus of Bethany, near Jerusalem, and of John, a priest from Jerusalem, who was also the beloved disciple in John's gospel and had contacts with such secret disciples in the Sanhedrin as Nicodemus and Joseph of Arimathaea; but they too remained in the dark concerning his plan. For the safety of all, Jesus needed the greatest possible secrecy and circumspection. Therefore, each one was to be informed and to carry out his task separately in order to help Jesus fulfill the prophecies as the rebuked and crucified Messiah. Lazarus, writes Schonfield, probably prepared the tethered foal of an ass used by Jesus for his entry into Jerusalem to fulfill, as Luke explains, the words of the Prophet Zechariah. The donkey was released only to messengers who knew the secret words: "The Master needs him." Jesus used Lazarus' home at Bethany for quick escapes from Jerusalem when in danger and for safety at night time; while John, the beloved disciple, provided Jesus his home for the enactment of the Last Supper.[9]

Judas Iskariot, whom John refers to as the son of Simon, probably Simon the Zealot, says Schonfield, was also to play his role in this divine drama, as Jesus desired. Jesus' strategy, writes Schonfield, was to heighten the pressure at the crucial moment and thus induce Judas to act. Jesus, therefore arranged the incident in which Mary anointed his feet (without her knowing of his intentions) so that he would be able to comment about his body's being anointed for burial. The ointment Mary used was very expensive, but the perfume's value, Schonfield asserts, was used to play on Judas' weakness, greed. Judas knew that Jesus expected to be betrayed. Suddenly, it occurred to him that he could make money by fulfilling Jesus' wish. He connected the ointment's cost with profit derived from his master's death. Thus, Judas' tempter came in the guise of his master. Jesus used only hints to induce Judas to perform the act of betrayal. When Jesus told Judas during the Last Supper to do quickly what he had to do, writes Schonfield, Judas understood that Jesus knew of his resolution and that he wanted him to fulfill it, and so he acted on it.[10]

Not only Judas, Schonfield asserts, but the Sanhedrin as well was simply led into the fulfillment of the Scriptures by Jesus' ability to predict their reactions whenever he applied the proper stimuli. The culprits might have thought that they were free to act, but in actuality, they were merely parties to Jesus' Passover plot. Thus, through them, Jesus saw to it that he would be arrested the night before the start of the Passover and be quickly crucified a few hours before the start of the Passover Sabbath. Thus, he would have to be brought down from the cross and buried in accordance with Jewish law, which did not permit unburied dead during the Sabbath. To hasten the process, Jesus admitted to Caiaphas that he was the Messiah. Schonfield agrees with Klausner that Jesus did not blaspheme against God, but committed a political crime against Rome. Fearing and anticipating a nationalistic demonstration, the Sanhedrin quickly turned Jesus over to Pilate on Friday morning, just as Jesus had desired. Pilate tried to save Jesus, Schonfield says, but the chief priests brought pressure to bear through the crowd within the praetorium courtyard, which went as far as to say to Pilate that if he freed Jesus, he was no friend of Ceasar, the Roman Emperor. He who claims to be king, the crowd shouted, opposes Ceasar. Becoming apprehensive, Pilate released Barabbas, condemned Jesus to death, and posted on the cross the words "Jesus the Nazorean, King of the Jews," as charged by the priests. He refused to change the words to "He said, I am king of the Jews," as the priests desired.[11]

Jesus all alone had carefully planned not only his crucifixion, but also his survival and recovery from the ordeal of the cross. Most likely, Schonfield says, he did not rely on an act of God alone to survive the ordeal of the cross, but he might have depended on the prophesies of Isaiah 53 and Psalms 2. He desired to be crucified on Friday, Schonfield asserts, in order to be taken down from the cross alive in a matter of a few hours, before the start of the Passover Sabbath that evening. Those crucified had to be buried before the Sabbath. Jesus was on the cross barely three hours, from a little after midday to about three o'clock in the afternoon. It took several days for a crucified man to die; a few hours could not have killed him. Because the Roman soldiers broke the bones of those crucified to hasten their death from shock and hemorrhage, if they were not already dead, or to confirm their death, Jesus, writes Schonfield, must have made previous arrangements with Joseph of Arimathaea to prevent breaking of his bones.

Joseph of Arimathaea, whose name is questionable, says Schonfield, is one of the great mysteries of the gospels. The gospels have very little to say about him except that he was wealthy and a member of the Sanhedrin. He suddenly appears on the scene, right after the crucifixion, with Nicodemus, another mysterious wealthy Jew and a member of the Sanhedrin, and then completely disappears from the New Testament records. He was probably, says Schonfield, a messianically-minded Pharisee whom Jesus had met through Nicodemus during his previous visit to Jerusalem.

Jesus, Schonfield hypothesizes, could have had assistance to help him survive the cross. He needed certain individuals who were members of the Sanhedrin, such as Joseph of Arimathaea, to give him information concerning the Sanhedrin's against him and also to advise him on procedures in political trials, relations between Sanhedrin and Pilate, and such other unfamiliar but pertinent matters. John tells us that Joseph was a secret disciple of Jesus, and Luke that he had not consented to the Jewish Council and the deed of the high priest. Evidently, writes Schonfield, Joseph had been greatly impressed by Jesus and was ready to cooperate with him and frustrate the intentions of the Sadducceean chief priests. He had property with a tomb and a garden near Golgotha, where Jesus was crucified. According to John (19:41), "in the place where he was crucified there was a garden and in the garden a new sepulchre, wherein never man yet laid." It is strongly suspected, therefore, that Jesus was crucified on Joseph's private property and that the crucifixion was a private one witnessed by the people, including the women, from "afar off" (Luke 23:49). Arrangements were made to have a drug administered to Jesus in the vinegar (sour wine) that was offered to him by an unnamed onlooker when Jesus said, "I am thirsty." This saying might have been the signal, Schonfield says, which Jesus derived from the prophetic words, "They gave me also gall for my meat; and in my thirst they gave me vinegar" (Psalms 69:21). Jesus drank it, fell unconscious, and immediately appeared to be dead (John 19:28-30; Mark 15:36-38; Matthew 27:48-50). According to anthropologist Michael J. Harweek, "wine made from the mandrake plant was used in Palestine to induce a deathlike state in persons who were being crucified."[12]

Joseph of Arimathaea would have had to act quickly to bring Jesus down from the cross. The unnamed onlooker, states Schonfield, right away informed Joseph of Jesus' state, and he quickly appeared before Pilate and requested to have Jesus' body taken down from the cross. As a member of the Sanhedrin, Joseph would have had standing permission to visit Pilate. Astonished to hear that Jesus was already dead, Pilate asked the centurion in charge of the crucifixion if this were true, and upon receiving a positive answer, he granted Joseph his request. Although the Roman soldiers broke the legs of the two thieves crucified with Jesus, they did not break Jesus' bones because he was already dead, something which they confirmed by thrusting a lance into his side and perceiving the flow of blood and water. This particular incident of the lance must have been doubted by individuals, since in John (19:34-37) an eyewitness had to avouch for its authenticity, writes Schonfield; and it might have been recorded only to confirm, as John indicates, that Old Testament prophecies were again fulfilled. The reported flow of blood from his wound reveals that Jesus was still alive, says Schonfield. However, if he were pierced by a lance, depending on how badly he was wounded, the chances for his recovery would have been severely diminished.[13]

Part of Jesus' plan, which was unknown to his disciples, must have been that he be taken out of the tomb and revived at the first opportunity. In reconstructing a hypothetical tomb scene, Schonfield writes that Jesus might have been brought out of the tomb and regained consciousness long enough to beg his friends present to tell his disciples that he would meet them in Galilee after his resurrection. However, he died from the unexpected wound in his side. Rather than return the body to the tomb, his friends buried it somewhere outside. Jesus, Schonfield says, might have understood that he would die in spite of all his secret plans, interpreting Isaiah 53, "He made his grave with the wicked and with the rich in his deaths [plural]," in this sense. He might have forseen, therefore, two deaths and two burials. Schonfield dismisses the story of the soldiers sent to guard the tomb of Jesus, recorded only by Matthew, as too fantastic and of later origin. However, he asserts that the man whom Mary Magdalene (Mary of Magdala) saw near the tomb was not Jesus, but, perhaps, that same unknown man who had given Jesus the drugged vinegar while on the cross and had probably also assisted in taking his body into and out of the tomb and in burying it when Jesus died. It was this man who had now attempted to deliver to Madgalene Jesus' message of his brief period of consciousness and who was mistaken for Jesus by Mary Magdalene because she was now distraught and unbalanced. However, Schonfield also indicates that the young man in a white robe in Mark's gospel (16:1-7), who met the women in the tomb and told them that Jesus was risen and that he would meet his disciples in Galilee, was that same man. Later on, as the story of the resurrection progressed, he became an angel, meaning messenger (Matt. 28:1-7), and then two angels (Luke 24:1-8; John 20:10-13). The stranger who talked to two of the disciples on the road to Emmaus and who was recognized as Jesus only after he briefly sat to eat with them was the same unknown man (Luke 24:13-32).

It is rather doubtful that anyone saw Jesus after his death on the cross. The gospels are ambiguous. Peter and John, the beloved disciple, saw only the empty tomb, writes Schonfield, and then John remembered that Jesus had said he would be resurrected. Both Luke and John report Jesus' appearance to his disciples in Jerusalem, where he reveals his wounds to them and eats with them, but this account is questionable. Matthew suggests that in Jerusalem the disciples remained unconvinced of Jesus' resurrection, but trusted that Jesus would reveal himself to them in Galilee, the appointed place. Even John (21:1-13) indicates that later on, at the Sea of Tiberias, when the disciples saw a man on the shore from the boat, they did not know that it was Jesus. They merely presumed that it was he. "None of the disciples dared ask him, Who are you? knowing it was the Master." However, says Schonfield, that is exactly what they did not know. Most likely, it was the same man who talked to the women at the tomb and to Mary Magdalene and to the two disciples on the road to Emmaus, and who was now seeking to make sure that Peter and the others had received the message of the resurrection. The disciples saw someone, but not Jesus, only a stranger who fulfilled their expectations.[14]

Although there has been and still is a controversy over Jesus' death and a variety of hypothetical explanations have been proposed, biblical scholarship has revealed that the Romans must undoubtedly have crucified Jesus for political reasons. The Jewish leaders, most of whom did not want any disturbance lest they feel the wrath of Roman retribution, delivered Jesus to Pontius Pilate. Jesus was a religious, social, and political agitator who attacked as hypocrites the Scribes and Pharisees, the members of the Jewish establishment, accusing them of religious dishonesty and moral deprivation. His religious criticisms and his aim at a new social order of equality and morality (albeit non-violent) could not but have irritated the Jewish hierarchy and have made them suspicious.[15] But by being proclaimed by the masses as King of Israel in the streets of Jerusalem, while riding on a donkey, and by posing and confessing to being the Messiah, the liberator of Palestine, Jesus united the Jewish leaders and the Roman governor against him in an effort to destroy him before he could cause a revolution and the slaughter of many Jews. The Zealot disturbance in Jerusalem at about the same time could only have excited the Jewish and Roman leaders, who directed their fear and anger toward Jesus. Schonfield's hypothesis that Jesus alone plotted his crucifixion is merely a hypothesis. Jesus did not have to plot in order to be crucified. His attacks on the Jewish leadership and the money changers in the Temple, and Jewish and Roman suspicion that he sought to stage a revolution to take over as the Messiah, the King of Israel, as proclaimed by the masses, were sufficient to bring about his crucifixion. Whether he personally plotted to fulfill the Old Testament prophecies concerning the Messiah or whether these acts of fulfillment were partly filled in or thought out later by the evangelists is debatable. In any case, if Jesus had plotted anything, it would have had to have been his return to his disciples alive and well after surviving the ordeal of the cross. What happened to Jesus following his crucifixion is the greatest mystery of biblical scholarship.

The Mysterious and Astounding Resurrection

The resurrection of Jesus, which attests to his divinity, has been questioned by many modern scholars. One reason is the difficulty of accepting such a miracle as genuine, but scholars have also been led to doubt by the accounts of the gospels. Great suspicion has been aroused by the sudden appearance in the gospels of Joseph of Arimathaea and Nicodemus, both secret disciples of Christ, wealthy members of the Sanhedrin, who took charge of the burial of Jesus, and also by the fact that the Romans did not break Jesus' bones to assure his death. It is suspected that they merely pierced Jesus' side, verifying his death by the flow of blood and water, which scholars claim, like Schonfield, reveals the opposite, that Jesus was still alive. His blood was still flowing, his heart, therefore, was still beating, and rigormortis had not set in. Also, as Schonfield indicated, the gospels are not in agreement concerning Jesus' resurrection.

Scholars have found many discrepancies, which are evidently the product not only of the evangelists, but also of later additions to the gospels. The gospel of Mark contains later additions by editors that any careful reader can detect. As A. Powell Davies writes, Mark's gospel ends rather abruptly, when the young white-robed man in the tomb announces to the women, Mary of Magdala, Mary, the mother of James, and Salome, that Jesus is resurrected, and asks them to tell Peter and the other disciples that Jesus will be waiting for them in Galilee (Mark 16:1-8). The rest of Mark's section (16:9-20) is universally accepted as a later addition. In this added section, Jesus appears to Mary of Magdala, to two disciples as they are walking, and to the eleven disciples as they are eating. He admonishes them for their "incredulity and dullness" for not believing in his resurrection, tells them to preach the "Good News" to all creation, and ascends to heaven. The gospel then continues with the story of the women delivering the message to Peter and his companions as instructed by the young man in the tomb, something that should have been stated earlier; the discrepancy reveals that someone tampered with the original.

Because the Jews claimed that Jesus' disciples stole his body, A. Powell Davies says, it became necessary for the other evangelists to elaborate on the story and to claim that Jesus had been seen and, therefore, had been resurrected. Matthew (28:1-20) has an earthquake take place and an angel descends from heaven to roll away the stone. He brings in witnesses to the resurrection, a Roman patrol, who see the angel and fall to the ground in terror. The young man in white robes becomes in Matthew the angel whose face shines as lightning and who has garments white as snow. Matthew mentions the two Marys, but not Salome, and the angel gives them the same message to tell the disciples that Jesus will meet them in Galilee. As they run excitedly away from the tomb, Jesus meets them and confirms the angel's message. The Roman soldiers run the the chief priests, who bribe them to say that Jesus' body was stolen by his disciples (an implausible story), and the disciples meet Jesus on a mountain in Galilee. Although some of the disciples are in doubt, Jesus speaks to them and tells them to convert, baptize, and teach all nations; and says that he will be with them till the end of time.

Luke (24:1-53), Davies says, attempts to make the story of the resurrection even more convincing. He does not mention an earthquake which cannot be accepted as resurrection evidence. Nor does he make any reference to Galilee, since he wants Christianity to begin at Jerusalem, the capital, better known to the Gentiles than Galilee. Therefore, in Luke, the two Marys and Joanna (not Salome) go to the tomb and meet not one but two men in dazzling garments, who tell them about Christ's resurrection but say nothing about a meeting in Galilee. There is also no mention of Jesus meeting these women. The women tell the eleven disciples what they heard, but the disciples do not believe them. However, on that same day, two of these disciples meet Jesus on the road to Emmaus village and talk to him, but something keeps them from seeing who it is. Even though Jesus converses with them and explains that the Messiah was to suffer as predicted by the prophets before being glorified, the two disciples do not realize who he is until he sits to eat with them and breaks and gives them the bread. As they recognize him, he quickly disappears. The two then hasten to Jerusalem, and as they are telling the other disciples what occurred, Jesus appears before them. He asks his disciples to touch him because they can not believe their own eyes, and he even eats a piece of fish before them. Jesus then explains to them that the prophecies have been fulfilled through his death and resurrection. He commands them to proclaim the message of salvation to all nations and to remain in Jerusalem until he sends to them his "Father's promised gift." Then he leads them out of Jerusalem as far as Bethany, blesses them and parts from them; while the disciples return to Jerusalem and praise God.[16]

Charles Foster Kent indicates that discrepancies are also to be found in the gospels concerning Jesus' meeting with his disciples after his crucifixion. Mark's gospel simply ends with Mary Magdalene, Mary the mother of James, and Salome receiving the message of the resurrection from the young man in the tomb, and with the comment that they were not able to convey this message to anyone because they were afraid. Both Mark and Matthew have Jesus going to Galilee, but

Luke places the resurrection stories in Jerusalem. Luke also defends the Pharisaic position, unacceptable to the Sadducees and the pagan Greeks, that the spirits of the dead will return to earth to repossess their physical bodies and that there will be a physical resurrection of the dead. Thus, in Luke's gospel, Jesus is able to become a physical being. He walks, eats, and is touched by his disciples.[17]

Alfred Firman Loisy maintains that Jesus has been carried by myths to the highest point in history. He dismisses the gospel narratives concerning Christ's arrest and trial, his burial by Joseph of Arimathaea and Nicodemus, and the story of the empty tomb as Christian inventions based on arbitrarily selected Old Testament prophecies and intended to satisfy Christian tradition. Only one genuine historical event is to be found in the gospels, says Loisy, and that is, the crucifixion and death of Jesus in agony without any witnesses to his passion, with the exception of his executioners, who also buried him. Because the disciples had fled to Galilee following Jesus' arrest, the evangelists bring in Joseph of Arimathaea and Nicodemus to bury him and the women of Galilee as witnesses to his burial, the empty tomb and resurrection. But gospel discrepancies concerning the disciples' whereabouts after the crucifixion, either Galilee or Jerusalem, reveal that the disciples had not remained in Jerusalem during their master's death. Jesus' disciples, writes Loisy, had only visions or revelations of Jesus' resurrection by which their faith and courage were rekindled in hopes of the future establishment of God's Kingdom with Jesus' second coming. Nothing is impossible to zealots, says Loisy. Rudolph Karl Bultmann agrees that the stories of the empty tomb, the resurrection and the ascension were traditional legends which were incorporated into the gospels. Matthew and Luke strengthened the mythical side of Mark's gospel by relating the miracle stories of Christ's birth and the resurrection. They used an historical tradition available to them but not to Mark. Bultmann finds no biographical or historical interest in the gospels, only indoctrination.[18]

Biblical scholars contend that discrepancies in the resurrection story are even greater when the Synoptic gospels are compared with John's gospel. In John (20:1-9), Mary of Magdala (Magdalene) alone goes to the tomb on Sunday morning, and upon finding the tomb empty, she runs and tells Simon (Peter) and John, "the other disciple, the one who Jesus Loved." Both disciples go and enter the tomb (although John hesitates and waits for Peter to go in first). Until now, John's gospel says, "they had not understood the scriptures, which showed that he must rise from the dead." After Peter and John leave, Mary Magdalene, who has followed the two to the tomb, remains weeping. She sees two angels in white sitting on either side of the tomb where Jesus had lain. While she converses with the angels, Jesus stands before her and speaks to her. But Mary, thinking he is the gardener, did not recognize him right away. When she does Jesus asks her, without any further explanation, not to cling to him because he has not ascended to the Father. Mary goes to the disciples and gives them the Lord's message that he is ascending to his Father. There is nothing in Jesus' message about meeting his disciples in Galilee. Thus, John appears to agree with Luke. Late that same Sunday, in the evening, Jesus appears before his disciples, who are behind locked doors, and shows them his wounds. A week later, he reappears to tell doubting Thomas, whom he had not seen the first time, to touch his wounds with his fingers and to believe (20:10-19).

John tells us that Jesus performed many other signs before his disciples, but that John did not record them. He merely wrote down a few so that his readers would believe that Jesus was the Son of God. Then, without any explanation, he shifts (21:1) from Jerusalem north to the Sea of Tiberias (Galilee), where Peter, Thomas "the Twin," and the other disciples, including John (Jesus' beloved disciple) are fishing in their boat at night, not able to catch anything. In the morning, they see Jesus on the shore, but do not recognize him until Jesus tells them to try fishing again, which they do, catching more than enough fish. Then the disciples sit and eat with him. However, John states (21:12-13): "None of the disciples dared to ask 'Who are you?' They knew it was the Lord." Why the disciples were not sure that he was Jesus, John does not explain. If they knew he was the Lord, why would there be any doubt any need to ask? Although, Schonfield maintains, as mentioned earlier, that the disciples did not really know, perhaps Jesus had undergone such a drastic transformation after his resurrection that he looked different. In any case, biblical scholarship maintains that John's chapter 21 is a later addition and not genuine. According to Rudolph Schnackenburg, this chapter predates the previous chapter on the resurrection and cannot be accepted as the intended continuation by the same author. Since it also reveals the importance of Peter, whom Jesus asks three times if he (Peter) loves him, and Peter's future martyrdom, the whole chapter was evidently written from the viewpoint of the Church editors who compiled it. It appears that critical scholars are right, says Schnackenburg, because this chapter reveals an adjustment of the claims of Rome for Peter and of the Church of Ephesus for the beloved disciple, John, who is also mentioned in this chapter.[19]

Floy Vivian Filson says that we can be sure that Jesus died, and was buried, and the disciples saw him. Whether they saw him in Jerusalem or in Galilee (a strong case can be made for Galilee), they did see him. Peter and the other disciples saw Jesus, writes Filson, and he appeared to them in a glorified body, as the gospels testify. He last appeared to Paul, as I Corinthians indicates. Early tradition confirms that Jewish opposition neither found his body nor denied the empty tomb, which attests to the truth concerning the empty tomb and the resurrection. However, how they saw him, Filson says, in what form, physical or spiritual, is debatable. The encounters in which the disciples failed to recognize him at once (Matt. 28:17; Luke 24:16; John 20:14, 21:4), Jesus' appearance in various places and mysterious disappearances (Luke 24:31, 36; John 20:19, 26), and Paul's clear argument that there are "heavenly bodies and earthly bodies" that are different in splendor (I Corinthians 15) are all indicative of Jesus' changed form of being, after his resurrection. Jesus was able to make his presence real to his followers and to communicate with them, states Filson, but free of the limitations of a flesh-and-blood body. Nevertheless, Filson admits that in Galatians 1:12 (a first-hand account, not a second as in Acts 9 and 22), Paul writes that he had only a revelation of Jesus, implying an experience that was internal and subjective.[20]

The question has risen, therefore, as to whether the disciples saw Jesus physically at all or whether they merely had a spiritual revelation. It is difficult not to accept a bodily resurrection because all the disciples saw Jesus and were evidently adamant about his resurrection. St. Paul might have had only a spiritual revelation of Jesus, but he states in I Corinthians 15:12-15 that Christ was certainly raised from the dead and that this constitutes the foundation upon which Christianity rests. In other words, Paul might not have physically seen Jesus, but the resurrection did take place as the disciples had said. Nevertheless, there have been at least three different scholarly interpretations of Jesus' resurrection. The first contends that Jesus did not die on the cross, but was hurriedly taken down and placed in the tomb, where he was revived during the night. After he was left alone, he became strong enough to roll away the stone blocking the entrance and to tell the women who came in the dark to embalm him that he would meet his disciples at Galilee. At Galilee, he bade his disciples farewell and died on the lone hilltop where he took leave of them. A second interpretation maintains that Jesus survived death and went far away from Palestine; and a third, that Peter was so emotionally distraught that he had a hallucination and thought he actually saw Jesus. He convinced the other disciples of this, but did not have any subsequent hallucinations.[21]

The story of Jesus' bodily ascension to heaven is not taken seriously by most scholars. None of the evangelists mention the ascension. Matthew and John say nothing about it. Matthew (28:16-20) has the disciples meeting Jesus at a mountain in Galilee, where Jesus commands them to make all nations his disciples and assures them that he will be with them till the end of time, and nothing further. John only records some of Jesus' appearances after his resurrection, and makes no mention of an ascension. Mark alone writes of the ascension, but only in the later addition (16:9-20), which is out of text and questionable, as already mentioned. It is obvious that Mark ended his gospel with the women delivering to Peter and his companions the message about a meeting in Galilee with Jesus, and with the comment: "Afterwards Jesus himself sent out by them from east to west the sacred and imperishable message of eternal salvation" (16:21). Luke (24:50-53) merely terminated his gospel by writing that Jesus led his disciples from Jerusalem as far as Bethany "and in the act of blessing he parted from them. And they returned to Jerusalem with great joy, and spent all the time in the temple praising God." The Acts of the Apostles (1:1-11), which traditionally is attributed to Luke and was written about the early second century A.D., does record that Jesus, after conversing with his disciples on the hill called Olivet near Jerusalem, "was lifted up, and a cloud removed him from their sight." And, as the disciples were intently gazing up, two men in white stood beside them and told them that Jesus would return in the same way. The story of the ascension, therefore, was obviously a later story of the Christian tradition, perhaps inspired by the story of the ascension of the prophet Elijah; and what happened to Jesus after his crucifixion alive or dead is one of the great mysteries.

Contemporary Doubts Concerning Jesus' Divinity

Biblical scholarship today is rather skeptical concerning Jesus' divinity and resurrection. Hans Kung of Tubingen, Germany, a Roman Catholic priest and theologian, in his best seller *Christ Sein* (published in 1976 in English with the title *On Being a Christian*), reinterpreted the dogmas of the Church's early ecumenical councils on Christ's nature, which he finds outdated, to meet today's prevailing mentality. He holds that Jesus' divinity simply implies that God was present in Jesus and revealed himself through Christ's work. By proclaiming that the Son "pre-existed" with the Father from eternity, Kung says, the Church Fathers merely meant to substantiate God's unique call made in and with Jesus. For Kung, Jesus had the same resurrection as every man who dies and goes to God because he has been saved. No physical resurrection took place contrary to the laws of nature, only a spiritual one in God's world. In 1978, the German Catholic bishops issued a warning that Kung's book created a "distressing insecurity of faith" and that Kung had failed to reveal how his Christology (theological interpretation of Christ) could be reconciled to the Nicene and Chalcedon creeds that Jesus is the pre-existing, eternal Son of God, one in being with the Father. Kung replied that same year with the publication of *Um Nights Als Die Warheit* (Nothing but the Truth). In this work, Kung tries to prove by documenting the dispute that he is the victim of an inquisition. Although he accepts the Chalcedon formula, he asserts that it must be interpreted in the light of modern scholarship, which holds that Jesus did not proclaim himself as the eternal Son of God, nor did the early Christians accept him as such. In addition, Kung maintains that the early dogmas were faulty because they were based on Greek concepts of man and nature that are now outdated. Kung says that he and other contemporary theologians, including Karl Rahner, started their Christology "from below" with Jesus the man and worked upward toward his divinity, a more sound approach, while the Church councils started "from above" with concepts about God's essence.[22]

The Church Fathers of the first two ecumenical councils at Nicea (325 and 381 A.D.) formulated by a simple majority vote the Nicene Creed, which proclaimed Jesus as "eternally begotten of the Father . . . light of light, true God of true God . . . of one essence with the Father." These councils took place because of disputes led by Arius, a priest at Alexandria, Egypt, who questioned Christ's divine nature, professing that Christ was created by God and, therefore, was man and not God in nature. Even though the Church bishops denounced Arius as a heretic, a deviate from true doctrine, and forced him into exile, Arius had many followers, including Constantine, the first Christian Roman emperor, and his sons. Arius' beliefs survived on among the German Goths into the 700's. A new controversy erupted in 428, caused by the Patriarch of Constantinople, Nestorius (428-431 A.D.), who claimed that Mary was not the "Theotokos," the mother of God, because Mary was only human. Jesus was the instrument of divinity but not divine in essence. He had two distinct natures, the human and the divine. However, Jesus, according to Nestorius, so closely united in himself these two natures that they could almost be regarded as one. The Council of Ephesus of 431 A.D. condemned Nestorius' teachings and forced Nestorius and his followers to go to the East, where they eventually established the Nestorian Church of Persia under the leadership of the Katholicos. In the 1500's, one group called the Chaldean Christians transferred their allegiance to the Pope of Rome and in 1830 united with the Roman Catholic Church. In 451 A.D., the Council of Chalcedon further clarified Christ's nature, adding that, although Jesus had two natures, divine and human, they merged without confusion or change in one person of the Holy Trinity.

Kung is only one representative of the New Christology, which first appeared at the University of Nijmegen, The Netherlands, in 1966. There, an Augustinian monk, the late Ansfield Hulsbosch, issued a challenge to the Council of Chalcedon, announcing that the Church should "no longer speak of a union of the divine and human nature in one pre-existing person." Jesuit Piet Schoonenberg, one of the Dutch movement's two leading figures and Hulbosch's colleague, in his 1969 work *The Christ*, also rejected Christ's two natures and accepted instead "God's complete presence in the human person Jesus Christ." Another Dutch liberal, Dominican Edward Schillenbeeckh, whose first volume on Christology was published in English in 1978, describes Jesus as a human being who gradually grew closer to God.[23]

Some proponents of the New Christology have been even more antagonistic toward the belief in Christ's divinity than these individuals. Jacque Pahier, a Dominican at the Institute Catholique in Paris, declared that it is absurd to say "that God makes himself into man. God cannot be anything other than God." Father Pierre-Marie Beaude of the Center for Theological Studies in Caen maintains that the early Church bishops had to "murder their founding father Jesus" to grow into maturity. Another Frenchman, father Michel Pinchon, editor of the magazine *Jesus*, writes that he was liberated from the "idolatry" of Jesus, who "does not present himself as an end or as an absolute." In Spain, Jose-Ramon Guerrero, director of catechetics at Madrid's Pastoral Institute and author of the 1976 book *El Otro Jesus* (The Other Jesus), and Jose Ignacio Gonzales Faus of the Jesuit theological school at Barcelona both rejected Jesus' divinity. So did Jon Sobrino, a German-trained Basque professor at the Universidad Jose Simeon Canos in El Salvador, in his *Christology at the Crossroads* (English edition, June, 1978), which is considered the most thorough study of Christ's nature based on Latin America's "liberation theology." Guerrero says that

Jesus was "a man elected and sent by God, and has been constituted by God as the Son of God." Faus insists that Jesus was not aware of his divinity and revealed traits of doubt and ignorance that are quite human; while Sobrino indicates that Jesus was mistaken in expecting the imminent appearance of God's Kingdom. Only gradually, says Sobrino, did Jesus become the Son of God, revealing "the way to the Father, not the Father himself." This view is no different from that of Arianism and Sobrino admits that it sounds like the old heresy of Adoptionism (that Jesus was eventually adopted by God), but he is convinced that it is in agreement with the Catholic Church's dogmas.[24]

Catholics are not alone among Christians in attacking Christ's divinity. Seven British theologians, six Anglicans and one member of the United Reform Church, in a collection of essays titled *The Myth of God Incarnate* have also attacked Jesus' divinity and the Nicene Creed. Among these contributors is Oxford Theologian Maurice Wiles, for five years chairman of the Church of England's influential Doctrinal Commission. The authors of this work dismiss Christ's own statements about his divinity, contained especially in John's gospel, as later interpretations rather than actual quotations. Since the divinity of Jesus has been attacked from the left for a century and a half, they make no claim to originality. But their work aroused controversy in England because of the general acceptance of Christ's divine incarnation and because of the importance of some of these theologians.[25] In the United States, Robert S. Alley, a Southern Baptist theologian and religion chairman at the University of Richmond, was suddenly transferred to another department after he told a group of atheists at a meeting that "Jesus never really claimed to be God, nor to be related to him as son."[26]

Jesus' divinity, of course, has many defenders. One of this century's greatest Protestant theologians, Karl Barth of Switzerland, has consistently maintained that God is a wholly other being who can be known by His self-revelation in the person of Jesus, as recorded in Scripture. Searching for God through human experience, Barth warns, one can only discover an idol and not God. The Catholic Church has its traditionalist proponents of Christ's divinity, including the Vatican and the Rev. Walter Kasper, a former colleague of Kung at Tubingen. In 1972, the Vatican's Congregation for the Doctrine of the Faith, in an attack aimed primarily at Schoonenberg, declared to be error the theory that God was only "present in the highest degree in the human person Jesus," including the version in which Jesus is "God" in the sense that in "his human person God is supremely present." Kasper, in his 1974

work titled *Jesus the Christ* (English edition, 1976), attacks Kung,
pointing out that the Church councils did not distort the Gospel with
Greek concepts, but rather "dehellenized" the Church, using Greek
philosophical terms to express beliefs that "shattered all of its
perspectives." Kasper does accept many findings of recent biblical
critics, but insists that the Church council dogmas are truths that Jesus
taught about himself as God, and any Christology developed solely
"from below," starting with Jesus as a man, is bound to fail. Kasper also
writes that the dogma upholding Jesus' divinity was a part of the earliest
material in the New Testament. Therefore, the Council of Chalcedon
correctly declared what the New Testament teaches that in Christ, "God
himself has entered human history."[27]

English theologians and the Anglican Church have also vigorously
defended the divinity of Jesus. The semi-official *Church Times* attacked
The Myth of God Incarnate as "a notably unconvincing contribution to
the cause of unbelief," while the *Daily Telegraph* referred to this work
as "a failure of ecclesiastical statesmanship" that will confuse the faithful.
The Archbishop of Canterbury thinks the book "has made more hubbub
than it is worth," and refused to allow a debate on it in a church General
Synod of July, 1977. However, the best rebuttal has come from Anglican
Evangelical Michael Green in his work *The Truth of God Incarnate*
(1977), which presents theological views by contributors from various
denominations. In it, Anglican Bishop Stephen Neill laments that the
fundamental problem of the liberals' theology is that it merely offers us
"a God who loved us a little, but not enough to become one of us."
Oxford Theologian John Macquarrie says that "Christian doctrines are
so closely interrelated that if you take one away, several others tend to
collapse;" while Roman Catholic Bishop-Theologian Christopher Butler
contends that Christianity is doomed, if the incarnation of God is
denied.[28]

Secularism's Attack on God and Jesus' Divinity

In the United States, a group of eighteen Christian theologians of
nine major denominations met in 1975 at the Hartford Seminary
Foundation in Connecticut, where they discussed and denounced thirteen
"false and debilitating" theses including those of Harvey Cox (*The
Secular City*), situation ethicist Joseph Fletcher, Britain's Bishop John
Robinson (*Honest to God*), and Catholic theologians who give the Bible
a Marxist reinterpretation, popularizing the ideas of the late Teilhard

de Chardin and "liberation theologians." In a statement of 1,150 words titled "Appeal for Theological Affirmation," they attacked ideas that undermine transcendence and seek to humanize God as though he were produced by man. Some of these false ideas are that modern thought is superior to all past forms of understanding reality, that religious language refers to human experience and nothing else (God being humanity's noblest creation), that Jesus can be understood only in terms of contemporary models of humanity, that an emphasis on God's transcendence is at least a hindrance to, and perhaps incompatible with, Christian social concern and action, and that the struggle for a better humanity will bring about the Kingdom of God. Exasperated by the influence of scientific rationalism and socialism, the Rev. Richard Newhaus and fellow Lutheran Peter Berger, iconoclastic author and sociologist at Rutgers University (New Jersey), wrote the original draft of this denunciation, sent it to churchmen for their reactions and summoned the Hartford meeting. The view from Hartford is that Christianity will not be able to sustain its attack of social evils or of anything else unless it first retains its belief in God's transcendence. As the Hartford Eighteen declared: "We did not invent God; God invented us."[29]

One reason for the rise of secularism and its emphasis on Jesus the man rather than on God has been the fact that some contemporary theologians themselves have attacked God's existence. The late Paul Johannes Tillich, for example, who taught first in Germany and then in America, declared such terms as God, Christ, Resurrection as symbols that must not be mistaken for the unknowable and transcendent things for which they stand, "the God above God." Christ and his resurrection are symbols of higher truths unknown to man, and the same, Tillich says, applies to all doctrines. On that basis, however, all doctrines evaporate into thin air. In his three-volume *Systematic Theology,* Tillich deals with Being (man's estranged actual nature) to which the theological answer is God and the triumph of God's Kingdom through the efforts of all good people of all religions and views, theists and atheists. Such views, however, can only lead to ethical humanism and the abandonment of salvation through Jesus. Tillich's starting point was from below, the human condition (situation or existence), and in this sense he was an existentialist philosopher. The key to salvation, he says, is courage, the courage to be, to exist in the face of life's uncertainties, dangers, and the dread possibilities of nonbeing. God, he maintains, was the "ground of being," the "ultimate concern" and sin is an estrangement from union with God. These themes recur in Tillich's popular books, such as *The Protestant Era*, *The Courage to Be*, and *The New Being*, in which he also bemoans man's attempt to find comfort in such idolatries as status, sex, nationalism, communism or even the church.[30]

Although Tillich humanized salvation and made God and the resurrection symbols, a small group of radical theologians of the 1960's, such as J. J. Altizer of Emory University, William Hamilton of Colgate Rochester Divinity School, and Paul Van Buren of Temple University, agreed with the German nineteenth century philosopher, Friederich Nietzsche, that God is dead, killed by self-centered striving man who no longer needs Him. Less radical theologians define God as one who touches man's emotions and influences man's mind, but they admit that God, in the image of a man sitting in heaven, is dead. Secularization, as a rebellion against the Judaeo-Christian God of faith, a personal God who created the world and sustains it with his love, has been on the rise for a long time. Harvey Cox of the Harvard Divinity School defines it in *The Secular City* as "the loosing of the world from religious and quasi-religious understandings of itself, the dispelling of all closed world views, the breaking of all supernatural myths and sacred symbols." Certain intellectuals slowly came to realize that they no longer needed God. In his book, *The Death of God*, Gabriel Vahanian of Syracuse University hints that medieval Christianity, by imposing its tenets and spirit on a culture, through art, politics, and even economics, unconsciously made God part of that culture; and when this milieu changed, belief in God was undermined. As Dominican Theologian Edward Schillenbeeckh says, "God has disappeared because of the image of him that the church used for many, many ages."[31]

A theological evolution has been taking place since the Middle Ages. At its worst the image of God propagated by the medieval Church was of a being who performs miracles, explains the world's mysteries and seems to have somewhat more interest in punishing men than in rewarding them. Not that medieval theologians were not controversial. During the faith versus reason controversy of the twelfth and thirteenth centuries, western theologians vigorously debated whether to follow the truths of the Bible and the Church or the dictates of their reason, especially the reason of the Greek philosopher Aristotle, who was rediscovered during the latter part of the twelfth century. The Dominican Friar Thomas Aquinas, in his *Summa Theologiae*, reconciled a great part of Aristotle's philosophy to the truths of Christianity and rationally defended the Bible and doctrines of the Church on the basis of past authorities; Aquinas' theology became official and his views were generally accepted. The rediscovery of pagan Greek knowledge during the Italian Renaissance of the fifteenth and sixteenth centuries and the dissemination throughout Europe of Greek ideas, with their emphasis on philosophy or rational inquiry, culminated in the eighteenth-century enlightenment, which rejected the divine-right theory that government and law come from above. The Age of Enlightenment espoused ethics, seeking to formulate sound laws by reason than revelation, and gave rise to Deism, a religion adopted by many intellectuals, including Thomas Jefferson and Benjamin Franklin. Deism declared that God is impersonal and outside the universe and rejected divine revelation, miracles and the Bible as the word of God.

Attempts to prove the existence of God by reason are no longer given serious consideration. Thomas Aquinas' five rational proofs for the existence of God, presented in his *Summa Theologiae* of the thirteenth century, have been rationally refuted and are no longer acceptable for many intellectuals. In addition, since the eighteenth century Enlightenment, there have been atheistic writers in philosophy and literature, from English empiricist David Hume and German materialists Ludwig Feuerbach and Frederick Nietzsche, to French existentialists and novelists Jean Paul Sartre and Albert Camus, and playwrights Samuel Becket and Michelangelo Antonioni, and many others who have denounced belief in God and have accentuated life's futility and hopelessness. Christianity's general acceptance of slavery, poverty, and factory slums and its general alliance with the rich and powerful helped to give rise to such nineteenth century atheists as Karl Marx and the anarchist Pierre Joseph Proudhon, who denounced God and religion, declared God the opium of the people, and called on man to liberate himself from the fetters of the clergy and the rich.

Although the Pope and Christian leaders in general have denounced communism and, in the recent past, socialism, unionism, and liberalism, today they are confronted with an even more formidable contender in shaping man's ideas and the most important agent in giving rise to secularization: science. The scientific method has helped man to explain much of nature and the universe, and thus to eliminate the godly mysteries of the past and man's fear of the unknown. In previous ages, it was the priest or the philosopher who held the leadership and the prestige in the field of ideas; now it is the scientist who has the method and the facts. Knowledge enables scientists to predict with a high degree of accuracy the course of the material world and to master nature for man's benefit; such progress eliminates for many the need for God. In addition, genetic engineering is enabling man to become master of himself and to hope for physical immortality, erasing the need for an immortal, non-physical soul and God.

Aided by developments in biblical scholarship and by the rise of secularism, modern writers of fiction have produced numerous imaginary biographies of Jesus depicting him as a good, incomparable and noble man, a human hero and a teacher of morals, but not as God. In 1863, the French writer Ernest Renan produced a best seller in *The Life of Jesus*, which caused an international controversy because it depicted Jesus as a great man rather than a miracle wonder. The book made a great impact on the public and influenced even Albert Schweitzer. *The Brook Kerith*, a fictionalized account of Jesus that appeared in 1916, written by the Anglo-Irish novelist George Moore, depicted Jesus as a man who survived the cross and was nursed back to health by Joseph of Arimathaea. It too caused a considerable scandal, as did D. H. Lawrence's *The Man who Died*, which had a similar theme. In 1946, Robert Graves produced a fictional portrait of Jesus who survived the cross in *King Jesus*, and in 1954, Nikos Kazantzakis, the Nobel-prize winning Greek author, humanized Jesus in his novel *The Last Temptation*, which caused a great disturbance. It was made into a motion picture (1988) and produced controversy. In it, Jesus, while dying on the cross, has a vision of how wonderful it might have been had he married his beloved Mary Magdalene and fathered children by her.[32] However, a Christ who is not divine cannot be any more important than other great historical figures, such as Socrates, Buddha, or even Leo Tolstoy, the famous Russian novelist. Rather than be confronted with such a dilemma and risk losing their faith most Christians seem to prefer to continue with the traditional divine revelation, and many conservative Christians, fundamentalists and others, believe in the relevance and true meaning of the Holy Scriptures. As the modern novelist John Updike stated it in the beginning of his poem, *Seven Stanzas at Easter*:

> Make no mistake: if He rose at all
>   it was as His body;
> if the cells' dissolution did not reverse,
>   the molecules reknit, the amino
>   acids rekindle,
> the Church will fall.[33]

It is apparent, however, that many Christians, even theologians and church leaders, have difficulty accepting biblical truths, especially Jesus' divinity. The resurrection of Jesus is one of the most controversial subjects, even for many who express belief in God, and the main reason for this is New Testament inconsistencies. Even though the disciples of Christ professed to have seen Jesus after his crucifixion, much doubt still exists and many questions are being asked as to what really did happen to Jesus. Did he die or not, and if so, what happened to his body? Was he resurrected or not, and if so, where did he go? If he could eat and drink, did he still have his physical body to nourish, and did he therefore remain on earth a while longer, especially since the ascension appears improbable? Is it possible that Jesus' body may still be with us, perhaps entombed in some unknown land where he lived out the rest of his life? To consider these questions, we must now turn to the Muslims and the eastern tradition which present us with surprisingly different answers.

3. Islam, the Ahmadiya Sect and Rozabal, the Tomb of Yuz Asaf (Jesus)

The Koran and Muhammad

Christian disagreements and polemics concerning the nature and resurrection of Jesus have given considerable aid not only to the Jews, but also to the Muslims (those having submitted to God's will), who have not accepted his resurrection or divinity. The Muslims, who accept that God produced the Koran (Qu'ran), their holy book, through the prophet Muhammad (ca. 570-632 A.D.), profess that the Koran (literally "recitation") confirms and replaces all earlier revealed books produced by a series of messengers of God from Adam through Abraham to Moses and Jesus. Muhammad is the last of these messengers, the "Seal of the Prophets."

The Koran, which is considered a masterpiece of Arabic writing, proclaims the religion of the Muslims, called Islam, apparently meaning submission or resignation to God (Allah in Arabic). It discusses God (the merciful and compassionate) and man, sin and salvation, angels and devils, paradise and hell, the resurrection of the dead and judgment day, but also the Jinn, both good and bad spirits created of fire. It is composed of one hundred and eleven chapters, or suras, written at Mecca and Medina in Saudi Arabia. The prophet Muhammad was born and raised in pagan Mecca, but his revelations from God (Allah), which he began to receive around the age of forty, were not accepted by the Meccans. In 622 (the year of the Hegira or Flight), he was forced to flee north to Medina where he won many followers, raised an army, defeated and exiled the local Jews, and eventually forced Mecca to accept his religion. In the beginning, before each revelation, Muhammad, who was sensitive to tastes, smells, and sounds, underwent a frightening ordeal. Before each revelation, he would have an attack of fever, whence he would turn red in the face, roll on the ground, and scream. Then he would break out in sweat (whereby, he always kept a towel over his head to collect the sweat) and speak as God's vehicle, while someone wrote down his pronouncements. The suras or chapters are arranged in a descending order according to their length; they are preceded by an opening prayer and concluded by two small charms for one's protection. Also usually the end of each sura includes the epithet, "Meccan" or "Medinan," indicating the place of revelation. The longest suras, which are first in the Koran, came from Medina and contain revealed instructions for organizing and meeting the social and political needs of the community of believers headed by Muhammad, while the shortest came earlier from Mecca, when Muhammad sought to acquire converts, and contain the moral teachings of Allah. The Koran consists of rhythmical, rhymed prose, and of beautiful poetic passages, and teaches that it is an unalterable reproduction of the original scriptures preserved in heaven. It also contains many non-Arabic words that apparently were taken from Hebrew or Syriac sources.[1]

Muhammad was greatly influenced by Judaeo-Christian ideas proclaiming one God in opposition to the Arabs' polytheism. Muhammad's knowledge of the Judaeo-Christian Bible increased, and he soon spoke of such famous biblical figures as Adam and Noah, Abraham and Isaac, Moses and Aaron, David and Solomon, Jesus and John the Baptist, and even Alexander the Great. He proclaimed himself to be the restorer of the religion of Abraham and maintained that Ishmael, Abraham's son by his servant Hagar, was the father of the Arabs. He also announced that Abraham and Ishmael were the founders of the Kaaba, a pagan temple at Mecca that contained statues of gods and a sacred meteorite stone. Muhammad destroyed the idols of the Kaaba, but not the black stone, which according to him was given to Abraham and Ishmael by the angel Gabriel. Thus, the Kaaba became the most sacred shrine of the Muslims.[2]

Although Muslim orthodoxy insists that Muhammad could not read or write, Koran scholarship in recent years has discovered that Muhammad could indeed write. In his later years at Medina, where he died and was buried, Muhammad was gathering and preparing in writing much of his material to be issued as the Book (Kitab), which was to supersede the Jewish Old Testament (which he called the Torah) or the Christian New Testament (which he referred to as the Injil). According to the Koran (2:291; 16:104) and the Muslim tradition, he was working with the help of the angel Gabriel, an emanation of the Holy Spirit, who over twenty years had revealed to him piecemeal the scriptures in heaven and was now making certain that Muhammad's written material was correct. But Muhammad died before he could accomplish his task. At his death, he left behind a large body of scattered material of revelations, some of it written even on bits of parchment, palm leaves, smooth stones, and the like. Several individuals soon compiled the revealed material, but each in a personal and incomplete codex form. Thus arose a need to produce an official authentic text of the faith. Abu Bakr (632-634), Muhammad's father-in-law, who succeeded him as the first caliph or leader, issued the first rendering of the Koran, edited by Zayd ibn-Thabit, Muhammad's former secretary. However, because of lexical difficulties that produced differences of interpretations and disputes over the Koran's contents, Zayd produced in 657 under Caliph Uthman (644-657) the official and final revision, while all other copies were ordered destroyed.[3]

The Koran and Jesus

The Koran makes several references to Jesus. It does not offer an account of Jesus' life, of his teachings, miracles, and death, but it does refer to and confirm the gospel or the truth, which it claims to protect against outside detractors and internal divisions. It discusses Jesus' birth, mission, and death in fifteen chapters or suras (ninety-three verses altogether), especially in suras three, five, and nineteen. It honors Jesus, referring to him as "a sign to all beings" (21:91), and points out that Jesus was sent "in order that We may make him a sign unto Me" (19:21). Jesus' mother, Mary, is continuously honored in the Koran as a special person, the mother of God's messenger; and the Koran also states (3:30-33) that Jesus' family was chosen "above the worlds." However, Christians are denounced as idolaters worshiping images, icons, and statues against God's commandment.

The Koran accepts Jesus' miraculous birth. The virgin Mary's miraculous conception of Jesus is declared with the statement (19:17): "We sent to her Our Spirit, who for her took the shape of a comely human" who informed Mary that he was a messenger of the Lord "sent to thee that I may give thee a pure son." Muslim commentators associate "Our Spirit" with the angel Gabriel, because he is mentioned in the New Testament as being God's messenger to Mary. When Mary asks him in the Koran, as she does in Luke (1:34), how the conception is possible since she is chaste, his reply is: "Thy Lord has said: 'It is easy for Me, and truly We shall make him a sign to the people, and a mercy from us. The matter has been decided.'" The Koran then continues: "So she conceived him and retired with him to a remote place." Mary's husband Joseph, evidently, played no role at all in the Koran. Sura 66:12 asserts that "she [Mary] was chosen and purified by God," while sura 21 states: "We breathed into her who was chaste of Our Spirit and We made her and her son a sign to the worlds." The reference to the Holy Spirit of the gospels is quite clear, and it would appear that Muhammad had accepted Jesus' divinity. However this is not the case at all.

The Koran denies the divinity of Jesus. It accepts the birth of Jesus as unusual and comparable only to that of Adam whom God created from dust by breathing into him His Spirit of life (3:59; 15:29). Jesus is the second Adam in that he was created by the immediate action of God through his breath and not by physical conception. But it cannot be said that in the Koran, the Holy Spirit, which is the breath or wind of God, is God himself. The Koran distinctly rejects Jesus as the son of God (4:171): "Allah is only One; far be it for His glory that He should have a son: whatever is in the heavens and whatever is in the earth is His and Allah is a sufficient protector." It declares (21:25-27) that "there is no God but Me, therefore, serve Me." The Christians, the Koran continues, say that "the beneficent God has taken to himself a son: glory be to Him. Nay they [the prophets] are honored servants. They do not precede Him in speech and [only] act according to His commandments. . . . If any one of them should say, 'I am a god besides Him,' such a one We should reward with Hell." The Koran also consistently rejects the Holy Trinity (4:171: 5:76). It refers to Jesus not only as a prophet, a messenger of God, and a successor of messengers and prophets of the Old Testament, but also as God's helper. Muhammad and the Arabs associated Nazarene not with Nazareth but with the Arabic verb, *nasara*, to aid. (This word, however, is one of reproach, and the Arabs use the word *masihi* for Christian.) In addition, the Koran (5:78) proclaims Jesus as the Messiah and an apostle of God. "The Messiah, son of Mary, is but an apostle: apostles before him have indeed passed away. . . . " Although several times it calls Jesus the Messiah, son of Mary, and pronounces that "a painful chastisement shall befall on those among them who disbelieve" that the "Messiah, son of Mary, is but an apostle," it offers no explanation for the title Messiah. Muslim scholars have offered over fifty interpretations of the term. It appears to have a number of special meanings, including the "anointed" or "blessed" one of God; he whose touch heals (from the Arabic root, *msh*, to touch); or he who travels (from the Arabic verb, *masih*, to travel). Jesus was reported to have travelled extensively or gone on pilgrimage, and for later Muslims, he became the model of pilgrims and mystics.[4]

The Koran is not clear concerning the death and resurrection of Jesus. The Meccan chapter or sura (19:33-34) states in reference to Jesus: "Peace is upon me the day of my birth, and the day of my death, and the day of my being raised up alive." However, an almost identical phrase appears earlier concerning John the Baptist (19:5) which indicates that the resurrection refers to the general resurrection of the dead when the world shall end and not to Jesus' resurrection in three days following his crucifixion. In the Medinan sura on Jesus' death that follows (3:48-55), the Koran is even more enigmatic. It states (3:55): "God said: 'O Jesus, I am going to bring thy term to an end and raise thee to myself, and purify thee from those who have disbelieved; and I am going to set those who have follwed thee above those who have disbelieved until the day of resurrection; then to me do ye return and I shall judge between you in regard to that in which ye have been differing.'" The phrases "bring thy term to an end" and "take thee to me" have been accepted by Muslim scholars to mean "to cause thee to die," or "it is I who am causing you to die." A similar statement is found later in the Koran (19:33-34), where Jesus says: "I am a witness over them as long as I remained amongst them, but when thou didst take me to thyself, it was thou who wert a watcher over them."[5]

However, another important and baffling passage in the Koran (4:154-159) states that Jesus did not die on the cross, that the Jews did not kill him, which contradicts other Koranic verses on this subject. This passage reads:

> As for their [Jews] violating their compact, and for their unbelief in the signs of God, their killing the prophets without justification, and for their unbelief, and their speaking against Mary a mighty slander; and for their saying: 'We killed the Messiah, Jesus, son of Mary, the messenger of God,' though they did not kill him and did not crucify him, but he was counterfeited for them [or, "one was made to resemble him," or perhaps, "they thought they did"]; verily those who differ about it are in doubt about him. They have no [real or revealed] knowledge about him but only follow opinion, for certainly they did not kill him. Nay, God raised him to himself. God is sublime, wise. There are none of the People of the Book [Jews] but will surely believe in him before his death, and on the day of the resurrection, he will be a witness against them.[6]

This passage has been subject to several interpretations. Traditionally, the Muslims maintain that the Jews were unable to kill Jesus. According to one story, Jesus hid in a niche in a wall, and one of his companions was killed in his place. Another asserts that God sent his angels to protect Jesus; a cloud of darkness came down and Judas was crucified in his place. However, God caused Jesus to die for three hours, and he was then raised to heaven. The idea of a substitute did not originate with the Muslims. The second century Gnostic Christian Basilides, from Egypt, is said to have taught that at the crucifixion Jesus changed appearance with Simon of Cyrene, who had helped him carry the cross, and it was Simon that the Jews nailed to the cross. Jesus, disguised, stood by deriding the Jews for their error before ascending to heaven. The founder of ancient Manicheanism Mani (crucified in 276 A.D. by the Persians), who believed in two gods, the god of goodness and light (identified with Jesus of the New Testament) and the god of evil and darkness (identified with Jehovah of the Old Testament), taught that Jesus' brother was crucified in his place and that he was Mary's son (the widow's son of Nain), whom Jesus had raised. A Manichean text, however, also manifests the belief that the devil and not Jesus was crucified, falling victim to his own schemes.[7]

The Muslims have offered several individuals as victims of the cross in place of Jesus. Not only Simon of Cyrene, but Judas, Pilate, a disciple of Jesus, and a Jewish leader called Joshua have been suggested as substitutes at the crucifixion. However, no educated Muslim accepts such a view today. The Koran assertion that "he [Jesus] was counterfeited for them" can better be interpreted as: "it appeared to them as such," not that a substitution actually took place. In his *City of Wrong*, Kamel Hussein explains that, according to the Koran, "the Jews thought they killed Christ but God raised him unto him in a way we can leave unexplained among the several mysteries which we have taken for granted on faith alone." Some Muslims maintain that Jesus will die after his second coming, while others indicate that, although the Jews bore the responsibility, they did not kill Jesus; the Romans did. In any case, as Jesus pointed out to Pilate neither Romans nor Jews had the power to kill him unless it was given to them by God. The prevalent Muslim view is that according to the Koran, Jesus died on the cross and, therefore, completely surrendered to God's will. This view is in agreement with the Islamic belief of self-surrender or resignation to the will of God. Jesus, being the servant of the servants of God, the Son of Man, the Messiah, very human but exalted, surrendered to

God's will to give his life as a ransom for many. Jesus did ascend to heaven like all past prophets. However, because of the Koran's ambiguity on this subject, many Muslims also maintain that Jesus was not actually crucified. He did not suffer the usual human death, but was bodily raised to heaven and will return to earth.[8]

The Muslim Sects and the Coming of the Mahdi

After Muhammad's death, the Muslim faith began to suffer divisions. Legends arose attributing to Muhammad a number of miracles and supernatural signs that took place during his birth and ministry. Since the middle ages, the Muslims have held Muhammad to be sinless, like all prophets, protected by God from wrongdoing and thus a perfect example (in contradiction to sura 48:2 of the Koran, which mentions Muhammad's shortcomings). They also have accepted him as the intercessor of the faithful on Judgment Day, pleading his own virtue before God in order to ward off punishment from his followers. Even though Muhammad's tomb is to be found in Medina, Muslims believe that Muhammad ascended to heaven, as all prophets have. Eventually, with the rise of Sufism (Muslim mysticism and asceticism), which developed into the Dervish orders, Muhammad was deified. The Sufis (or Dervish), sought union with God and a glimpse at immortality much like the neo-Platonists, Gnostics and Christian mystics by whom they were influenced. In the twelfth and thirteenth centuries, particularly under Ibn Arabi, the Spaniard (1165-1240), the Sufis declared Muhammad as pre-existent, the eternal manifestation of the Divine Light, the very force that created and sustains the universe and the intercessor through whom God may be approached and known. Many Dervish leaders and their followers arose with different theological concepts. One of these, al-Hallaj, taught that man is God incarnate and accepted Jesus rather than Muhammad as the supreme example of glorified humanity. He went too far, however, when he declared: "I am God—I am the truth" and was crucified in 922 A.D. The Persian Sufi, Abu-Said (d. 1049), rejected the Islamic Law (Shariah), which calls for praying when the muezzin sounds the call to prayer from the minaret at the Mosque (Muhammad disliked the sound of bells) and for making at least one pilgrimage to Mecca. Gradually, the Dervish suffered persecution as heretics. Only a few Dervish sects survive today, primarily in Africa, where they still practice their methods in attaining the *gnosis* (mystic knowledge) through union with God and carry on their rituals of rhythmical, hypnotic, and exhausting dances and superhuman feats, such as eating live burning coals to reach God.[9]

Sufiism was only one of the movements that arose in the Muslim world. Many other sects sprang up, primarily for political rather than theological reasons, and many are no longer in existence. One of the largest of these sects, the Shia (party) movement, composed mostly of non-Arabs and concentrated today primarily in Iran, arose in opposition to the Sunnis (traditionalists or orthodox). The Sunnis, who constitute the largest body of Muslims, remained followers of the Ummayad dynasty, which took the leadership away from the fourth caliph, Ali (Muhammad's cousin and son-in-law), and killed his son Husayn (today a great Shiite martyr). The Shia soon split into a large number of sects, the most important being the Twelvers or Imamites, who accept the twelve Imams or spiritual-secular leaders of Ali's line ending with Muhammad, surnamed al-Mahdi (the guide or guided one). Unlike the Caliph, whom the Sunnis recognize as the spiritual and secular head accepted by the Muslim community, the Shiites recognize only the Imamate of the House of Muhammad, the descendants of Ali, whom Muhammad, the Prophet himself, designated as his successor; and they consider the Imam's authority as coming directly from God and not the people. Certain extremists (Alawites, Ghulah, and Ali-Ilahis, Qizil-bash and Bektashis) accept Ali as the incarnation of God and place him above Muhammad. The Twelvers believe that Muhammad al-Mahdi, who disappeared in 880, will return on his second coming as the Mahdi, the last Imam, who will restore righteousness and justice.

All of the Shiite sects—including the Zaydis of Yemen named after the fourth Imam, Zayd (Husayn's grandson); the Ishmailis of India-Pakistan, who regard Ismail (died in 760) rather than his younger brother Musa (whom the Shiites accept) as the seventh Imam; and the Druzes of Lebanon, who proclaim the divinity of the Fatimid caliph of Egypt, Hakim (who disappeared in 1021 and whose return they are waiting)— uphold this hope of the second coming, undoubtedly influenced by Jewish and Christian Messianic concepts. Interestingly, some Indians, Mongolians, Peruvians, Chinese and others hold the same hope, making the idea of a returning Messiah almost a worldwide phenomenon. Mahdis have appeared in Muslim countries in the past, and the British army had to fight at least two: "the Mad Mullah of Somaliland" and "the Mahdi of Sudan." Although this belief in the Mahdi's second coming is much stronger among the Shiites, later Suni tradition holds that the Mahdi is Jesus, who will slay the anti-Christ when he returns to earth. One of the greatest Islam thinkers, Ibn Khaldum, says that this belief in the Mahdi is not found in any trustworthy authority and must be of a popular origin. However, the Koran (9:33) contains a promise that, in later times, a prophet will appear to establish Islam's superiority throughout the world. The Koran states: "He it is Who sent His Messenger with guidance and the religion of Truth, that he may make it prevail over every other religion, even though the pagans may dislike it."

On March 23, 1844, Sayyid Ali Muhammad from Shiraz, Persia warned his followers of the coming of the "great promised One," "Him whom God shall manifest,"—the "Latter Day Revelator," and established a sect called Babi after his own name the "Bab," meaning the gateway to divine truth. The Bab was executed in 1850 for inciting violence and his followers were persecuted; but the Bab's disciple, Bahaullah, converted this Muslim sect into the Bahai religion, combining several religious teachings into one and preaching pacifism and humanitarianism. The early converts to Bahai accepted Bab as the promised Mahdi and Bahaullah as Christ (God's spirit or revelation). The Bahai religion has universal scope and appeal, seeking to satisfy the belief in the long-awaited one, not only of the Muslims and Christians, but also of the Hindus, Buddhists, and of the Zoroastrians.[10]

The Ahmadiyya Sect

The latest Muslim sect to appear from the Mahdi tradition is the Ahmadiyya movement. A Muslim belief arose that the Mahdi-Messiah would appear at the beginning of the fourteenth century of the Hegira, or about the last decade of the nineteenth century A.D., while some Christians also believed that Jesus' second coming was due at that time. In 1889, Hazrat Mirza Ghulam Ahmad (1835-1908) of the village of Qadian, India, proclaimed himself to be "the real and true Promised Messiah who is also the real Mahdi, tidings of whose appearance are to be found in the Bible and the Quran. . . . " Thus originated the Ahmadiyya movement, named as such about ten years later. Eventually, in an attempt to gain universal appeal, Ahmad also claimed to be the god Krishna of the Hindus. Informed by God that he was the Mahdi, Ahmad proclaimed himself "the light of this dark age" who was to lead the people of the world through peace and humility to the true God. He also claimed to have had, while fully awake, several visions of Jesus, of some of the prophets, and of the "Chief, Master and Leader, the Prophet Muhammad." He continued to have such visions, he said, whenever he devoted his attention to them, because he was endowed with new senses, a gift from heaven.[11]

Gulam Ahmad's followers, the Ahmadis, defend their founder's claim as the Mahdi. They maintain that the advent of their founder was predicted in the Koran in several suras—(which actually appear to be references to Muhammad, the prophet, and not the Mahdi). Also, Muhammad himself said that the appearance of the Mahdi would be manifested by two signs, an eclipse of the moon and an eclipse of the sun during the same month of Ramadan (the Muslim lunar month for fasting, when the Koran was sent down). The eclipses did take place on April 6, 1894 and were repeated in the United States in 1895. His followers also claim that he was a true prophet and a spiritual reflection of Muhammad because he was sinless; God revealed to him hidden truths; he made many prophecies, many of which have come to pass; and his message, as he predicted, has been carried throughout the world. In addition, Ghulam Ahmad was protected by God as the Prophet Muhammad had been before him. If he were an impostor, God would have destroyed him and would not have allowed him to succeed.[12]

The Ahmadis are considered heretics and are not accepted by other Muslims. Ghulam Ahmad accepted the superiority of the Koran and the Islamic law. He interpreted the jihad or the Muslim holy war against the infidels as a nonviolent struggle waged by the pen and not by the sword. However, he was influenced by Sufiism, especially by the medieval Sufi, Ibn Arabi. Therefore, in contradiction to the orthodox Muslims, he believed in the continuance of divine revelation, in understanding the truths of the Koran through divine assistance, and in championing the cause of Islam by mysticism and not by reason. Although the Ahmadis defend the mystical Sufis as the true expounders of Islam and the beacons of true Islamism, they also promote the study and use of science and are willing to use reason whenever necessary in defense of their ideas. To the vast body of orthodox Muslims, Sunni and others, the Ahmadiyya claims are an anathema, because no other prophets are to appear after Muhammad. Yet, as the Ahmadis indicate in their own defense, the orthodox do claim that, when Jesus bodily returns to earth, the same way that God raised him to heaven, he will have the status of a prophet. Therefore, obviously, other prophets are to appear.

The Ahmadiyya movement was not able to retain its unity. After Ahmad's first successor (caliph) died in 1914, the movement split into two groups. The majority, called the Qadianis, elected Ahmad's son, Mahmud Mirza Bashir-ud-Din, as their caliph or successor. He proved himself a capable organizer, but a minority known as the Lahore Ahmadiyya refused to recognize Mahmud Mirza as caliph or Ghulam Ahmad as a prophet and withdrew to Lahore, Pakistan. Both sects, found primarily in Pakistan, are relatively small in numbers, and both have been active missionaries in the West, including the United States and Africa. The Qadianis do not designate Islam to their converts as a sectarian movement but only as the religion of the Prophet Muhammad. But in Pakistan, they denounce as unbelievers all Muslims who do not accept Ghulam Ahmad as the Mahdi-Messiah. The Lahore Ahmadis have been striving to become reconciled with the orthodox or Sunni Muslims, but the authorities (ulama) of Sunni Islam have been reluctant to accept them.[13]

The Ahmadi Claim that Jesus Did Not Die on the Cross

One of the major disagreements between the orthodox Muslims and the Ahmadis is on the question of Jesus' status after his crucifixion. Unlike the orthodox Muslims, who accept that Jesus, like all prophets, was raised to heaven, the Ahmadis claim that Jesus was brought down alive from the cross and simply left Palestine to preach elsewhere. In 1890, after being divinely inspired, Ghulam Ahmad announced that Jesus did not die on the cross, and in 1899, he published a book titled *Jesus in India (Masih Hindustan mein)*, asserting that Jesus survived the cross and traveled to the East looking for the lost tribes of Israel until he settled in Kashmir. There, said Ghulam Ahmad, he died of old age and was buried in the Khanyar quarter of the city of Srinagar, where his tomb is still to be found. Since then, certain Ahmadis have produced several works and pamphlets, including the well-documented *Jesus in Heaven on Earth* (1951) by Al-Haj Kwaja Nazir Ahmad and the *Qabr-i-Masih* by Mufti Muhammad Sadiq of Shapur, which support Ghulam Ahmad's thesis with additional evidence. However, for the most part, all of these works are based on Al-Haj Kwaja Nazir Ahmad's book, which according to Muhammad Yasin, falls short of sound scholarship, because many of his references are incorrect, his bibliographical data incomplete, and his citations at fault. All these Ahmadi authors have combined religious beliefs with historical facts, says Yasin, and have evoked criticism from the scholarly world. In 1957, Aziz Ahmad Qureshi published *Assar-i-Kashmir*, based on *Masih*

Hindustan mein, Qabr-i-Masih, and *Jesus in Heaven on Earth,* but he claimed to be the originator of the thesis that Jesus went to India. He also announced that he was the Imam-i-Zaman, the Prophet of the Age, and that he knew this on the basis of divine revelation and spiritual guidance.[14]

The Ahmadis have relied on western biblical scholarship and on eastern tradition, not just divine revelation, to prove that Jesus undoubtedly survived the cross, recovered from his wounds, and went on to the East to settle in Kashmir in northern India. Since they accept Jesus as a prophet, as all Muslims do, they indicate that Jesus prophesied in Matthew (28:38-40) to the Scribes and Pharisees, who asked for a sign from him, that there would be no sign, but that, just as the prophet Jonas spent three days and nights in the whale's belly, so would the Son of Man be for three days and three nights in the heart of the earth. The Ahmadis interpret this to mean that Jesus would enter the earth alive and come out alive. He would not die. Therefore, they assert that Jesus, who remained crucified for only three to six hours at the most, could not have died. They correctly assert that, in the past, individuals remained on the cross for as long as six days before dying from exposure to the weather, exhaustion and suffocation, thirst and hunger, and attacks of wild beasts and birds of prey. Death was at times accelerated by burning, stoning, or breaking the bones of those crucified, or by the thrust of a spear. The thieves crucified with Jesus were not dead, say the Ahmadis, and neither was Jesus. In any case, there are many recorded instances of individuals who survived the ordeal of the cross after one and even three days and who were removed and treated in time to be saved. Pilate, who had been warned by God through his wife of Jesus' innocence, did his best to save him from death by seeing to it that he remained on the cross for only a short time.[15]

The Ahmadis are certain that Jesus was alive when taken down from the cross. Jesus was spared death because in the garden of Gethsemane he prayed tearfully to God to spare him from an accursed death ("Anyone hanged on a tree is cursed by God."—Deuteronomy 21:23), and as Luke states, God heard him and sent an angel to visit him (22:43). God could not have allowed him to suffer such a disgraceful death. Pilate, they point out, was surprised to hear that Jesus was dead (Mark 15:44-45). He could not believe that he had died so quickly. The fact is that Pilate, along with two Essenes, Joseph of Arimathaea and Nicodemus, a physician, saw to it that Jesus' legs were not broken. Although some have attributed the death of Jesus to the small wound inflicted by the thrust of the Roman soldier's spear, the flow of blood and water from Jesus' side reveals that coagulation had not taken place and that his heart was still beating. According to Nazir Ahmad, *The Crucifixion by an Eye-witness* (p. 71), which is the title of a letter written seven years after Jesus' crucifixion to an Essene in Alexandria, Egypt, by a personal friend of Jesus (a Tharapeut of the highest rank of Essenes), the Roman soldier's spear "passed over the hip of Jesus into the side." There were no convulsions, this letter indicates, "and this was taken by the centurion as a sure sign that he (Jesus) was actually dead," and he hurried to tell Pilate. From this rather insignificant wound, the letter continues, "blood and water flowed at which John (the evangelist who was a member of the Order, as a noviciate) wondered for even John knew, from the knowledge of our Brotherhood, that from a wound in a dead body flows nothing but a few drops of thickened blood." This letter, writes Nazir Ahmad, was translated from Latin to English and published in America in 1873. However, all copies of it and plates in English were deliberately destroyed (presumably by Christians who did not care for its contents), except for one that was republished in English in 1907, after it had been compared for accuracy with its Latin manuscript still in existence in Germany.[16]

Relying on western sources, the Ahmadis persistently cast doubt on Jesus' death. They agree with such writers as F. W. Farrar, William Stroud, Ernest Renan, Frederick Strauss, William Hannah, and others that Christ did not die on the cross. Although Jesus appeared to be dead, they say, he had merely fallen into a comatose state, "a syncope." The Roman soldier's spear did not pierce his heart because it only wounded him on the side, right or left, but somewhere from the shoulder to the hip, not in front of the chest. None of the evangelists, the Ahmadis assert, claimed that any of the disciples saw Jesus dead when they brought him down from the cross and placed him in the tomb. Only some of the women were there watching from a distance, say all the gospels except John's, not close enough to really know what was happening. According to the Ahmadis, Jesus was taken down from the cross alive by his fellow Essene members, to whose order he belonged, as confirmed by *The Crucifixion of an Eye-witness.* They found the opportunity to do this during the confusion caused by a storm that had just erupted, which made it easier to conceal the fact that Jesus was still breathing. The Jewish leaders, who thought of Jesus as a pretender and had rejected his divine origin and mission, had doubts about his dying on the cross after such a short while on it, and since his bones were not broken. Therefore, they asked Pilate to secure and seal the sepulchre, not so that his disciples might not steal his body and say that he was resurrected, as the gospels assert, but most likely to make sure that if buried alive, he would die in the tomb of suffocation. The Jews, according to Matthew (27:64), did not want the last error of burying Jesus without sealing and securing his tomb to make worse than "the first error," which obviously, say the Ahmadis, was that of not breaking his bones and sealing his death. It is true that Matthew does not explain what he meant by "the first error." [17]

Like all Muslims, the Ahmadis refute the story of the resurrection. Once Jesus was taken down from the cross alive by his fellow Essenes and placed in the private tomb of Joseph of Arimathaea, who was also an Essene, Jesus' wounds were treated with special herbs, and Nicodemus (a physician) spread balm on both pierced hands. They applied to Jesus' bruised body spices and the famous ointment called Marham-i-Isa (the Ointment of Isa) or Marham-i-Rasul (the Ointment of the Prophet), which is well known in eastern history and mentioned in oriental medical texts, including the world reknown medieval *Canon of Avicenna* (Vol. V., Discourse No. 11 on Ointment and Plasters). With the aid of his Essene friends, Jesus was able to recover from the ordeal of the cross, and to show himself to the women, with some of his Essene friends, dressed in white, the color of the garments of the Essenic order. Therefore, eventually, he was also able to show himself to his disciples, to exhibit the healing wounds to doubting Thomas, and to eat and converse with them. There was no resurrection. The gospel stories are full of disscrepancies and cannot be taken seriously, say the Ahmadis. Also, the resurrection stories, as western scholars have revealed, were not a part of the early Christian tradition or Logia (Q) used by the evangelists, but a later addition. Jesus still had his physical body and not anything different. The Koran is quite clear in its message. Allah exalted Jesus over his enemies by saving him from the death of the cross and the plotting of his enemies to kill him, but Jesus did die a natural death later on. Even though St. Paul wrote twenty-five years after the event that Jesus' resurrected body was spiritual, incorruptible, and immortal, the fact is that Jesus was afraid to show himself to his enemies. He went into hiding among the Essenes, revealing himself infrequently and suddenly to his disciples, who knew nothing of what had taken place since Jesus had been taken to Joseph's tomb. The fact is that Jesus was as physically vulnerable as any man, and he obviously feared for his life. [18]

Jesus Travelled to India

The Ahmadis emphasize that one of Jesus' missions was to find and save the lost tribes of Israel. (Israel was Jacob's second name, given to him by God, after Jacob wrestled well with Him—Genesis 32: 22-32.) Just as there was no resurrection, there was also no ascension. Relying on western scholarship, the Ahmadis indicate that the gospels say nothing of an ascension except in later editions of Mark, Luke, and Acts. The popularity of pagan gods who also ascended into heaven, like Adonis, Dionysus, Heracles, Mithras, Krishna and the Hebrew prophet Elijah, might have influenced the Christians to have their Lord also ascend into heaven. In any case, the gospels do not agree about where Jesus met his disciples, Jerusalem or Galilee, or from where he ascended. They do agree, the Ahmadis assert, that Jesus' desire was to save the lost sheep of Israel. In Matthew (15:24-26) Jesus says: "I was sent to the lost sheep of the house of Israel." He only reluctantly consented to heal the daughter of the Canaanite woman, the Ahmadis correctly state, and only after he referred to the gentiles as dogs. In Luke (22:29-30), he speaks of his kingdom where his disciples will sit on thrones, judging the twelve tribes of Israel. Jesus never did command his disciples to preach to the Gentiles, but only to the lost children of Israel. In Matthew (10:5-6), he instructs his disciples not to teach to the Gentiles or to the Samaritans, but to the lost sheep of the house of Israel. Later on, the Ahmadis indicate, the disciples only reluctantly gave in to St. Paul's wish and preached to the Gentiles as he did.[19]

Jesus fulfilled his mission to preach to the lost children of the house of Israel, the Ahmadis claim, by going to the East. Only two of the twelve tribes of Israel were in Palestine, during the time of Jesus; the rest were to be found in present-day Afghanistan, Pakistan, and northern India. Because of the oppressive rule of King Solomon and of his son and successor, Rahboam, the ten northern tribes of Israel under King Jeroboam formed the kingdom of Israel in the north, while the tribes of Judah and Benjamin constituted the Kingdom of Judah in the south. The ten tribes in the north were conquered in 722 B.C. by the semitic Assyrians from northern Mesopotamia, who moved them beyond the Euphrates river; while in 586 B.C., the Chaldeans or Neo-Babylonians under Nebuchadnezzar conquered the southern kingdom and moved the Jews to Babylon. Although in 537 B.C. the Persians who had conquered the Neo-Babylonians and all of Meso-potamia, allowed the Jews to return to Palestine and to rebuild the

Temple of Solomon, the wealthiest and most influential Jews remained behind. The Jews who did return came for the most part from the southern tribes of Judah and Benjamin. Those of the northern ten tribes, exiled earlier under the Assyrians, never did return. II Kings 17:23 states: "So were the Israelites carried away out of their own land to Assyria unto this day." According to the Old Testament apocryphal book of II Esdras (13:39-46), they migrated further to the east and settled in a region called Assareth (or Arzareth). The Ahmadis maintain that in ancient times Assareth was the Hazara district of northern Pakistan stretching over the Indus River into the present-day Kashmir province of northern India.[20]

The Ahmadis are not entirely correct in this account of the tribes. In 721 B.C., the Assyrians exiled only the upper classes of Israel to lands elsewhere within the Assyrian Empire, while mainly the lower classes remained behind. At the same time, however, the Assyrians brought into Israel other foreigners, including some Babylonians and Syrians, whom they had conquered. It appears that more foreigners were brought into Israel in 676 B.C. by the Assyrians and between 660 and 630 B.C. by the Elamites. Although some of these Gentiles probably intermarried with the native Israelites, around 620 B.C. a remnant of Israel, genuine Jews, survived in the tribal lands of Menesseh and Ephraim, two of the twenty northern tribes (II Chronicles 34:9). After 530 B.C., these northern Israelites were commonly called Samaritans because Samaria was the capital of the former northern kingdom of Israel. The established Jewish authorities in Jerusalem attacked them as heretics, but they claimed to be the true descendants of the ten lost tribes. They further asserted that all their exiled members had long since returned, a claim which was not accepted by the rest of the Jews. They also set up a rival temple at Mt. Gerizim and maintained their own version of the Old Testament (Luke 10:25-37; John 4:4-42). These Jews constitute to this day a relatively small but distinct religious community in Samaria, Israel. According to Jewish tradition, the ten lost tribes must return in order to fulfill the Old Testament prophecies that predict the restoration of the exiled Samarians to the land of Israel, either as a separate nation or in union with the two southern tribes of the kingdom of Judah (Nahum 2:2, Jeremiah 31:31, Ezekiel 37, and Zechariah 10:6, 7). This return will serve as a preparation for the coming of the Messiah for whose first coming the Jews are still waiting. Although the Old Testament indicates that the Assyrians exiled the Jewish aristocracy to lands elsewhere within the Assyrian Empire, such as the regions of

Gozen (today's northwest Iraq), Assyria (northern Iraq), and Media (Iran), the Jews have believed (based on the Old Testament and the Mishnah and the Talmud) that the descendants of the lost tribes are to be found mostly in Syria or Africa. This is why in 1984, the two chief rabbis of the modern state of Israel declared the Jewish tribe of Falasha in drought-stricken Ethiopia as descendants of Dan, one of the ten lost tribes, and allowed them to migrate to Israel. Speculations concerning the fate and location of the lost tribes have existed for a long time, but they remain as mere speculations to this day. No one knows what has happened to these people, evidently because they have left no historical evidence, no histories or literature; and their historical continuity has to a large extent disappeared.

The Ahmadis have produced much evidence revealing that the Jews migrated to Pakistan, Kashmir, and Afganistan. During the later part of the first century, the Jewish historian, Josephus, says that the ten tribes composed of a great multitude were still to be found beyond the Euphrates. (Josephus also mentions [*Jewish War*, p. 21] that there was close contact between Jerusalem and the Jews of northern Mesopotamia, for whom he wrote his original book in Aramaic.) The Ahmadis further point out that a large number of eastern and western works, including James Frazer's *An Historical and Descriptive Account of Persia and Afghanistan* (1843), report that the people of Afghanistan and Kashmir are the descendants of Jews of the lost tribes, who now call themselves the Bani Israel (the Children of Israel). Although the Jews of Palestine, Arabia, Turkey, Mesopotamia, and Persia (Iran) call themselves Jews, those residing east of Persia refer to themselves as Bani Israel. Many of these works make this claim of Jewish origin for the peoples of Afghanistan and Kashmir on the basis of their physiognomy, a claim that is questionable. However, the Ahmadis have also produced a long list of tribal, caste (class), and place names found in Kashmir and neighboring lands that have linguistic parallels in the Bible. It is pointed out that the name Moses is common among the Kashmiris. In addition, the Ahmadis write that customs, rituals, and the habits of the Afghans and Kashmiris on birth, marriage, mourning and burial, food and festivals, etc., are similar to those of the Jews. There can be no doubt of Jewish presence in the areas indicated by the Ahmadis, but letters and documents excavated at Gozen (in northwest Iraq) and dated about 600 B.C. contain names of officials and citizens that appear to be Hebrew, indicating that they might still have preserved their religion and culture in this area as well.[21]

The Ahmadis assert that Jesus undoubtedly went to preach to the lost children of Israel in the East where he knew they were to be found. To avoid apprehension, he frequently traveled in disguise so that his own disciples had difficulty recognizing him whenever he appeared to them. However, he did not travel alone. He had with him his mother, Mary, and his twin brother, Judas Thomas. Robert M. Grant indicates that, on the basis of Oriental sources, both eastern and western scholars identify Thomas with Judas, the brother of Jesus (Matt. 13:53; Mark 6:3). In the gospel of John (11:16; 20:24, 29; 21:2), the only canonical gospel to mention Thomas, Thomas is referred to as "Thomas called Didymus," or "Thomas (Didymus)." Didymus is Greek for "twin," but the very name Thomas means "twin" in Aramaic. Therefore, in his gospel, John is merely translating Thomas' Aramaic name into Greek. Besides the apocryphal Gospel of Thomas, says Grant, two documents use the full name Judas Thomas Didymus or speak of Judas Thomas as the twin—of Jesus. The latter form is to be found in the Book of Thomas the Athlete, part of the Nag Hammadi collection, while the first appears in the apocryphal Acts of Thomas, written in Syria or perhaps in the city of Edessa in the second or third century. Al-Haj Nazir Ahmad indicates that The Acts of Thomas is called in Syriac The Acts of Judas Thomas, and was written by Leucius, who evidently wrote several apocryphal Acts. He based this particular work on letters from Thomas himself and on information sent by an embassy from southern India via Edessa to Jerusalem and Rome. This work was read and used along with the Gospel of Thomas by all the Christian churches until the Decree of Pope Gelasius (495 A.D.). It was declared heretical because it rejected the virgin birth and divinity of Jesus and established Jesus' physical presence in Taxila (in Pakistan) long after his resurrection. The early Christian fathers attacked the view that Thomas was Jesus' twin brother, and in the Clementine *Homilies* (II, 1) Thomas is mentioned as the twin brother of Eleezir; but there was already a widespread tradition that Thomas was Jesus' twin brother. Therefore, Eusebius refers to him as Judas Thomas and identifies him as Judas of James which according to Al-Haj Nazir Ahmad, means brother, not son of James. James, we know, was Jesus' brother.[22]

Jesus and his family left Jerusalem and traveled via Samaria and Galilee to Damascus, Syria. He remained at a place called today Maqam-i-Isa (Jesus' place of stay), located two miles from this city. There, he remained long enough to make Ananias a disciple and to meet and convert Saul of Tarsus, his persecutor, who changed his name to

Paul. While in Damascus, he received a letter from the ruler or Abgar of Nisibis (or Nasibain) near Edessa (Urfa, Turkey), asking him to hasten there to cure him of a grave illness. There were three Nasibis, one near Mosul (a commercial center on the upper Tigris River in Iraq), one on the banks of the Euphrates River, and one near Jalalabad, Afghanistan. Since volume 8 of the *Majma-ul-Bul-dan* (1207) by Shaikh-ul-Imam of Persia indicates that it is situated six days' journey from Mosul, Nisibis might have been the modern town of Nusaybin, Turkey, near the Syrian border. Through Judas Thomas, who acted as his secretary, Jesus sent word to the Abgar that he would send a disciple to him.[23] However, the arrival of Jewish authorities to arrest Paul forced Jesus to go to Nisibis, where there were also to be found Jews of the lost tribes of Israel, something which is mentioned in Josephus' *Antiquities of the Jews* (XVIII, 1-8, 9). Because of the absence of any western records of Jesus' travels from Nisibis and on, the Ahmadis rely on the Acts of Thomas and Muslim sources written primarily since the fifteenth century in their endeavor to trace Jesus' journey to the East. These works record the eastern oral tradition or legends, some of which deal with Jesus (Isa). According to the Persian historical classic *Rauzat-us-Safa* (The Gardens of Purity) by Mir Khwand published in 1417, Jesus went to preach to Nisibis, ruled by a cruel and arrogant monarch who cut off the hands and feet of Thomas and Jacob (a companion) because they had angered the people with their preaching. Jesus, who had remained in the city's outskirts, was invited by Shamun, one of the King's ministers, to demonstrate his power; and he did so by restoring the dismembered parts of both Thomas and Jacob. Then, Jesus quietly left the city. *Tafsir-Ibn-i-Jarir at Tabrir* by Ibn-i-Jarir records that he ran away, not only because the King of Nisibis was cruel, but because the people there tried to kill him. *Jami-ut-Tawarick*, by Faqir Muhammad, describes the traveling Jesus as holding a staff in his hand to facilitate his walk and wearing a turban and clothes of white fleece. The *Rauzat-us-Safa*, which depicts him holding a rod (asa) and traveling on foot, also asserts that he slept on the ground with a stone under his head for a pillow.[24]

Jesus left Nisibis without Thomas. According to the Acts of Thomas, while Jesus was in Magdonia, which is another name for Nisibis, King Gondaphares (or Gopadatta) of India (49-109 A.D.) asked the King of Magdonia (Nisibis) through his emissary Abanes (or Abdagases) to send him a skilled builder to construct a Roman-style palace. Jesus, who was with the King of Magdonia when Abanes arrived, suggested to the

King that he send his brother Thomas, who was a mason and a carpenter; and Thomas was sent about 48-49 A.D. via Mesopotamia, the sea, and the Indus river to Taxila (in northern Pakistan), where he built a palace within six months. According to the Anglo-Saxon life of Thomas, written perhaps by Elfaric, Jesus himself saw Thomas and ordered him to go to India, however The Acts of Thomas does not record this.[25]

After leaving Nisibis, Jesus seems to have travelled incognito under the alias Yuz Asaf, which is revealed in the writings and oral traditions of the regions through which he passed. According to Al-Haj Nasir Ahmad, Yuz came from the Hebrew word Yusu, translated Jesus, while Asaf in Hebrew means the gatherer. But there is confusion concerning the meaning of the name Yuz Asaf. In two eastern works (*Farhang-i-Jahangiri* [p. 108], and *Anjuman-i-Asac Nasiri*, XXIV, Col. 1), we read that Asaf was one of the grandees or great noblemen of non-Arab (Ajami) countries. In two other works (*Ghias-ud-Lughat* [Vol. I:11], and *Burhan-i-Qate*, 34, Col. 2), Asaf is the name of a son of Barkhia who was one of the learned men of Bani Israel. Muhammad Badshah's *Farhang-i-Anand Raj* (Vol. VIII, 487 [Col. 3] and Strigass' *Persian-English Dictionary* define Yuz as seeker or leader, but they do not say what Yuz Asaf signified. The most probable explanation is given by the reputable *Farhang-i-Asafia* (Vol. I, 91), which states that lepers cured by Hazrat Isa (Honorable Jesus) were called Asaf. Therefore, if Yuz means leader, Yuz Asaf must have meant the leader of cured lepers. Faizi, the poet at the court of Akbar (1560-1605 A.D.), the Mogul emperor of India, thought that the two names indicated the same person, and he addressed Jesus as "Ai Ki Nam-i to: Yus o Kristo" (You whose name is Yus and Christ).[26]

Gradually, Yuz Asaf (Jesus) arrived on foot, first in Iran (Persia) and then in Afghanistan. Local tradition in Iran says that Yuz Asaf arrived in this country from the West, preaching and converting many; and according to Agha Mustafai's *Ahwali Ahalian-i-Paras* (p. 219), the traditional Iranian sayings of Yuz Asaf are similar to those of Jesus. One of these sayings, inscribed on a city gate of an unidentified town (perhaps traditional Kashan), states: "The palaces of kings are devoid of three virtues: Wisdom, Patience and Religious Wealth." Traces of Jesus are also to be found in Ghazni (eastern Afghanistan) and in Jalalabad (in northeastern Afghanistan). Both of these cities contain a platform called Yuz Asaf because at these two different spots Yuz Asaf sat and preached. One of the Amirs of Afghanistan appointed a caretaker for the Jalalabad platform, which is called Ziarat and provided funds for its maintenance.[27]

Jesus met Thomas, according to the Ahmadis, at Attock or Taxila (not far from the Kashmir border) and attended the marriage feast of Abanes (Habban or Abdagases), the former emissary, who was the son of Gad, one of Gondaphares' brothers. The Acts of Thomas does not say that Jesus joined Thomas at Taxila, but it does indicate that they were both at this wedding. It also records that, although Thomas left the place after the ceremonies, when the bridegroom lifted the curtain that separated him from his bride, he thought he saw Thomas conversing with her. The bridegroom asked him in surprise: "How canst thou be found here. Did I not see thee go out before all?" To which the Lord (Jesus) replied: "I am not Thomas, but his brother." The point is thus made that, being twins, Thomas and Jesus looked alike.[28]

Jesus and Thomas could not have remained very long at Taxila. Around 50 A.D., the Kushans crossed the Indus River and within ten years conquered this area. The Acts say that, before leaving for southern India, Thomas went to another kingdom that is not specified. Yus Asaf and Thomas left with their mother, Mary, for the adjoining hills and the present town of Murree close to the Indian border, a distance of about forty-five miles from Taxila or thirty from Rawalpindi, Pakistan. Jesus' mother died on the way and was buried at Pindi Point in Murree. Until 1875, Al-Haj Nazir Ahmad says, Muree was called Mari in her honor, and her tomb is known to the local residents as "the resting place of Mother Mary" (Mai Mari da Asthan). Her grave lies in an East-to-West direction in the Jewish burial fashion, and is venerated by both Muslims and Hindus as a miracle worker in bringing rain during droughts. The Hindus, who are superstitious by nature and worship many deities, seeing the new tomb at the top of the hill, began to pray there, giving the tomb recognition, while the Muslims, coming later on into this area and recognizing that the person buried in the tomb must have been a Jew or a Christian (one of the people of the Book), began also to venerate Mary's tomb and to make their offerings there. After building in 1898 a defense tower next to this tomb, the British decided in 1916-17 for security reasons to demolish Mary's tomb in order to terminate the people's visits to her tomb, but the people protested so vigorously that the British had to give up their plan. Later on, when the engineer of the British garrison at the tower was fatally injured in an accident, some thought that this mishap was the result of divine judgment. According to a document at the Muree

Muncipal Council (file 118) dated July 30, 1917, dozens of established residents confirmed that the tomb of Pindi Point, which is the sanctuary of a person of saintly qualities, venerated by Hindus and Muslims, generally succeeded in bringing relief in times of drought after prayers and offerings were made there. In 1950, Mary's tomb was repaired through the efforts of Al-Haj Nazir Ahmad, the author of *Jesus in Heaven on Earth*. Eventually, the defense tower became obsolete and was destroyed, and a television tower was erected in its place.[29]

Jesus in Kashmir, India

Jesus' trip ended in Kashmir, India, say the Ahmadis, and there are many indications of this. Jesus entered Kashmir between 60 to 87 A.D. through a beautiful green valley with wooded slopes called Yusmarg (Meadow of Jesus), named after him. Kashmir is a land of streams and rivers, and the prophecies of Isaiah (62:4) and Malachi (3:12), says Al-Haj Nazir Ahmad, predict that the Messiah would live in green pastures. As the Koran declares (23:50): "And We made the son of Mary and his mother a sign, and We gave them shelter on lofty meadows." About forty-five miles from the city of Srinagar in Kashmir, not far but eastward from Yusmarg, another place bore the name of Jesus, Aishmuqam (Jesus' place of rest). According to the *Nur Nama*, Aishmuqam was named after a prince, and Aish or Ashush is a prefix derived from Isa (Jesus). Eventually, Aishmuqam was renamed Mohammedan, and found there today are the horns of the Ram of God, which are preserved under lock and key, and the staff of Jesus or of Moses, which is made of olive wood and has the power to produce rain. There are conflicting statements regarding to whom it belonged, but custodians of the staff confidently assert that it belonged to Moses and not Jesus. Kashmir also contains many places bearing the name of Jesus and attesting to Jesus' presence in Kashmir, including Issa-Brari, Isa-Kush, Isa-Ta, Arya-Issa, Kal-Issa, Yusu, Yusu-dha, Yusu-raja, and Yus-marg.[30]

Many eastern works, says Al-Haj Nazir Ahmad, record Yuz Asaf's stay and death in Kashmir. The most important of these works is *Tarikh-i-Kashmir* (History of Kashmir), written in Persian 1413 A.D. by Mulla Nadiri, Kashmir's first Muslim historian. It states that Yuz Asaf was alive and preaching in Kashmir in 78 A.D., during the reign of Gopadatta, who built and restored many temples. Gopadatta appointed Sulaiman of Persia, one of his ministers, to undertake the necessary repairs to the Throne of Solomon, a temple on the top of Mount Solomon in east Srinagar. The dome of this temple had cracked. Interestingly, it was not the Jews but the Hindus who, according to this work, objected to Sulaiman's repairing this holy tomb because he was not a Hindu. Gopadatta referred the decision to Yuz Asaf, the prophet, whom the people trusted, and he ruled in favor of Sulaiman's repairing the dome. Yuz Asaf, this work continues, having come from the Holy Land to this holy valley, had devoted himself day and night to prayers to God. Having attained the heights of piety and virtue, he proclaimed himself to be God's messenger and invited the people of the valley to his religion. Upon completing the restoration of the temple's cracked dome in 78 A.D., Suleiman erected four pillars supporting the roof of the temple. On two of these pillars, writes Al-Haj Ahmad, there are still legible today inscriptions in Persian which read: "The mason of this pillar [is] the suppliant Bihisti Zargar. Year fifty and four [probably, 78 A.D., but no particular calendar is given]," and "Khwaja Rukun son of Murjan erected this pillar." Two more inscriptions in the same script on the flank walls encasing the staircase read: "At this time Yuz Asaf proclaimed his prophethood. Year fifty and four [perhaps, 78 A.D.]," and "He is Yusu, Prophet of Bani Israel." The last two inscriptions were mutilated after the Sikhs' conquest of Kashmir, but markings are still there on these walls, even though they are not intelligible. Nevertheless, the contents of these mutilated inscriptions have been preserved in two eastern works. Mulla Nadiri's *Tarikh-i-Kashmir* comments on and records in quotes only the last two scripts on Yuz Asaf, probably because he considered their historical value to be greater. Khwaja Hassan Malik's *Tarikh-i-Kashmir* also writes of and quotes these inscriptions, confirming that they declared Yuz Asaf's ministry in Kashmir. Evidently, when these men wrote their works, the inscriptions on Yuz Asaf had not been destroyed. Mulla Nadiri also says that he had seen in a Hindu book that this prophet, Yuz Asaf, was really Hazra Isa (Honorable Jesus) and that after his death he was laid to rest in Mohalla Anzmara. He adds: "It is also said that lights (anwar) of prophethood used to emanate from the tomb (Rauza) of this Prophet."[31]

Al-Haj Nazir Ahmad writes that this Hindu book mentioned by Nadiri must be the *Bhavishya Maha Purana* by Sutta, written in 115 A.D. in Sanskrit and printed for the first time in Bombay, India, in 1910. It describes how raja (ruler) Shalewahin of India, an able warrior, met in the Himalaya mountains at Wien (or Voyen), about ten miles northeast of Srinagar, "Yusashaphat" (Yuz Asaf), who was fair complexioned and dressed in white. When the Raja asked him what his religion was, he replied: "O Raja! When truth had disappeared and there was no limit [to evil practices] in the meleech country [the country of the infidels beyond the Indus River], I appeared there and through my work the guilty and the wicked suffered, and I also suffered at their hands." When the Raja asked a second time what his religion was, he answered: "'It is love, truth and purity of heart and for this I am called *Isa Masih* [Jesus, the Messiah].' The Raja returned [to his capital] after promising obedience to him. . . . "[32]

Two Arabic works also mention Jesus' work in India. The prolific Arab historian, Shaikh Al-Said-us-Sadiq (d. 962), wrote in detail of Jesus' mission in Kashmir in his work *Kamal-ud-Din*. (Published in 1782 in Iran and later on in Germany, where it was translated by Professor Muller of Heidelburg University, it was found to be valuable by western Orientalists.) According to *Kamal-ud-Din*, Jesus' message in Kashmir, where he traveled and taught, is similar to that found in the gospels. Yuz Asaf taught not to seek this earthly kingdom but heaven, because this earthly kingdom and its happiness will vanish along with those who seek after it. The end of time is at hand. Just as the birds have no hold over their enemies, you do not either without faith and good works. Travel in the light of virtue, Yuz Asaf said, but be discreet about your good works. Treat others as you would like to be treated, Yuz Asaf taught, but reject desires, slander, hate and gossip. Keep your minds and actions identically pure. In addition, *Kamal-ud-Din* contains the famous parable of the sower, which is almost identical to that found in the gospels. This parable is also to be found in *Ain-ul-Hayat* (Vol. II, 177-178) by Ibn-i-Muhammad Hadi Muhammad Ismail, which devotes a whole chapter to Yuz Asaf. It attritubes over fifteen parables to him and describes his travels and teachings.

Both of these works mention the death of Yuz Asaf in Kashmir and the presence of Thomas (Ba'bad) there on this particular occasion. According to *Kamal-ud-Din*, eventually death overtook Yuz Asaf, "and he left the earthly body and was elevated toward the Light." Before dying, Yuz Asaf "sent for a disciple of his, Ba'bad [Thomas] by name, who used to serve him and was well versed in all matters." Yuz Asaf expressed his last wishes to Ba'bad and said: "My time for departing from this world has come. Carry on your duties properly and turn not back from truth and say your prayers regularly." He then directed Ba'bad to prepare a tomb over him at the very place where he died. He stretched his legs toward the West and head towards the East and died. *Ain-ul-Hayat* indicates that Yuz Asaf resided in "the city of Kashmir . . . till death approached him, and his holy spirit departed from his earthly body and went to rest with God." It too mentions Thomas in reference to Yuz Asaf's death and burial. It states that before his death, Yuz Asaf "called his companion Ba'bad and made a will . . . and directed him to construct a tomb for him. He laid himself with his head towards the East and stretched his legs towards the West, and went to the place of eternity."[33] Since Yuz Asaf (Jesus) was still alive in 78 A.D. at the age of 85 (Jesus was born in 7 B.C.), he must have died at a very old age; but some have declared him to have been 125 years of age when he died.

Thomas' Missionary Work in India

After burying Jesus, writes Al-Haj Nazir Ahmad, Thomas retraced his journey, going back to Taxila; and according to the apocryphal Acts of Thomas, he reached the mouth of the Indus River. Having heard, probably from Jesus, who had earlier visited southern India, of the Bani Israel of Malabar and Sri Lanka, Thomas desired to preach to the Jews there. However, finding that no ship would sail to southern India, because of a war fought in this area between King Mazdai and a neighboring ruler, Thomas first sailed to the island of Socotra of South Arabia, east of the Gulf of Aden and the Somali Republic of Africa, and proceeded to preach in Abyssinia (Ethiopia). But he soon left Africa for southern India, landing first on the island of Kerala near Crangonore and preaching at India's western coast of Malabar, where he established seven churches. From the city of Andra (not as mistakenly mentioned in the Acts of Thomas, Andrapolis, which has been confused with Andrapolis by the Nile River in Egypt), says Al-Haj Nazir Ahmad, Thomas went to India's eastern coast, where at Maelapore (Madras), he converted Queen Tertia to Christianity. However, her conversion so enraged King Mazdai and his Hindu subjects that four soldiers struck and killed Thomas with their spears.[34]

The Ahmadis rather accurately indicate that according to Christian tradition the apostle Thomas went to preach the gospel to India. Hippolytus, bishop of Portus, one of the earliest Christian historians, wrote that "Thomas preached to the Parthians, Medes, Persians, Bacterians, Indians, Hyrcaneans and was thrust with a spear at Calamania the city of India and was buried there." Early Christian writers Origen,

Rufinus, and Socrates mention Parthia (an ancient empire between the Indus and Euphrates rivers and extending from the Indian Ocean to the Caspian sea) as the scene of Thomas' work, while Ephrem, Gregory Nazianzen (who even mentions King Gondaphares or Gopadatta), Ambros, Jerome, Sophronius, and Gregory, bishop of Tours, refer to India as the scene of Thomas' martyrdom. In the ninth century, King Alfred of England sent an embassy under Bishop Sherbourn to the shrine of St. Thomas in India, while the Greek traveler of the sixth century, Cosmas, who traveled throughout most of the Christian world of his time, found the Christians of St. Thomas in southern India and on the island of Ceylon (Sri Lanka) as well as in northwestern India. He wrote that their bishops were ordained by the Nestorian Patriarch of Antioch. About 1294 A.D., Marco Polo wrote of St. Thomas' martyrdom near Madras, while in 1436, Count Nicolo of Venice, and in 1670, Friar Vincenzo Maria also mentioned various tablets found in southern India as the artifacts of St. Thomas.[35]

The converts of St. Thomas, who called themselves The Christians of St. Thomas, underwent persecutions from their fellow Christians. Evidently, at first the Churches of Parthia and India were led by Edessa, but after 325, the leadership of these eastern churches was taken over by the patriarch of Antioch. Eventually, the Christians of St. Thomas united with the Nestorian branch of the Assyrian Church in Iran. As indicated earlier, Patriarch Nestorius of Constantinople, who held that Jesus was the instrument of God but not divine, was condemned by the Council of Ephesus in 431 as a heretic and forced to go to the East, where he gradually established the Nestorian Church of Persia headed by the Katholikos. The Nestorians carried on missionary activities in India, Tibet, Turkestan, and China, and even in Egypt. In the sixteenth century, one group of Nestorians called the Chaldean Christians transferred their allegiance to the Roman Catholic Church. The Christians of St. Thomas discovered that their beliefs and practices were similar to those of the Nestorians. Originally, they did not believe in praying to saints and did not have guardian angels. They accepted only two sacraments, baptism and the Lord's supper, solemnized with holy water, bread, or wine. They did not believe in Jesus' divinity or in his virgin birth, and they did not adore Mary as the Theotokos, the mother of God. They held St. Thomas to be the twin brother of Jesus. Their services were held in Syriac without any instrumental music, and their churches were void of icons or paintings. Their priests married, and they had no monks or nuns. According to Edward Gibbon's *Decline and Fall*

(VI, 52), when the Portuguese arrived in India and presented them with an icon of Mary, these Christians of St. Thomas refused it, protesting that they were not idolaters. They were eventually persecuted as heretics by the Catholics who killed their priests and forced them to accept their faith.[36]

Buddhist Evidence of Jesus' Presence in India

The Ahmadis maintain that while in Kashmir, Yuz Asaf made an impact on Tibet's Buddhism, which is further evidence of Jesus' presence in India. Ancient Buddhist records, they say, contain stories on the life and teachings of Buddha and reveal traditions that are similar to those recorded in the New Testament writings concerning the life of Jesus. Like Jesus, Gautama Buddha was divinely born of a virgin and welcomed by angels. He was "received by an old saint who was endowed with prophetic vision, presented in a temple, baptized with water and afterwards baptized with fire." He astonished the most learned doctors with his answers and understanding, and after being led by the spirit into the wilderness and tempted by Satan, Buddha went about preaching and performing wonders. The friend of publicans and sinners, he was transfigured on a mount, descended to hell, and ascended to heaven. "In short with the exception of Christ's crucifixion, almost every characteristic incident in Christ's life is to be found narrated in the Buddhistic traditions of the life of Sakya Nuni, Gautama Buddha."[37]

In the seventeenth century, the Jesuit father Grueber, who traveled through Tibet with his fellow Jesuit father Dorville, while returning from China, was amazed by the similarities of the doctrines and rituals of the Buddhists of Lassa to those of his Catholic faith. The garments of the Buddhist Lamas or priests corresponded with those of Christ's apostles portrayed in paintings. The different orders of the Lamas resembled those of the Roman Catholic Church, and so did their beliefs in incarnation, paradise, and purgatory, and their practices of using holy water and praying for the dead. Like the Catholics, the Buddhist monks near Lassa, numbering about thirty thousand, took the three vows of poverty, chastity, and obedience along with other vows. Superior Lamas or Buddhist bishops authorized confessors to receive confessions, impose penances and give absolution much as did the different orders of the Catholic Church. The Jesuits, therefore, concluded that the ancient books of the Lamas contained traces of Christianity, which must have been taught in Tibet during the time of Christ's apostles. A Professor Seydel of Germany presented fifty-one examples of harmony between Buddhist and Christian writings, revealing that these religions had an influence on each other.[38]

The Ahmadis point out that according to Dwight Goddard's work, *Was Jesus Influenced by Buddhism?*, Jesus' heavenly kingdom closely resembles that of Buddha's earthly kingdom made possible by love. Quoting Goddard, they indicate that Jesus' parables are all colored with Buddhist thought and sentiment. The parable of the Good Samaritan reveals a similarity to the Buddhist emphasis on kindness, especially toward the sick and poor; and the parable of the Prodigal Son manifests a similarity with Buddhist concepts of altruism and forgiveness. It is true that Goddard did discover resemblances between Buddha's teachings and those of Jesus. Jesus commanded love of God, not the Jewish notion of fear of God, and Jesus' emphasis on selfless love and his willingness to suffer the cross for others were distinct Buddhist rather than Jewish ideas, says Goddard. Although the Christian idea of an immortal soul was foreign to the Buddhist doctrine of an enduring and suffering conscious soul that must be eradicated in order to terminate its reincarnation, both Jesus and Buddha proclaimed ascetic values denouncing interest in material things. In any case, the notion of an immortal soul, Goddard maintains, had its origin with Paul, not with the Jews and Jesus, who believed that physical death terminated all.[39]

The Ahmadi contention concerning Goddard, however, is not quite accurate. Goddard maintains that Buddhist ideas had permeated Jewish thought before Jesus. Therefore, "Jesus unconsciously had been influenced by Buddha" to accept God as love rather than as the Jewish Jehovah, Lord God Almighty; and he also unwittingly followed Gautama Buddha's Golden Eight-fold Path which calls for right thinking, speaking, and living as the way of love. Goddard indicates that, when Buddha died in 483 B.C., India was the center of one of the four major civilizations: China, India, Assyria-Persia, and Egypt-Greece. The ideas of their great philosophical and religious thinkers were carried far by merchants, wandering scholars, ascetics, prisoners of war, and conquerors like Alexander the Great. Buddhist and Persian ideas can be detected, not only in Pythagoreanism, Stoicism, Platonism, Gnosticism, the cult of the Theraputae of Alexandria, and the Hermetic and Kabalistic literature of Egypt, but also in the ideas and practices of the Essenes. Like the Buddhists, Goddard says, the Essences, to whose organization Jesus belonged, tried to follow the middle path between extremes, aimed at self-control, lived in communities as brothers, practiced celibate lives of equality, shunned earthly possessions, and opposed violence. Historians have maintained that the Essenes heard of Buddhist concepts only from the Greeks and their fellow Jews. However, recent linguistic research, says Goddard, "strongly confirms that there were stronger influences, than had hitherto been supposed, of oriental ideas at work among the early Jewish sects, especially among the followers of John the Baptist" or the Mandaeans, who also called themselves Nasoreans and who were, evidently, Essenes.[40]

The Ahmadis, however, maintain that Jesus was influenced directly by the Buddhists long before he came to stay in Kashmir. They point to Nicolas Notovich, a Russian traveler who at the end of the nineteenth century explored the region called Little Tibet, which borders Kashmir and Ladakh. At the lamasary (Buddhist monastery) of Hemis, which contains a large library of religious books, the head lama told Notovich that their library had among its 84,000 scrolls the life and work of the prophet Isa (Jesus), written in the Pali language of Tibet. This work had been acquired from the lamasary of Lhasa that housed all the original scrolls. The head lama said that Isa, whose sacred doctrines spread in India and among the sons of Israel, was not recognized by the Buddhists as a principal saint, and his doctrines did not constitute an essential part of Buddhism. During Notovich's second stay at the lamasary of Hemis, the head lama showed to Notovich two big volumes of yellow leaves in cardboard covers containing the life of Isa, which Notovich copied while the head lama translated. Notovich points out that this strange work is written in verses that often do not form a continuous narrative. Notovich attempted to have the work published in Russia and western Europe, but after being discouraged from doing so by the Metropolitan of Kiev and by certain Catholic cardinals at Rome and Paris, he had it published in New York in 1890 under the title *Life of Saint Isa* and again in 1894 and 1926 as *The Unknown Life of Jesus Christ*. The publication of this work aroused a great controversy, and Notovich was attacked as an American atheist who had never left America. It appears that Notovich was sincere. Others later on saw and translated these Pali scrolls on Isa, but Holger Kersten, who visited the Hemis monastery in 1973, was informed by the lama that these scrolls could not be found.[41]

According to this Tibetan Buddhist biography, Isa (Jesus), who was an excellent child divinely conceived, after reaching the marital age of thirteen, secretly left his home to go to the Far East. Joining a caravan of merchants, he came to India to study the laws of the gurus, the teachers of the East. For six years, he lived and studied the Hindu holy scriptures in various holy cities of India, including Jagonnoth, Jajagriba, and Benares. Like Gautama Buddha before him, he got himself into trouble with the Hindu priests, the Brahmans, because he denied the divine origin of the Vedas (sacred books of the Hindus) and attacked India's caste (class) system, which upheld the supremacy of the Brahmans and the exploitation of India's two lower classes (farmers and laborers) by the two upper classes (priests and warriors). Isa taught that God loves everyone equally and no man should exploit another man. Because the Brahmans and the warriors desired to destroy him, Isa, with the help of the class of shudras (slaves), escaped to Nepal, the land of the Buddhists. There, he learned the Pali language and studied the Buddhist scrolls. After residing six years in Nepal, he left to go back to his homeland in the west, where he returned at the age of twenty-nine.[42]

There has been a written and oral tradition that Jesus went to the East during his missing years between the ages of thirteen and thirty. Except for describing Jesus' visit to the Temple at Jerusalem and his discourse with the priests, the gospels tell us nothing about him during this time, except for Luke (2:40), who, after relating his birth, merely mentions that "the child grew and waxed strong in spirit, and was in the desert till the day of his showing into Israel." Again, after narrating the visit at the Temple and just before mentioning his baptism by John the Baptist, Luke writes (2:52), "as Jesus grew up, he increased in wisdom and stature and in favor with God and man." Jesus' absence of sixteen years has given rise to various stories as to how he acquired his wisdom. According to Al-Haj Nazir Ahmad, in the tenth century, Shaik Al-Said (mentioned earlier) described in *Kamal-ud-Din* Jesus' visits, first to India and later to Kashmir, not separately but in a continuous narrative that is not clear. Concerning Jesus' first trip to India, he mentions Hindu legends, including his visit to the island of Ceylon (Sri Lanka) in southern India. At the time of Jesus, there were to be found on India's western coast from the north to the south, including in Bombay and even in Sri Lanka, communities of the Jews of Bani Israel, who were in touch with each other. Therefore, had he traveled to India, Jesus would not have found himself in a completely strange land. Al-Haj Nazir Ahmad maintains that Jesus visited India twice, both before and after his crucifixion. Nicolas Notovich thought that Jesus did go to the East as a young man to study Hinduism and Buddhism, but no great attention was paid to him until after he left India and became famous back in Palestine. The Buddhist monks did keep chronicles before, during and after Christ, says Notovich, but it was not until after Christ's fame spread that the Buddhist monks investigated every detail of his life. The two manuscripts containing the life of Isa that the lama read to him were compiled from various copies written in the Tibetan language on scrolls brought to the monastery of Lassa from India, Nepal and Maghada. They contained information about Christ that was "oddly mixed, without relations or coherence with other events of that period."[43]

Hazrat Mirza Ghulam Ahmad, the founder of the Ahmadya movement, asserts that Jesus made only one trip to India after his crucifixion. He refutes the stories that Jesus went to India between the ages of thirteen and twenty-nine to study Hinduism and Buddhism as myths coming from Buddhist monasteries. Hazrat Ghulam Ahmad says that the events of Buddha's life were not recorded by his followers until the time of Jesus in the first century A.D. The Buddhist monks, therefore, had ample opportunity to ascribe to Buddha's life and teaching whatever they wished. The stories about Jesus, his work and teachings, came out first, and then they were incorporated into writings concerning the life of Buddha. Thus, Buddha received titles similar to those of Jesus, like "King," "Light," "Master," "Blessed," and "Prince." Events in the life of Buddha, says Hazrat Mirza Ghulam Ahmad, were also made to resemble those in the life of Jesus. Thus, Buddha was tempted by the devil but did not obey him, just as Jesus did not, but Buddha's temptation was made more elaborate. Just as Jesus sent out his disciples with instructions to teach the world to love, performed many miracles, and delivered a sermon, so did Buddha. Jesus taught in parables and advocated love of heaven, renunciation of worldly things, compassion, goodness, the golden rule, and love of enemies, and so did Buddha.[44]

In support of H. M. Ghulam Ahmad's thesis, the Ahmadis present an impressive list of western scholars who agree that Buddhist writings were influenced by Christian works and not the other way around. They indicate that there is no evidence of any direct communication of ideas common to Buddhism and Christianity from the East to the West. Not a single ancient original manuscript of Buddhist authorities has survived the ravages of time, they say, and no ancient biography of Buddha existed prior to the Pali or Tibetan texts. Buddha's life and teachings were not recorded until 30 B.C. or perhaps 80 B.C. One of the main reasons the Buddhist monks became interested in Jesus, say these scholars, was they they too were waiting for the coming of the Messiah, or Metteyya in the Pali language of Tibet, as prophesied by the Buddha. The Ahmadis interpret the word Metteyya to mean Messiah, because, as Henry T. Princep indicates, it does bear a close resemblance to Messiah. When a word is transferred from one language to the next, it is often changed; for example, the English "th" becomes "s" in Arabic and Persian. Thus, the word Messiah obviously became Metteyya in the Pali language. According to Princep, Gautama declared himself to be the twenty-fifth Buddha and said that the "Bagwa [White] Metteyya is yet to come." One of the oldest Buddhist sources, "The Dhigha Ninaya," mentions that, when Gautama's religion will have been forgotten, the Metteyya will appear in order to reveal again the true path to man. Chinese books of the Chang Yang period (785-804 A.D.) on Buddhism, containing the word Messiah and the Buddhist prophecy, state that the new Buddha Messiah, who will be bagwa or of light complexion, will appear five hundred years after the time of Buddha to restore Buddhism from a state of decay to a state of purity. Jesus did appear five hundred years later, and he was light-complexioned. The Ahmadis maintain, therefore, that since the Tibetan Buddhists were waiting for the Messiah to receive the blessings of salvation, and since Jesus' teachings affected Tibetan Buddhism, Jesus must have visited Tibet in person while residing in Kashmir after his crucifixion. The Ahmadis also think that the Christian-Greek medieval popular story of Barlaam and Joasaph, the origin of which was Indian and which was thought to be based on the life of Buddha, was an old version of the life of Yuz Asaf or Yuzasaph, meaning Joasaph. Supposedly, Yuz Asaf was the appearance of the new Buddha. But since Joasaph was an Indian prince converted to Christianity, one fails to see the connection.[45]

Notovich's *Unknown Life of Jesus Christ* does not shed any light on this subject. It merely states that it seeks to convey information on the torture and execution of Isa (Jesus) given by "the merchants who have come from Israel" (p. 99). Before taking up this theme, it very briefly discusses the history of the Israelites, starting with Moses (Mosa). In contradiction to the Old Testament, it explains that Prince Moses was the younger of the Pharaoh's two sons, not an adopted Jewish child. The Pharaoh of Egypt oppressed the Israelites with hard work as slaves, but Moses, who believed in the God of the Jews, pleaded with his father to ameliorate their condition. Because he refused, a great plague struck Egypt, forcing the Pharaoh to send Moses to lead the Israelite slaves out of Egypt to find another capital at a far distance, and to remain with them. Then it briefly discusses the conquest of the Israelites by the Romans, because they had deviated from the law of Moses, and tells the story of the birth of Isa, who was the incarnation of the Supreme Judge, the Eternal Spirit. After discussing Isa's journey to India and his return to Palestine, it narrates his teaching, which was mainly that the human heart is the temple of God in which abide love, justice, and compassion that can be manifested through a renunciation of material wealth. Acts for profit, said Jesus (p. 126), can only cause the world to "fall into a state of moral degradation in which theft, falsehood, and murder, seem like generous actions."

The Unknown Life of Jesus Christ also contradicts the New Testament concerning the reason for Jesus' crucifixion. It states that it was not the Jewish priest and learned men that wanted to destroy Jesus, but Pilate, the Roman governor. Pilate had heard of Jesus' claims that the Jews would soon "be rid of their intruders." Becoming alarmed at Jesus' popularity and hearing that he desired to become king, Pilate had him arrested and tortured. The priests and learned men of the Jews begged Pilate to free Isa because of an approaching great feast, but Pilate refused. He told the priests and elders to judge Jesus and to condemn him to death. However, the priests refused to do so because Isa merely desired to become king of heaven and taught nothing that was illegal. When Pilate furiously insisted that they carry out his orders and that they also release two thieves, the Jewish leaders courageously answered him: "We will not take upon our heads the great sin of condemning an innocent man and acquitting two thieves, a thing contrary to our laws. Do therefore as thou pleases." Then, they went out and washed their hands in a sacred vessel, saying (pp. 143-144): "We are innocent of the death of a just man." Betrayed by one of his disciples as aspiring to become a king, Isa was crucified along with the two thieves and died at sunset. However, being apprehensive over this act, Pilate turned over the body of Isa to his relatives, who buried him near the place of his execution. Three days later Pilate sent his soldiers to bury Isa's body elsewhere, but the tomb was found to be open and empty. Therefore, the rumor spread that "the Supreme Judge had sent his angels to take way the mortal remains of the saint in whom dwelt on earth a part of the Divine Spirit" (p. 145).

This work does not mention Jesus' reappearance to his disciples following his crucifixion or ascension. It does state, however, that Jesus' disciples left Israel and went out in all directions to spread his message to the pagans, their kings and soldiers, who accepted his teachings and "abandoned their absurd beliefs . . . to sing the praises of the all-wise Creator of the universe, the King of kings, whose heart is filled with infinite mercy" (p. 146). Neither is there in this work any mention of Jesus traveling to and preaching in Kashmir, Tibet, or Afghanistan. If the Ahmadis are correct that Jesus went to live in Kashmir and directly influenced the Tibetan Buddhists, surely these Tibetan Buddhists, who were expecting the imminent coming of the Bagwa Metteyya, would have recorded in their scrolls such an important event. But, on the contrary, this work reveals that whatever the Tibetan Buddhists knew about Jesus, their information came from Jewish merchants who were traveling between Palestine and Kashmir-Tibet to sell their goods. Thus, it contains a Jewish narrative of Jesus' crucifixion, colored by Buddhist ideas and spiced by an account of young Jesus' trip to India between the ages of thirteen and twenty-nine. Obviously, the Jewish merchants wanted to absolve the Jews from any guilt in Christ's crucifixion and squarely place the blame on Pilate; while the Tibetan monks desired to make Jesus a student of Buddhism.

The Tomb of Jesus in Srinagar

The Ahmadis are confident, however, that Jesus lived in Kashmir because in Srinagar, Kashmir, they have the tomb of Yuz Asaf, the Prophet whom the local population calls the Shahzada Nabi (The Prince Prophet) and Hazrat Isa Sahib (The Honorable Noble Jesus). This tomb is also called Rauzabal or Rozabal (The Prophet's Tomb). Rauza signifies a prophet's tomb, as opposed to ziarat, which indicates the tomb of a saint. A few Occidental and Oriental writers have mentioned this tomb, including Francis Younghusband, former British resident at Kashmir, who wrote in his work *Kashmir* that the tomb of Yuz Asaf is in Srinagar and that in theory it is the tomb of Jesus; and Captain C. M. Enrique, who indicated that during his stay in Srinagar, he encountered some strange traditions concerning some of the tombs there, including one which was said to be the tomb of Christ. Some westerners say that the tomb is that of a disciple of Jesus. However, most Europeans writing on Kashmir have preferred not to mention the tomb of Yuz Asaf, perhaps because of their own religious convictions. Among the oriental writers who wrote of this tomb there is Kwaja Muhammad Azam of Deedamari, who wrote in his *Waqiat-i-Kashmir* (or *Tarakh-i-Azami*) that besides the grave of Seyed Nasir-ud-Din, a Muslim saint buried in Khaniyar (Srinagar), there is the resting place of a prophet who, after great tribulations, had come to Kashmir in ancient times from a great distance and had become God's messenger to the people of Kashmir. Yuz Asaf's tomb is also mentioned in *Wajeez-ut-Tawarikh*, Mir Saadullah Shah's *Baqh-i-Suleman*, Abdul Ali Khan's *Hashmat-i-Kashmir*, Amir-ud-Din Pakhliwal's *Tahqiqat-i-Amiri*, Mizra Said-ud-Din Baig's *Khulasa-tut-Tawarikh*, and others. *Wajeez-ut-Tawarikh* states that the tomb of Seyed Nasir-ud-Din in Mohalla Khaniyar is also called Rauzabal, and that the tomb of Yuz Asaf, the prophet, who had come as a messenger to the people of Kashmir, is also to be found there. An aroma of musk used to emanate from a hole in its wall, this work says, until a woman with an infant visited the tomb. The child accidentally relieved itself, and the urine entered the tomb's hole.[46]

In 1776, five muftis (judges) of Srinagar confirmed that the tomb of Rozabal belongs to Rahman Mir and his descendants. The tomb of Yuz Asaf, therefore, is the private property of the Mir family. According to a photocopy of an old document shown to Al Haj Nazir Ahmad by a custodian of this tomb, Mir declared in the Court of Justice and in the Department of Instruction and religion that nobles, kings, and the general public came from everywhere to pay their respects to Yuz Asaf and make their offerings, "that he is absolutely authorized to receive and utilize these offerings, and that no one else has this right. . . . " This document also goes on to state that, based on confirmed evidence, Yuz Asaf arrived here during the reign of the ruler Gopadatta who repaired the building on Mount Solomon and built numerous temples. Yuz Asaf, a law-giver, who renounced all material cares, was of a royal lineage. He constantly prayed to God and meditated mostly while alone. He came to Kashmir as a prophet after the Great flood, and until his death, he taught that God was one. He was buried on the side of the lake in Mohallah Khaniyar in the Rozabal tomb, and next to him is buried Seyed Nasir-ud-Din Rizvi, who died in 1451. Rahman Mir is the hereditary custodian of this place, continues this document, and "is entitled to receive the offerings" deposited in it and no one else has this right.[47]

Andreas Faber-Kaiser, who visited this tomb recently writes that the tomb is contained in a rectangular building. Behind it is a Muslim cemetery in which the graves are aligned in a north-south direction in accordance with Muslim tradition. Outside the tomb, says Faber-Kaiser, a blue notice attached to a post contains the name Rozabal in white letters, a contraction of Rauza Bal, signifying a prophet's tomb. A small

entrance hall, where one must remove his shoes, leads first to a gallery
that surrounds the inner chamber, entered through a small opening,
on the left of which an inscription on a wooden tablet is headed by
the words "Ziarat Yuza Asaf Khanyar." This is rather curious. The
Department of Archaeology of the state of Kashmir, which presented
this tablet, used the word ziarat designating the tomb of a saint rather
than rozabal designating that of a prophet. The rest of the inscription
indicates that Yuz Asaf came to Kashmir centuries ago and preached
the truth. On the floor of the inner chamber, one sees two tombstones
enclosed by a wooden framework. The largest one at the further end
of the chamber is that of Yuz Asaf, while the other, near the entrance,
is that of Seyed Nasir-ud-Din Rizvi, a fifteenth-century Muslim saint
and a devotee of Yuz Asaf who wished to be buried next to him. Behind
Yuz Asaf's tomb in the northeast corner of the inner chamber, a stone
block is used as a base on which to place candles; on it are carvings of
footprints bearing traces of crucifixion wounds. These footprints were
exposed some time ago when the thick candle-wax was removed from
the stone, revealing first a crucifix and then a rosary. Whoever fashioned
these footprints, says Faber-Kaiser, evidently held Asaf and Jesus to be
the same person because of the crucifixion wounds. And he could have
added that, evidently, Christian worshipers had been there previously
and might have venerated Yuz Asaf as Jesus. Perhaps they left their
crucifix and rosary behind, or simply dropped them by accident. When
questioning the custodian of Rozabal, who was quite ignorant of the
history of this tomb, Faber-Kaiser was told that many people of different
denominations have visited the tomb, including Prime Minister Indira
Ghandi's uncle and famous movie stars, perhaps also Christian priests,
because there were various Christian schools in Srinagar. Faber-Kaiser
discovered that the people of Kashmir who visit the tomb speak of it
as the tomb of Hazrat (Honorable) Yuz Asaf, of the Nabi Sahib (the
Lord Prophet), of the Shahzada Nabi (the Prince Prophet), or of Hazrat
Isa Sahib (the Honorable Master Jesus).

Holger Kersten, who also visited Rozabal, and Faber-Kaiser write
that the real tomb of Yuz Asaf or Jesus is not shown. Both tombstones
in the inner chamber are aligned in a north-south Muslim burial fashion.
However, the true tomb of Yuz Asaf, which lies in a crypt underneath,
is aligned in the east-west Jewish burial manner. This real crypt underneath, says Faber-Kaiser, could be previously reached from the street
by a stairway on the west side of the building. But this entrance was
blocked, except for a small opening or window, which window, according
to Al-Haj Nazir Ahmad, proves that the tomb was constructed in a

Jewish fashion reminding one of the door of Jesus' tomb in Jerusalem. None of these men report whether they were allowed to see the real tomb of Yuz Asaf, whether one can actually see it through the aperture, or how they learned that it is aligned in the east-west Jewish burial custom. Faber-Kaiser does not explain when and why the stairway entrance to the real crypt was blocked, while Al-Haj Nazir Ahmad and Kersten do not mention at all that such an entrance existed. Nor do these men describe the tomb's geometric dimensions or speculate on the size or probable height of its deceased occupant.[48]

Not only did Faber-Kaiser visit Jesus' tomb in Srinagar, but he also met and conversed with one of Jesus' descendants, by the name of Sahibzada Basharat Saleem. While in Srinagar, Jesus or Yuz Asaf did marry. According to the old Persian book *Negari-Tan-i-Kashmir*, previously mentioned, King Shalewahin, who had conversed with Yuz Asaf in the Tibetan mountains and had asked him twice what his religion was, also advised Yuz Asaf to have a woman take care of him and offered to let him choose one from among fifty. Yuz Asaf refused the offer because he had no need for a woman, nor did he want one to work for him. However, Shalewahin insisted, until Yuz Asaf agreed to have a woman look after him. Yuz Asaf chose Maryan, who, eventually, bore him children. Faber-Kaiser found Saleem, who is "a keen photographer, an art lover and a poet," to be a very sensitive man of high integrity and altruism. He told Faber-Kaiser that, according to his father, the Muslim saint buried in Rozabal, Seyed Nasir-ud-Din Rizvi, was nothing when compared to the prophet in it. His father used to respond to those who asked him whether he was a descendant of Jesus that he was but, that "we call him Yuz Asaf." Saleem, says Faber-Kaiser, keeps a genealogical table that traces his ancestry back to Jesus. When Faber-Kaiser asked him who the mother of Jesus' children was, he responded that it was Maryan (also Mirjan or Marjon) from one of the shepherd villages in the valley of Pahalgam, Kashmir. Saleem's father and grandfather are remembered for their exceptional healing powers. By tradition, the Saleem family's oldest son is in charge of the maintenance of Rozabal. But Sahibzada, who is the oldest, is occupied as a hotelier (previously, as editor of a daily newspaper and, during the Indo-Pakistan conflict of 1965, as a political leader), so he has been hiring different men to look after Rozabal and to serve its visitors. Sahibjada Busharat Saleem, who was born on August 14, 1934, is a political activist who has been arrested and imprisoned many times in the past for his political convictions.[49]

4. Was Yuz Asaf Jesus?

Did Jesus Ever Go to Kashmir With Thomas?

Hazrat Mirza Ghulam Ahmad, the founder of the Ahmadiyya movement, discovered through divine revelation that the tomb of Yuz Asaf was the tomb of Jesus. Divine guidance in various forms in the past has enabled Christians to discover buried icons, relics, and even churches. God certainly works in mysterious ways. The Ahmadis, therefore, especially Al-Haj Nazir Ahmad, devoted themselves to the task of using works written in the past, both by westerners and especially easterners, to prove that Yuz Asaf was Jesus. However, almost all of the eastern works have been written since the fifteenth century and are based on an oral tradition, on hearsay, which most likely continued to evolve long after the supposed facts occurred. Unfortunately, the eastern works cited are not reliable because their authors repeated stories that were either exaggerated truth or myths simply because they were a part of an oral tradition that people believed to be true. Hazra Ghulam Ahmad admitted, for example, that the *Rauzat-us-Safa* contains exaggerations about Jesus, ascribing "many an absurd and irrational miracle to Jesus."[1] The ancient world was undoubtedly filled with myths through which individuals sought to convince and entertain a public always ready, for the most part and for many reasons, to accept them. India and the eastern world in general were certainly filled with such myths and legends, which became a part of Hinduism, Buddhism, and Jainism and other religions as well; and for the ignorant masses these exaggerated tales were real events.[2]

Not only the works used by the Ahmadis, but also their scholarship is questionable. They seem to have selected passages and to have presented them inaccurately and out of context in order to prove that Jesus traveled to Kashmir. For example, The Acts of Judas Thomas (Or the Twin), which is a Christian Gnostic work of the end of the second century, probably produced by three successive writers, seeks to promote celibacy through the supposed teachings and acts of the Apostle Thomas. This work is not an historical narrative, but a doctrinal defense of celibacy and virginity with little concern for historical and geographical accuracy. Thomas travels to the East to the court of

97

King "Gudnaphar" (Gondophares or Gopadatta) and later to that of King Mazdai, and he attacks sexual union and marriage while performing all kinds of spectacular if not unbelievable miracles. Compared to the gospels and the New Testament writings in general, The Acts of Thomas appears naive, seeking to impress the gullible. In order to demonstrate that Jesus, himself, was against sexual union, this work occasionally and abruptly brings Jesus in to speak. Jesus does not travel with Thomas to the East in this work as Al-Hag Nazir Ahmad has us to believe. After the Apostle Thomas was selected by lot in Jerusalem to go to India and he declined, Jesus appeared to him at night to calm his fears; but Thomas was still adamant about not going to India because he was a Hewbrew, and as a foreigner could not speak to the Indians. When Habban (Abanes), a merchant, happened to come "into the south country," according to the Acts, the work does not say where exactly; certainly it does not mention Magdonia (Nisibis), as the Ahmadis claim. Habban was sent there by King "Gudnaphar" to find a skillful carpenter. Then, suddenly, without an explanation, the Acts brings Jesus into the story with the comment "our Lord saw him [Habban] walking in the street," and Jesus sold Judas Thomas (as his supposed slave) to Habban for twenty pieces of silver. The Acts contains no reference to Jesus being with the King of Magdonia and advising him to send his brother Thomas with Habban to Gondophares, as the Ahmadis maintain. Judas Thomas quietly and without any protests complied with Jesus' wish. Jesus did not keep the pieces of silver but gave them to Thomas, who went on with Habban to Sandaruk (in Greek, Andrapolis) and was present at the marriage of the King's daughter. (The King's name is not given nor the name of his kingdom.) Although Al-Haj Nazir Ahmad (p. 352) claims that this wedding took place at Taxila and that Thomas went on to Andra (not Andrapolis) much later, the Acts record that from Sandaruk, Thomas and Habban went to the court of Godnophares at Taxila. After revealing his prophetic power and singing, and blessing the married couple (whose names are not given), as the unnamed king at Sandaruk had asked, Thomas left. Soon after, when the bridegroom saw his bride with Judas Thomas in the bedchamber and asked him how he could still be there, since he had left earlier, Jesus answered the groom that he was not Judas but his twin brother. How Jesus appeared there, the Acts does not say, but it is rather obvious that Jesus was not with Thomas. He was merely performing more miracles as mentioned in the New Testament after his resurrection. Although the point is made in Acts that Thomas and Jesus looked alike, the author obviously brought Jesus into his story primarily to give the married couple a sermon against "filthy intercourse" and against begetting children, which "are the cause of many pains; for either the king falls upon them, or a demon lays hold of them, or paralysis befalls them."[3] The married couple agreed not to consummate their marriage. When the King heard of their agreement, he became angry and gave orders for Thomas' arrest; but, Thomas had already left for King Gudnaphar's court in India, where he performed miracles throughout this country and even conversed with a talking black snake and a wild jackass. Although King Gudnaphar (Gondophares) hired him to build a palace and gave him the money, Thomas merely preached, healed the sick, and gave to the poor. But after he resurrected Gad, King Gudnaphar's brother, the King did not kill Thomas as he had planned. Although Al-Haj Nazir Ahmad writes that Jesus and Thomas attended the marriage feast of Abanes (Habban), who was Gad's son, no such feast is reported in the Acts. Jesus does not appear again to Thomas (except once in a dream). When King Mazdai's General Sifur asked Thomas to come to heal his wife and daughter, Thomas left the deacon Xanthipus to care for his converts in the land of King Gudnaphar and went on a chariot to the country of King Mazdai (presumably in southern India; the work does not say, nor does it mention a divergence to Africa). There, Thomas healed the sick and those possessed by demons, performed all kinds of wondrous miracles, but also preached against matrimony and sex, and converted even the King's wife, Tertia, to his belief, along with her friend, Mygdonia, a noble lady. Therefore, the frustrated, angry King Mazdai had him jailed and executed with spears by his soldiers. But, as Jesus had returned after his death, Judas Thomas appeared to his converts to comfort them and even to King Mazdai to remove a devil from his possessed son. Mazdai had tried to find Thomas' bones, intending to place them on his son and thus to cure him. The bones, however, had been removed. Thomas subsequently appeared to Mazdai and advised him to throw some dust on his boy from Thomas' grave, which he did, and his son was cured. Repentant Mazdai now became a Christian.[4]

The Acts of Thomas reveals that Thomas did go to northwestern India during the reign of Gondophares (Gopadatta) in the first century A.D. Gondophares is an historical figure, an Indo-Parthian king who ruled northwestern India, comprising the eastern Punjab (Kashmir), as coins of this period reveal. He was, however, a king independent of the Emperor of Parthia or Persia, who ruled from Ctesiphon.[5] The

Ahmadi contention that Jesus was present with Thomas in India as Yuz Asaf is not in any way supported by The Acts of Thomas. Therefore, the Ahmadi thesis can rest only on eastern legends recorded in oriental works, which for the most part are not reliable, not only because they were written long after the facts, but also because their stories of Yuz Asaf are different and in contradiction.

The Question of Thomas' Presence in India

St. Thomas the Apostle may have gone to India, as the Ahmadis maintain. But there is also much doubt about this. Local Christian tradition claims that St. Thomas appeared in southern India. After landing and preaching first at Malankara island near Cranganore, India, Thomas went on to establish seven churches on India's Malabar coast in the west before departing for Mailapore (Mylapore) on the Coromandel coast in the east, where he converted its king and all its people. From there, according to southern India's local tradition, he traveled to China with the same results and returned to Mailapore, India, near the city of Madras, where he suffered martyrdom. Aroused to anger by Brahmans, who were jealous of Thomas' success in converting many individuals to Christianity, the local people stoned him to death. However, early Christian tradition maintains that he was killed by soldiers who struck him with their lances. In 1517, Portuguese adventurers arriving at Mailapore were informed that the local ruined Christian church, of which only a part was still standing, was the burial place of St. Thomas and of some of his converts. Therefore, in 1522, by orders of King John III of Portugal, the viceroy of Goa, India, sent a commission to Mailapore, which discovered beneath the ancient ruined church what they believed to be the bones of St. Thomas, together with the remains of the king whom he converted. Believing that the bones of the apostle could be known by their superior whiteness, while the head could be detected by the fatal lance which killed him, the commission easily identified the apostle's remains and brought them to Goa, where they were deposited in the Church of St. Thomas. However, the Roman Catholic Cathedral at Mailapore still claims to have some of the ashes and bones of this apostle. Perhaps a portion of the relics was left at Mailapore.[6]

Interestingly, no such relics of St. Thomas existed in India in the sixteenth century. The Syriac version of The Acts of Judas Thomas states that one of the brethren had secretly taken away the bones of

Thomas and brought them to the West during the lifetime of the king (Mazdai) under whom he was killed, while the Greek version says that one of the brethren, having stolen his remains, brought them to Mesopotamia. St. Ephraem, who moved to Edessa from Nisibis in 363 and remained there till his death in 373, makes several references in his hymns to a merchant who brought the bones of Thomas to Edessa from India, but does not mention the merchant by name. The Nestorians or Eastern Syrian Christians mention in their calendar that the body of St. Thomas was brought from India to Urfa (Edessa) by the merchant Khabin. Evidently, in 163, the bones of St. Thomas were brought from Madras, India, to Edessa. The transfer of the Apostles' bones to Edessa is celebrated by the Syrian Church on July 3. On August 22, 394, under bishop Cyrus, the relics of St. Thomas were removed to a new church in Edessa erected in his honor, and in 442 or 443, General Anatolius donated a silver casket suspended by silver chains from the roof of the church to hold the bones of St. Thomas. St. Thomas' relics remained in Edessa even after the Muslim Arabs took that city from the Byzantines. They were still there when the western crusaders took over Edessa during the First Crusade of 1095-99 and when the Emir of Mosul, Zenghi, captured and sacked this city in 1142. However, after the son of the deceased Zenghi also plundered Edessa a year later, some of the surviving Christians removed the Apostles' relics for safe keeping to the Greek island of Chios and placed them in a tomb with his name and the figure of a bust engraved on it. On June 17, 1258, by the order of the Prince of Taranto, Manfred, a fleet under Admiral Philip Leonard sailed for Chios, removed St. Thomas' relics and the covering stone and on Setptember 6 brought them to Ortona a Mare, Italy, where they were placed in a chapel within the church of St. Mary, the name of which was changed to St. Thomas. Although on August 1, 1566, a Turkish fleet plundered Ortona a Mare and damaged St. Thomas' tomb, his relics are still there in the same church today. By this time, it seems, the history of the relics of St. Thomas had been forgotten by most writers and Christians. Therefore, the Portuguese thought they had been discovered in the church at Mailapore, India, where many other western Christians also thought they were to be found.[7]

Tradition reveals, as the Ahmadis assert, that Christians have always maintained that St. Thomas went to and died in India. Many of the fourth-century Church Fathers, including St. Ambrose and St. Jerome, Gregory Nazianzos and John Chrysostom, refer in their writings to Thomas' presence and martyrdom in India. Such references to Thomas are also found in the writings of the Greek, Roman, and Ethiopian Churches. An exception is Heracleon, cited by Clement of Alexandria (200 A.D.), who wrote that Thomas was one of the Apostles who were not martyred. Sokrates Scholastikos in the fifth century and other writers mention Thomas' relics as being enshrined at Edessa, where a magnificent memorial church was built. Many Christians of the West certainly held that Thomas had died in India. Relying on eyewitnesses who had visited the holy places in the East, Bishop Gregory of Tours (France) wrote in his *In Gloria Martyrum* (which he revised in 590, three years before his death) about St. Thomas, who had died in India and whose bones were removed to Edessa. Even the English in Anglo-Saxon times knew of St. Thomas' martyrdom in India. The *Anglo-Saxon Chronicle* records that in 883, King Alfred, in fulfillment of a vow that he had made while defending London from the Danes, sent an embassy to Rome and to India with gifts for the Pope and for the Christians of St. Thomas and Bartholomew. This interesting event is also mentioned in the *Chronicle* of Florence of Worchester, who died in 1117, and in the fourteenth-century *History of England* by William of Malmesbury.[8]

An historical confusion, however, has caused George Milne Rae and other scholars such as J. Hough (*History of Christianity in India* [London, 1859]) and John Kaye (*Christianity in India* [London, 1859]) to deny that Thomas ever traveled to India. One reason for this is that the Christianity established by St. Thomas on the eastern coast of India did not survive an early persecution, when many of these Christians fled to India's western coast. This is known through the ancient tradition of the west coast Christians, reported by Portuguese writers and mentioned in a British Report of 1604 now found in the British Museum. There remained, therefore, no continuous permanent Church at Mylapore. However, the Church on the western coast did survive. According to Philostorgius and Photius (in 354), Theophilus, while on a mission to India on behalf of the Roman Emperor Constantine the Great, evidently visited the Malabar coast and found there a Christian church fully established and probably unadulterated with the Arian belief that the Son was not of the same substance as the Father. When the Alexandrian merchant Cosmas the Indicopleustes (Indian Voyager), a Nestorian, visited the Malabar coast around 522, he found a fully established Church there as well as on the island of Sri Lanka (Ceylon), but it was by then Nestorian. Cosmas' *Universal Christian Topography* provides us with the earliest proof that the Christians of St. Thomas (also referred to as the Syrian Church) in southern India belonged by this time to the Nestorian Church of Persia (named in 498 by the Synod of Seleucia, the Chaldean Church). Founded by the heretical former Patriarch Nestorius of Constantinople and his followers, this heretical Church was run by the Patriarchate of Babylon and was completely separate from the Church of the Roman Empire. Its territory was vast, covering not only southern India and Ceylon, but also central Asia, eastern Tartary, and northern China. The Christians of St. Thomas received their bishops from the Patriarchate of Babylon, which claimed its apostolic succession from St. Thomas via Edessa. Thus, these Christians of southern India had a Nestorian or Eastern Syrian Church calendar, ritual, and beliefs, and as mentioned earlier, were persecuted by the Roman Catholics as heretics until they and their fellow Chaldean Christians aligned with the Catholic Church of Rome.[9]

Those who claim that St. Thomas did not go to India indicate that Nestorianism and St. Thomas went together. They also claim that no proof exists that St. Thomas ever visited Edessa because only the apostle Thaddaeus did so. Located on the banks of the Daisan, which supplies the Belik, a left-hand tributary of the upper Euphrates River, Edessa was the capital of the small kingdom of Osrohene in the higher latitude of Mesopotamia. It was ruled by a series of elective monarchs, who each held the title of Abgar, just as the rulers of Egypt were called pharaohs. The Abgars were tributary vessels, dependent monarchs, of the Parthian (Persian) Empire, a rival of the Roman Empire. The Parthian Empire extended from the Indus River to the Euphrates and from the Indian Ocean to the Caspian Sea and the Hindu Kush. It appears that Christianity had been well established in Edessa by the second century, and a Syriac translation of the New Testament was first made in this city. The earliest document from the archives of Edessa connect St. Thomas with this city contains two letters written in the fifteenth year of the Roman Emperor Tiberius (14-37 A.D.), obtained from an Egyptian monastery by the British Museum in the nineteenth century. These letters were also used by Eusebius in his *History of the Church.* They relate that Abgar Uchomo (the Black), after falling grievously sick, sent a letter to Jesus, of whose healing miracles he had heard asking him to come to cure him and offering him protection from the Jews. One of the two letters contains Jesus' reply to Abgar Uchomo to the effect that he had work to do and could not leave Jerusalem, but that, after being "received up," he would send one of his disciples to cure him and to give eternal life to those with him.

It was Judas Thomas (as the apostle is almost always called in Edessan literature) who wrote Jesus' answer to the king of Edessa, and it was Judas Thomas who "by divine impulse" sent to that city, after Jesus' ascension, one of the twelve disciples whom Matthew and Mark refer to as Thaddaeus. (Luke calls him Judas son of James, and others refer to him as Lebbaeus or Jude. Thaddaeus is thought to have authored the Epistle of St. Jude.) Thaddaeus cured the Abgar and spread Christianity throughout his realm with the help of his disciple Aggaeus, maker of golden chains. The authenticity of the Edessan document is questioned because it has Jesus correponding with this Abgar, an occurence not recorded in the New Testament, and because it reveals that Christianity had spread as far as Edessa and beyond during the apostolic era, a claim that is suspect. But Christianity could have extended during the first century to Edessa, which is located only 180 miles from Antioch. After all, it did spread at this time to Rome, a distance of over 1000 miles, and to Spain 2000 miles away. According to the eastern tradition, Mar (St.) Maris, a disciple of Thaddaeus at Edessa, traveled to Ctesiphon, the capital of Parthia, and to Seleucia across the Tigris River from Ctesiphon, twelve or thirteen miles below modern Bagdad, where arose the vast Patriarchate of the East. This eastern church had ties with the Church of Antioch, from which it received its bishops, thus maintaining its apostolic succession, which had been interrupted by persecutions and the martyrdom of its bishops by infidels.[10]

There is no evidence that St. Thomas himself traveled through the Parthian Empire via Edessa and on into Kashmir. The earliest Christian documents, incuding the ancient Syriac document titled "The Doctrine of the Apostles" of the early third century, indicate that it was Thaddaeus (referred to as Addaeus in the Syriac) and his disciples who preached the gospel within the regions of the Parthian Empire "even to the borders of the Indians." No evidence exists that Thomas went to the court of King Gondophares and thus came into contact with the northwestern corner of India. If Thomas traveled himself through Parthia and into the Punjab—as A. E. Medlycott suspects he did on his first trip to the East, before his trip to southern India via Egypt, Ethiopia and the island of Socotra (which took place after Mary's dormition)—then, as Medlycott himself admits, his first trip belongs to the omitted part of Thomas' history. The mention of a real figure such as Gondophares in The Acts of Judas Thomas, a figure eventually forgotten by history, is no indication, as Medlycott maintains, that Thomas visited Gondophares' domain. After all, The Acts was written in the third century A.D., perhaps, less than one hundred years after Gondophares' rule (21 (ca.)-60 A.D.). The Acts of Thomas presents only some incidents dealing with Thomas' mission to Parthia and India, not the history of his apostolic career to the East. It misplaces events from southern India to Parthia and moves from the court of King Gondophares in Parthia to King Mazdai in southern India without identifying the location of Mazdai's kingdom. The story of Thomas and the geography as presented in the Acts appear to be more mythical than real. It might be that Christianity arrived in the Punjab during the reign of Gondophares, and his name was subsequently remembered by early Christians. Eusebius writes that according to Origen and Church tradition, Parthia fell to Thomas, but this is no indication that Thomas appeared there in person. The use in the Acts of Thomas of a historical figure such as Gondophares does not in any way imply, as the Ahmadis assert, that the story must be true. In spite of the story in the Acts that Thomas left the deacon Xanthipus to look after the converts there, no historical evidence exists that a Christian community had been established in Gondophares' kingdom. No trace remains of the survival of such a Christian community in northwestern India under Xanthipus.[11]

Confusion about Thomas' presence in northern India is a result of a wide or loose territorial application of the names Parthia and India. The word Parthia was used loosely, denoting also India, and India in turn also covered Arabia and Ethiopia. Thus, in the fourth century, St. Jerome and St. Clement reported that the learned Pantaenus was sent from Alexandria to India where he found that Bartholomew, one of the twelve Apostles, had already preached and had left the Gospel of Matthew written in Aramaic to a people using this language. The India that they were writing about turned out to be neither India nor Parthia but Yemen in the southern part of the Arabian Peninsula, where there were many Jews. This was considered to be a part of India at the time. Rufinus of Italy in the fourth century mentions Meropius, a philosopher from Tyre, and his pupils Frumentius and Edesius, who preached in India, but who were actually in Abyssinia (Ethiopia), Africa. Even Ethiopia was referred to occasionally as India. Thus, Philostorgius, a fourth-century native of Cappadocia (a province in Asia Minor), writes that Theophilus went on a mission to India, but he refers to Yemen and Arabia Felix as well as Ethiopia or Abyssinia as India. Thus, Theophilus visited Yemen and the Christians of St. Thomas on the Malabar Coast of India, returned to Arabia, and went on to Axum, Abyssinia, where he visited Frumentius, all on a mission to India.[12]

If Thomas did not go to Parthia, but only Thaddaeus did, then there is hardly any chance that Jesus went to Kashmir as Yuz Asaf, as the Ahmadis contend. However, since Origen and Eusebius and others referred to Thomas' mission in Parthia and India and gave no details of any such mission to the court of Gondophares or to Kashmir, it is possible that they might have been seeking to hide something, perhaps the fact that Thomas did not go alone but that Jesus was with him physically, and not merely spiritually through miraculous appearances as in The Acts. Although the chance that this actually occurred is remote, it cannot be ascertained until Yuz Asaf's identity is known.

Questionable Ahmadi Claims Concerning Moses and Solomon

It is rather difficult, however, to be persuaded by the Ahmadis that Jesus died in India. They make several other contentions which only cast doubt upon and thus discredit their thesis concerning Yuz Asaf's identity. They claim that they have not only the Tomb of Jesus in Kashmir, but also the Tomb of Moses, and they maintain that the Promised Land in Deuteronomy (4:44-49) is not Palestine but Kashmir. They indicate that such biblical places as Beth-peor, Heshbon, Pisgah, the Moab valley, and Mount Nebo are in Kashmir. They identify Beth-peor with Bandipur, which was earlier called Behatpoor, and Hesbon, which had pools of fish, with the village of Hashba, twelve miles southwest of Bandipur. Pisgah they claim is a village whose name is synonymously used with Mount Abarim, located three miles from Hashba, at the foot of Niltoop (Naboo Hill or Baal Nabu), which they maintain is Mount Nebo. Niltoop is a single peak of Mount Abarim from which one can see the fertile valley of Kashmir. Unlike Palestine, which is arid, say the Ahmadis, the Promised Land of Deuteronomy (11:11) has plenty of rains and water and "extends even up to the sea of the plain, under the springs of Pisgah" (Deut. 4:49). No other land east of the Jordan or Euphrates rivers contains the springs, the rivers, the "sea of the plain," which is the large Lake Walar near Bandipur, and thus fulfills the Bible's description of the Promised Land as a "heaven on earth." There is a Mount Abarim in Palestine, say the Ahmadis, but the view reveals only an arid land and not the fertile valley that one observes from Mount Abarim in Kashmir. Genesis (14:18) describes the borders of Palestine or of the Holy Land as extending from the river of Egypt to the great river, the river Euphrates. But Palestine is not the Promised Land, say the Ahmadis. They contend that Moses went east of the Euphrates, Palestine's eastern border, in search of the Promised Land, Kashmir.[13]

As convincing proof of Moses' presence in Kashmir, the Ahmadis offer the tomb of Moses on the top of Niltoop, which they claim is Mount Nebo. A small Jewish community located nearby takes care of this tomb, which is in a square enclosure off the main path with a wooden gate containing the name of successive custodians for the past 900 years. (Since Moses lived about 1300 B.C., why were not the names of previous custodians recorded?) Three Muslim tombs are within the enclosure, but Moses' tomb, which is oriented in the east-west direction traditional for Jews is given prominence by two trees on either of its sides. The Ahmadis are confident that this is the tomb of Moses because of Kashmir's written and oral tradition, which affirms that Moses died and was buried there. However, the writings that they refer to date from the sixteenth century and after and are by Muslims. They also mention John Chrysostom's Homily 26 on Hebrews, in which he asks, "Does not Moses' body lie buried in some far away place in the East?" and the works of European travelers, including those of the French physician Francis Bernier (*Travels in the Mughul Empire*) and of George Moore (*The Lost Tribes*), who merely mention that there are legends in Kashmir that Moses lived, taught, and died there. These two authors discuss the legends, which they found among the Muslims, but do not confirm them. In addition, the Ahmadis point out that at least four places in Kashmir are called Moses' Resting Place. The name Moses is common and therefore popular among the Kashmiris, who have the 8′ 3″ rod or staff of Moses in Mohammedan, mentioned earlier, and the stone that Moses struck with this staff in order to bring forth, according to the Persian work *Rauzat-us Saufa*, four streams of water from its four sides. This 110-pound Stone of Moses, the Ahmadis assert, which is also called the Ka Ka Pal, is located twenty-seven miles south of Srinagar; and if eleven people sit around it and place one finger each at the lower edge of the stone and together call out "*Ka, Ka, Ka, Ka*," the stone will lift itself from the ground. The number eleven, according to the local residents, represents the twelve tribes who inherited the land of Israel minus one, Levi, who had been disinherited. In Ladakh, the people call Moses as Ka Ka, while the Pathans refer to a saintly or an elderly person as Ka Ka. Although the Ahmadis attest to the truth concerning the miraculous ability of the Ka Ka Pal to rise by itself, they admit that the Kashmiris often refer to the staff of Moses as the staff of Jesus and are confused about its ownership. The fact is that Moses' staff was also supposedly to be found in medieval Europe.[14]

As though all this evidence were not convincing enough that Kashmir is truly the Promised Land, the Ahmadis also assert that, during his reign, King Solomon of the Hebrews visited Kashmir by air because, as stated in the Koran (21:81; 38:36), God gave Solomon the power to command the wind and to go wherever he desired. Thus, Solomon flew to Kashmir, and there, where he rested on the hill in Srinagar, 1500 feet high, stands the Temple or Throne of Solomon (Takht-i-Sulaiman), built prior to 250 B.C. According to Al-Haj Nazir Ahmad, it is an exact replica of the tomb of Absalom (King David's third son) in the valley of Josephat not far from Jerusalem. Thus, the Ahmadis are certain that, since he could fly anywhere, Solomon was able to rule not only Palestine but also the Promised Land or Kashmir. Al-Haj Nazir Ahmad asserts that Solomon also landed via air on the Hindu Kush, where there stands another Throne of Solomon. The Temple of Solomon, says Ahmad, and other ancient monuments of Kashmir, including that of Martand, eight miles from Islamabad, reveal a Jewish type of architecture, and thus Jewish influence. However, contradicting Ahmad, Aziz Kashmiri (an Ahmadi) indicates that Martand is Greek in its architecture.[15]

Since they accept that Solomon flew through the air to visit Kashmir and other places, it is rather difficult to take the Ahmadis seriously in their insistence that Kashmir is the Promised Land. The thesis has several serious flaws. The Ahmadis have merely interpreted the names of Kashmiri towns to be the same as the biblical names of towns in Palestine. But such interpretations are improbable. The Ahmadis quote Deuteronomy (32:48-52) to make the point that Moses died on Mount Nebo. In it, God tells Moses:

> Go up this Mount Abarim, Mount Nebo in Moab, to the east of Jericho, and look out over the land of Canaan that I am giving to the Israelites for their possession. On this mountain you shall die and be gathered to your father's kin, as Aaron your brother died on Mount Hor and was gathered to his father's kin. This is because both of you were unfaithful to me at the waters of Meribah-by-Kadesh in the wilderness of Zin, when you did not uphold my holiness among the Israelites. You shall see the land from a distance, but may not enter the land I am giving to the Israelites.

However, in contradiction to the Ahmadi thesis, Deuteronomy (34:1-4) indicates that the Promised Land is Canaan, east of Jericho, which can be none other than Palestine and not Kashmir. It states: "Then Moses went up from the lowlands of Moab to Mount Nebo, to the top of Pisgah, eastwards from Jericho, and the Lord showed him the whole land: Gilead as far as Dan; the whole of Naphtali; the territory of Ephraim and Manasseh, and all Judah as far as the western sea; the Negeb and the Plain; the valley of Jericho; the Valley of Palm Trees, as far as Zoar." Thus, Moses is not in Pisgah observing Kashmir, but is looking at Palestine from Dan to Negeb and at the Mediterannean Sea. The fact is that Pisgah is a mountain range just east of the Jordan River, and its highest peak is Mount Nebo, located almost directly east of Jericho; while the Moab Valley is south of Mount Nebo and east of the Dead Sea. Palestine might be dry compared to Kashmir, but it is fertile and a heaven on earth when compared with the Negev Desert and other arid places, including Sinai.

Although the Ahmadis maintain that Moses died on the top of Mount Niltoop (Nebo) in Kashmir and was buried there, they have made no scientific examination of his supposed tomb. They rely on legends and the names of likely places to confirm that Moses was entombed in this location. If they had consulted Deuteronomy (34:6), they would have read: "There in the land of Moab Moses the servant of the Lord died, as the Lord had said. He was buried in a valley in Moab opposite Beth-peor, but to this day no one knows his burial place." Obviously, then, Moses was buried in a valley, not on the top of Mount Nebo or Niltoop, and as Deuteronomy (34:8) further affirms: "The Israelites wept for Moses in the lawlands of the Moab for thirty days." Thus, Moses' tomb was definitely not to be found on a mountain, but somewhere in the Moab valley of the Transjordan. When God tells Moses in Deuteronomy (3:27) to "go to the top of Pisgah and look west and north, south and east; look well at what you see, for you shall not cross this river Jordan," he is not referring to the Indus River or any of its tributaries in Kashmir. And even if God were speaking of the Euphrates river as this Jordan, which the Ahmadis indicate is Palestine's eastern border, he would not have been discussing Kashmir, since it is hundreds of miles away. In any case, many Muslims accept that Moses (Musa in Arabic) was buried in the Moab Valley of the Transjordan where they visit his supposed tomb.[16]

Contradictory Accounts Concerning Yuz Asaf

Who then is Yuz Asaf? The Ahmadis interpret the names Yuz and Asaf to be of Hebrew origin, but they have no clear evidence that this is the case. The semitic word for Jesus is Isa and not Yuz. The Ahmadis have made the point that Yuz Asaf was also called Isa, but only in the later eastern writings coming from legends. Although Al-Haj Nazir Ahmad insists that Yuz Asaf means Jesus, he also indicates that Yuz Asaf appears to mean a leader of healed lepers. Ahmad maintains that this identifies Yuz Asaf with Jesus, who healed lepers, as the gospels indicate; but as Ahmad himself also reveals, no one knows the exact meaning of this name, and that is why several interpretations exist.

As Al-Haz Nazir Ahmad reveals, confusion also exists in eastern writings concerning Yuz Asaf's past. Pirzada Ghulam Hasan writes in *Tarikh-i-Hassan* (1891), in the third of three volumes, that the inscription on the north wall staircase stone of the Throne of Solomon reads: "In this time a young man Yuz Asaf by name came from Egypt, claimed to be a descendant of a prophet. Year fifty and four." He does not mention any inscription identifying Yuz Asaf with Jesus. In his first volume, however, he writes that his father told him once that on one of the stone walls of the stairs of the Throne of Solomon, he saw the following inscribed in a Persian sulus script: "In this time a young man Yus Asap by name came from Egypt and claimed to be a descendant of a prophet. Year fifty and four Kashmiri era [1378 A.D.]." According to Al-Haj Nazir Ahmad, this author seems to be confused on his dates and deliberately avoided mentioning the inscription that identifies Yus Asaf with Jesus. In addition, says Ahmad, he seems to be intentionally confusing Yus Asap with Yuz Asaf in order to mislead his readers. He states in his first volume that adjoining the tomb of Seyed Nasir-ud-Din is the tomb of Yuz Asaf, a prophet from ancient times. Therefore, Yuz Asaf, being a prophet, had to come earlier than Muhammad, the last of the prophets. However, *Tarikh-i-Kabir-i-Kashmir*, published in 1903, says that, according to an Arabic book, Yuz Asaf was a prince who had come from Sholebeth [Sri Lanka] and resided here and died when Raja Gopanand was the ruler.[17] A third book titled *Kashir* (1949) by G. M. D. Sufi adds to the confusion concerning Yuz Asaf. It says that Sadhimati Aryaraja, minister of Kashmir to Jayendra (61 B.C.-24 A.D.), led a life of poverty, suffered imprisonment and death, but was resurrected, and by the request of the people ruled

Kashmir for forty-seven years. The same work continues that there is a persistent tradition occasionally perpetuated by writers that Christ was buried in Srinagar. Some even call him Hazrat Yuz Asaf and mention his burial place at Khanyar in Srinagar. However, Yuz Asaf, a supposed descendant of Moses, was sent by Egypt's ruler as ambassador to the court of Bad Shah. In Arabic writing, Yuz Asaf can be also read as Bodhisattva. There is no positive proof that Christ came to India, but it is indeed strange "that Christ should have had a resurrection similar to that of Samdhimati" and that both these men should also have "almost identical" dates.[18] Al-Haj Nazir Ahmad indicates that Sufi's *Kashir* is an admirable and exhaustive work in its investigation of the Islamic period of Kashmir, but that if the author had probed further into the life of Yuz Asaf, he would have reached a different conclusion.[19] However, this is merely the opinion of Ahmad whose evidence is in doubt.

Even the Persian writings in the khat-i-sulus script on the walls of the staircase of the Throne of Solomon are subject to questioning. As indicated previously, one of these inscriptions states: "At this time Yuz Asaf proclaimed his prophethood. Year fifty and four," the same year that the carvings were made; and the other states: "He is Yusu, Prophet of the Children of Israel" (Aishan Yusu Paighambar-i-Bani Israil ast). However, no calendar name is given for the year 54, and thus the exact date is subject to interpretation. The Indians used many different calendar eras, depending where and when they lived. It is believed that the calendar used for this particular inscription was that of the Laukika era, by which 1 A.D. equals 3076 B.C. The Laukika era was used by the Kashmiris prior to the establishment of Islam in Kashmir in 1324 A.D., after which the Kashmiri era was used. The Kashmiri era was introduced by the Sultan Shams-ud-Din, who set its starting date with the conversion of Kashmir's ruler Ratanju (Sultan Sadr-ud-Din). The year 54 is, therefore, probably 3054 Laukika era or 22 B.C. But, this does not suit Al-Haj Nazir Ahmad and others, and therefore, they fall back on Pirzada Ghulam Hasan's *Tarikh-i-Hasan*, whose dates they already discredited, in order to indicate that the date is 54 or 154 and therefore 3154 Laukika era or 78 A.D. This date may make linking Yuz Asaf with Jesus more plausible, but *Tarikh-i-Hasan* (Vol. I) connected 54 or 154 with the Kashmiri Era and claimed that the year refers to the reign of Sultan Zain-ul-Abidin (1424-1471 A.D.). Here again, Ahmad points out, Hasan was wrong, because whether the year is Kashmiri Era 54 (1378 A.D.) or 154 (1478 A.D.), it does not fall within the reign of this Sultan. Zain-ul-Abidin repaired the temple of the Panj Mukhia (Five Doors) in Srinagar but not that of the Throne of Solomon. Why, however, the Ahmadis are willing to accept Pirzada Ghulam Hasan's date of 154, when the date carved on the flank walls encasing the staircase of the Throne of Solomon is 54, they do not say. Hasan, it seems, arbitrarily accepted 54 and 154 merely to connect the year 54 and the repairs with the reign of Sultan Zain-ul-Abidin. The absence of a calendar for 54 has produced many other interpretations of dates. Al-Haj Nazir Ahmad indicates that H. H. Cole (*Illustrations of Ancient Buildings in Kashmir*, p. 8), without giving any reasons, claims that the year meant was 1054 of the Muslim Era or 1676 A.D., and Pandit Ram Chandra Kak (*Ancient Monuments of Kasmir*, p. 74) is of the same opinion. However, no record indicates that repairs were made to the Throne of Solomon temple in 1676 A.D., during the reign of the Mongol ruler Shah-Yahan. The historian Chaduarah Khwaja Hasan Malak in his *Tarikh-i-Kashmir* simply identifies 54 with the Muslim era or 676 A.D., but he says that the pillars to the Throne of Solomon were erected during the reign of Ghazi Shah Chak which cannot be, since the Chaks did not take over Kashmir until 1554 A.D.[20]

Since the exact date of the repairs on the Throne of Solomon is not known, it is difficult to say that they were carried out during the reign of Gondophares. Here, we have only the word of eastern historians, who wrote that the repairs on the Throne of Solomon occurred during the reign of Gondophares (Gopadatta). Pandit Narayan Kaul Ajiz's *Tarikh-i-Kashmir* states that "Thousands of years ago Rajah Gopadatta repaired the temple of Koh-i-Solaiman" and Haider Malak's *Tarakh-i-Kashmir* says that "Rajah Gopadatta . . . built many temples and repaired Koh-i-Sulaiman. Two thousand years have passed but the temple is intact. He governed for seventy years." The *Tarikh-i-Jadul* asserts that Gopadatta "repaired the temple called Zishi Shore" or the Koh-i-Sulaiman, and that Gopadatta's minister Sulaiman (Sandiman) was appointed to do the restoration. Similar remarks are also made in *Wajee-ul-Tawarikh*, Vol. I, by Mufti Ghulam Nabi Khaniyari and in *Khulasat-ut-Tawarikh* by Miraza Saif-ud-Din Baig. Pirzada Ghulam Hasan makes the same assertion concerning Gondophares, but his accuracy concerning the temple's inscriptions, as mentioned earlier, leaves much to be desired. The most important of these works, as previously indicated, is Mulla Nadiri's *Tarikh-i-Kashmir*, written in 1413 A.D. in Persian; and other eastern works agree that these repairs took place during the reign of Gondophares, but they are not necessarily correct. After all, these histories were written long after events had taken place, and they relied on an oral tradition. Only legends had survived, and whatever these historians recorded could not have been based on accurate accounts. India's early history is so full of mythical figures, evil spirits, and fairies, that many western scholars mistook them for real figures and arrived at contradictory conclusions. Ancient Indian writers used, even in the same work, many different eras, some of which are obscure in their origin and application; and many of these historians generally followed the custom of not mentioning eras or centuries at all. With the exception of inscriptions and coins, says Al-Haj Nazir Ahmad, the only other guide to chronological accuracy is Pandit Khulana's *Rajatarangini* (River of Kings), written in 1148-49 A.D. in Sanskrit as a didactic poem. But even Khulana's work, which according to Ahmad most western scholars agree is chronologically somewhat regular and consistent up to 589 A.D., employs three different eras, the Laukika era and, after 78 A.D., the Shalawahin and the Kalyugi eras (to which latter two it makes only occasional references). Prithivi Bamzai indicates in his *History of Kashmir* that Khulana's valuable work is a reliable record only from the seventh century and on. It has serious gaps in its chronology and does not distinguish legend from history. Sunil Chandra Ray, in his *Early History and Culture of Kashmir*, does not find Khulana (Kalhana), who was a non-Muslim, to be accurate in his early history of India. His account, he says, is full of myths and exaggerations without a clear and reliable chronology. In addition, Ram Chandra Kak writes in his *Ancient Monuments of Kashmir* that Khulana's chronology is hopelessly confusing and at variance with India's accepted chronology. He was the best of historians during his era, says Kak, but unable to distinguish between the legendary and the factual in tradition, and he also confused great foreign conquerors with local kings. Obviously, therefore, Indian writers before the nineteenth century did not know when Gondophares ruled, but some light has been recently shed on his reign by the discovery of coins and a stone inscription recovered in Taxila.[21]

Concerning the reign of this Indo-Parthian ruler the Ahmadis present us with inaccurate dates that conveniently place Yuz Asaf in Kashmir during this ruler's reign. Al-Haj Nazir Ahmad confidently asserts in *Jesus in Heaven on Earth* (pp. 384-385) that Gondophares ruled for sixty years and two month, from 49 A.D. to 109, and that Yuz Asaf appeared in Kashmir in 78 A.D. (3154 Laukika Era) and not in 22 B.C. (3054 Laukika Era). However, in this same work (p. 380),

Ahmad refers to Vincent A. Smith's *Early History of India* (p. 217 in 2nd ed. of 1908), which states that Gondophares succeeded King Azes II to the throne about 20 A.D. and died about 60 A.D. Then, Ahmad concludes on this same page of his work: "It is obvious, therefore, that Jesus and Thomas were in Taxila before 60 C.E. [A.D.] and, if Prof. Rapson is correct, before 50 C.E. [A.D.]." But this is a complete contradiction of his later conclusion in his same work, *Jesus in Heaven on Earth* (pp. 384-385), mentioned above, that Yuz Asaf began his career in Kashmir in 78 A.D., which obviously occurred after the death of Gondophares. In the fourth edition (1957) of his work *Early History of India*, Vincent A. Smith changed the date of Gondophares' death from 60 to 48 A.D. (p. 244). According to A. E. Medlycott's *India and the Apostle Thomas* (pp. 10-15), the Taht-i-Bahi stone (found in Taxila, Pakistan, and now preserved in the Lahore museum) contains an inscription which commemorates Gondophares in the twenty-sixth year of his reign (46 A.D.); therefore, Gondophares' rule must have begun twenty-five years earlier, or in 25 A.D., and must have lasted until his death about 50 or 60 A.D., a period of about thirty to forty years. Al-Haj Nazir Ahmad does refer (p. 380) to the Taht-i-Bahi stone's inscription commemorating Gondophares' twenty-sixth year as ruler (46 A.D.), and he admits that Gondophares' rule must have begun in 20 A.D. He even quotes from E. J. Rapson's *Ancient India* (p. 174), which states: "Gondophares, King of North-West India or 'Greater India,' combining the earlier kingdoms of the Parthians and Sakas ruled from 21 to 50 A.D."[22] This quotation is questionable. The date of 1911 given by Ahmad for the publication of Rapson's work cannot be correct, because both the first and second editions of this work appeared in 1914. The first and third editions, published in 1914 and 1916, state (pp. 144-145) that "towards the end of the first quarter of the first century A.D., the two kingdoms were united under the sway of the Pahlava Gondopharnes, as to the Parthian character of whose name there can be no doubt. The evidence is almost entirely numismatic. . . . " Rapson does not indicate the date of Gondophares' death. He refers to Gondophares as Gondopharnes, and does not use the names Parthians and Sakas in this particular passage as indicated in Ahmad's quotation. (Rapson calls the Sakas, Cakas.) However, in spite of these western writings and numismatic evidence, Ahmad prefers the eastern work *Tariht-i-Kashmir* (1617 A.D.) by Chadaura Haidar Malak, which states that Gondophares, who erected many temples and repaired the throne of Solomon, ruled for sixty years. And he also partly accepts H. H. Wilson's *History of*

Kashmir, Indian Researches (in *Asiatic Researches* [1841], Vol. XV). Although Wilson himself admits in his preface to his work that his chronology is off by fifty years, Ahmad declares that Wilson is off by 131 years and, after making allowance for Wilson's error, he dates Gondophares' rule from 49 A.D. to 109 A.D. He is obviously not willing to accept the chronology based on the most recent numismatic and inscription findings, and thus, he conveniently asserts that Yuz Asaf entered Kashmir in 78 A.D. (in any case, he says, after 60 A.D., but before 78 A.D.), and that Gondophares was the ruler responsible for the repairs in that same year (78) on the temple of Solomon. However, since Jesus and Thomas supposedly left Taxila around 50 A.D. because of the Kushan invasion of the Punjab (mentioned earlier), which anyway occurred after Gondophares' death, one has to accept that Jesus or Yuz Asaf had wandered for at least twenty-five years before reaching Kashmir even though Taxila is only about forty miles from the Kashmir border.[23]

Al-Haj Nazir Ahmad also concludes that the meeting between Yuz Asaf and Shalewahin must have taken place about 78 A.D. He indicates (p. 381) that about 60 A.D. (or in the 50's), Kadephsis I of the Kushans, from central Asia, conquered northern India and merely forced the rulers of this area to pay tribute to him and give him homage. It was about this time that the ruler Shalewahin, says Ahmad, championed the cause of the Brahmans against the Sakas, whom he drove out of northern India, which included Kashmir. He celebrated this victory by proclaiming a new calendar era, starting with March 14, 78 A.D., which he named after himself (the Shalewahin era). However, about 78 A.D., he left northern India for the Deccan in the south to crush a rebellion there. Therefore, he must have met Yuz Asaf in Wien (Voyen) near Srinagar shortly before his departure for the Deccan during that same year. But how could Shalewahin have waged war in Kashmir, when supposedly King Gondophares, who was the sole master of this area, was still the ruler? Gondophares ruled before the Kushan invasion under Kadephsis I, and there is no indication that he ruled under Kadephsis, although his successors did so. Al-Haj Nazir Ahmad's work, *Jesus in Heaven on Earth*, which constitutes the Ahmadis' best historical defense of Jesus' presence in Kashmir as Yuz Asaf, appears to be full of flaws, especially concerning Gondophares' reign.[24]

It is almost impossible to identify Yuz Asaf with Jesus. If he entered Kashmir after 60 A.D. and began his prophethood in 78 A.D., he was not in northern India during the reign of Gondophares and cannot

be connected in any way with the apostle Thomas, who supposedly was
there during this ruler's reign. Obviously, there is considerable doubt
that St. Thomas ever went to northern India. Even if one were to
consider the various Indian eras, it would be impossible to place Yuz
Asaf in India during the reign of Gondophares or during the first
century A.D., when Jesus might have been still living, unless one
changes the date on the wall of the Throne of Solomon from 54 to
any suitable date. Evidently, others have tried it, but unconvincingly,
because even 154 of the Laukika era does not fall within Gondophares'
reign, with the exception of the Kalyugi era, whereby 154 is equivalent
to 53 A.D. But, as indicated previously, the Kalyugi era is rejected by
Ahmad in favor of the Laukika (Haptrakesh-waran) era only because
Mullah Ahmad, the fifteenth-century historian of the court of Sultan
Zain-ul-Abidin, maintained that this era was used in Kashmir until
the conversion of Ratanju (Sultan Sadr-ud-Din) to Islam in 1324 A.D.
In any case, one would still have to use the date 154 rather than 54
to bring it within the reign of Gondophares. Looking at the Indian
eras listed by Al-Haj Nazir Ahmad clarifies the problem:

Muslim era	1 A.D. = 622 A.D.	54 =	676 A.D.
		154 =	776 A.D.
Kashmir era	1 A.D. = 1324 A.D.	54 =	1378 A.D.
		154 =	1478 A.D.
Shalewahin era	1 A.D. = 78 A.D.	54 =	132 A.D.
		154 =	232 A.D.
Bikrami era	1 A.D. = 57 B.C.	54 =	3 B.C.
		154 =	97 A.D.
Laukika era	1 A.D. = 3076 B.C.	54 =	22 B.C.
		154 =	78 A.D.
Kalyugi era	1 A.D. = 3101 B.C.	54 =	47 B.C.
		154 =	53 A.D.[25]

If Yuz Asaf was Jesus, he evidently did not reveal any supernatural
powers. Except for being called perhaps leader of lepers, with the
implication that he cured lepers rather than was one of them, it does
not appear that Yuz Asaf performed any other great miracles and
wonders. Obviously, his efforts in Kashmir must have failed because

he was not able to establish a new religion or a new Jewish sect by gaining enough followers to perpetuate his teaching till the present. Neither did he acquire dynamic disciples as he had in Palestine, able to expand his religion throughout India and beyond. He is remembered today primarily because of the Ahmadis and his tomb in Srinagar; but, interestingly, archaeologist Ram Chandra Kak in his *Ancient Monuments of Kashmir* does not mention Rauzabal or the Throne of Solomon. It is hard to believe that a tomb of such importance to both Muslims and Ahmadis would be left out by the former director of the department of archaeology and research of the state of Jammu and Kashmir. In addition, Prithivi Bamzai in his *History of Kashmir* also does not mention anything concerning Yuz Asaf, or the Jews of Kashmir or Rauzabal, which is most curious.

If Yuz Asaf arrived in Kashmir in 54 Laukika or 22 B.C., he most likely was a Jewish Essene whose teachings resembled those of Jesus. If he did arrive in Kashmir in the first century A.D., he could have been a Christian missionary or even an impostor. As already indicated earlier (Chapt. I), many individuals of the Gnostic sects during the first and second centuries after Christ, such as Dositheus, Simon Magus, and his disciple Menander made the claim that they were divine Messiahs, and were worshipped as such by their followers after they died. Clever magicians like Simon caused troubles for the early Christians, claiming that they were also divine and could perform great miracles like Jesus. There was also Apollonius of Tyana, famous in the second half of the first century A.D., who, according to Philostratus' *Life of Apollonius of Tyana* (216 A.D.), traveled to the East, living a saintly life, teaching, healing the sick, and raising the dead. He too was divine, the son of Proteus, a god of Egypt. His life and work so closely resembled Jesus' that some writers identified him with Jesus.[26]

Jesus the World Traveler

If one were to accept all of the legends concerning Jesus that have been circulating since his time, Jesus must have traveled around the world and preached everywhere. Not only are legends to be found throughout Asia, but an oral tradition has also existed among the North and South American Indians concerning a white man wearing white garments and called Kate-Zahl (the Prophet), Mahnt-Azoma, and other names. After sailing through the Pacific Ocean and apparently visiting the Polynesians, he arrived on the west coast of South America, where Peru is located today, and visited many tribes of Indians both in North and South America, east and west, before sailing toward the western Pacific. Similar legends have been found among many tribes of Indians concerning the pale prophet who taught them love and peace and performed all kinds of miracles. In the town of Cocha, Peru, when the sacrificing priests and the army decided to kill him, the Prophet performed the miracle producing lightning on a clear day and thus was able to escape death. A similar incident occurred in another Peruvian town, Caba Clos, on the Coba Clos River, where a jealous priesthood, with the army's compliance, tried to kill him. However, a miraculous curtain flame sent by God saved him from the arrows thrown at him. While in Paracas of Peru, he told the people of his crucifixion between two thieves. The Cherokee in West Virginia had a legend about the white prophet that healed a wounded doe for the sake of her fawn, and in Oklahoma, the Indians have a legend about the Healer who was born of a virgin across the ocean, while a star shone brightly and winged beings sang beautiful chants. The O'Chippewa by the shores of Mishe-gahme in Michigan have a legend of a divine white man, a pale god, who had a beard and green eyes and came to them alone. He performed miracles of healing, taught them to live in peace by resolving their problems in council, and went on into Canada with a couple of wolves. He had a strange power over animals. Many such legends abound among the Indian tribes of North, Central and South America, and some attribute to the white prophet changes in their ceremonies, including the abolition of animal and perhaps human sacrifices.

An amazing number of Christian concepts were held by the Mayans of Central America when they were pagans, including those of sin, trinity, and the virgin birth of the prophet. A number of works which record these concepts, such as *Documentos Ineditos Relaciones de Yucatan*, a volume compiled shortly after the Spanish conquest of these Indians, and *Historia General de Las Casas de Nueve Espana*, Vol. V (1938) and *Historia Apologetica*, both written by the same saintly monk, Las Casas, who suspected a mystery in the Indian legends and did not approve of what he was forced to observe. The last work has been lost, but Hubert H. Bancroft used it in his five volumes, *Antiquities* (1875), which is an important source of information on Indian legends because Bancroft quotes from ancient works now lost or impossible to obtain. One such work used by Bancroft is *Sur de Voyage Isthmus Tehuant-pec*, in *Archaeological Studies: History of Ancient Civilizations* (Paris, 1861-64), which contains a translation of ancient Mayan scripts.

L. Taylor Hansen suspects that this pale Prophet (Kate-zahl) was probably an Essene, and like the Essenes, wore a white garment, did not cover his head, and spoke of God as "My Father." The Indians seem to be familiar with the word Essene, which they pronounce Eessee-Nee and which is the name of their Wind God. Certain Mexican archaeologists think that this might have been "The Master" or "The Great Teacher," a saintly man mentioned in the Dead Sea Scrolls, crucified but apparently saved by fellow Essenes present in the crowd that surrounded him.[27]

Similar legends concerning a fair god who arrived with other men in three ships of the Mediterranean or Roman type, wearing apparently Mediterranean garments, are also to be found among natives of China and of Japan. On August 16, 1988, *The Globe* reported that Toyoji Sawacuchi, a 67-year-old garlic farmer in the remote northeast Japanese village of Shingo, was told in 1935 by Japanese scholars, who discovered that year certain ancient scrolls, that he was a direct descendant of Jesus Christ. Although the original scrolls, it is said, were destroyed during World War II, a supposed copy written in old Japanese states that "Jesus married a Japanese woman named Yumiko and had three daughters by her." According to this copy, Jesus made two trips to Japan. At the age of twenty-one, he arrived in Japan for the first time to study theology and live an ascetic life near Mount Fuji. Ten years later, he returned to Palestine, only to face the danger of execution. However, Jesus' brother Iskiri was crucified in his place, and Jesus returned to Japan after a difficult journey through Siberia. Tomekichi Shimotochidana, a village councilman, who saw the original scrolls, said that Jesus "traveled overland to Shingo where he remained for the rest of his life." The people of the village of Shingo are convinced that Jesus fled from the Romans in Palestine who tried to crucify him and came to their village, where he lived until his death at the age of 106. They believe that a burial mound on Sawaguchi's farm marked by a wooden cross is the burial place of Jesus, and supposedly buried there with Jesus is Iskiri's ear and some of his hair. However, because they fear divine retribution against Sawaguchi and his family, the villagers are unwilling to excavate the stone crypt. Interestingly, reports *The Globe*, the villagers of Shingo have for centuries had strange customs unknown elsewhere in Japan. They are not Christians, but they wrap their newborn babies in swaddling clothes embroidered with a Star of David and paint crosses on their foreheads. They also use such non-Japanese words as "apa" for father and "aya" for mother, which they think came from Jesus' language. In addition, each spring they hold a

Christ festival in which the women in kimonos dance around the burial mound singing in the supposed language of Jesus, while priests of the ancient Japanese religion Shinto bless the soul of Jesus. According to Frank Buck's *Vikings of the Sunrise*, the Japanese have a mountain called Wako-yama (yama is the Japanese word for mountain) where, according to legend, a white god is supposed to have taught.[28]

Rather recently, members of the media, Michael Baigent, Richard Leigh, and Henry Lincoln in their popular and sensational work *Holy Blood, Holy Grail* proposed that southern France might have been the hiding place of Jesus' family and perhaps of Jesus himself. (Perhaps his mummified corpse was taken there because documents in cryptic code from southern France state, "He is there Dead".) According to Australian journalist D. Joyce's *The Jesus Scroll* (London, 1975, 22), a scroll from Masada, written and signed by Jesus of Gennesareth, son of Jacob, which Joyce was asked to smuggle out of Israel, indicates that Jesus was eighty years old and the last of the rightful kings of Israel; therefore, Jesus must have died at Masada in 74 A.D., when that fortress fell to the Romans. However, the authors of *Holy Blood, Holy Grail* propose that Jesus' family—his wife Mary Magdaline and their several children; his brother-in-law Lazarus, whom he resurrected, probably symbolically, in Bethany and who might be St. John, the evangelist and the "beloved disciple"; his sister-in-law Martha; his friend and probably relative Joseph of Arimathaea, and perhaps Jesus himself (who may not have gone to Masada)—traveled to southern France at Rennes-le-Chateau. A Jewish community in this place offered them protection and preserved their lineage as descendants of King David. There is no evidence, say the authors, that John, the beloved disciple, remained with Jesus' mother Mary (who later tradition claims died in Ephesus) for the remainder of her life. Joseph of Arimathaea is depicted in medieval tradition as a custodian of the Holy Grail and related by blood to Jesus and his family. After being transported by ship to Marseilles, France, he was ordained by the Apostle Philip and was sent to England, where he founded a church at Glastonbury. According to Barbara W. Tuchman's *Bible and Sword* (New York, 1984, 13-21), the English claimed that Joseph of Arimathaea established the Church of England via Glastonbury, a fable to which they tenaciously adhered and which was eventually recorded in Thomas Malory's *Le Mort Darthur* (*The Death of Arthur*, 1469). Not to be left out, Spain claimed James as her apostle; Rome, Peter; and France, Philip. In any case, according to tradition, say the authors of *Holy Blood, Holy Grail*, Magdaline remained in France and died either at Aix-en-Provence or at Saint

Baume, while Lazarus died at Marseilles, where he had founded the first bishopric. The legendary Holy Grail of medieval tales, the authors speculate, symbolized Jesus' blood line from both King David and Mary Magdaline, from whose womb the Davidic bloodline was propagated.

Baigent, Leigh, and Lincoln think that they have evidence for their hypothesis. When the Romans under Titus sacked the Temple of Solomon at Jerusalem in 70 A.D., during the Zealot rebellion, the vast treasure of gold and diamonds seized by the Roman soldiers ended in the hands of the Prieure de Sion (Priory of Sion or Order of Zion), which still exists and has the treasure in its possession. But the Temple of Jerusalem may also have had detailed information concerning Jesus' Messianic aims and his family of royal blood, and perhaps a source revealing that Jesus survived the cross. In addition, it might have contained Jesus' body or his second tomb after his body was removed from the temporary tomb of the gospels. These might have been spared the Roman pillage because they were hidden and because of over-whelming Roman interest in the treasure.

The aim of the Prieure de Sion, say the authors of *Holy Blood, Holy Grail,* is evidently the establishment of Jesus' royal line on the throne of a united Europe. Jesus' royal line is identified with the Mero-vingian dynasty of the early Middle Ages, whose bloodline still survives today. The Merovingian family of King Clovis of the Franks, who became a Christian in 496 A.D., evidently intermarried with Jesus' heirs in the fifth century. This explains why the Church of Rome pledged its support of the Merovingian bloodline and why Clovis was created king but recognized only as the new Constantine or Holy Roman Emperor. (One would think that the Roman Church, which had accepted the divinity of Jesus, would never want to recognize Jesus' family or in any way perpetuate it.) However, the truth about Jesus' family was kept secret by the Church. Although in the eighth century, with Rome's consent, the Merovingian dynasty was replaced by the Carolingian, it survived because of Carolingian intermarriages with Merovingian princesses aimed at legitimatizing the Carolingian dynasty and because of the survival of King Dagobert II's son, Sigisbert IV, whose descen-dants included Godfroi de Bouillon, who captured Jerusalem in 1099, and the members of the Hapsburg-Lorraine family. The Prieure de Sion, say the authors of *Holy Blood, Holy Grail,* which appeared by the twelfth century, set up in 1118 the Knights Templar and sent them to Jerusalem to find something beneath the Temple in the so-called Stables of Solomon. They did find it, with the aid of German miners imported for this purpose, and they brought it back to Rennes-le-Chateau.

No one knows what this might have been, but the authors speculate that it could have been the mummified body of Jesus, Jesus' marriage license or the birth certificates of his children; in any case something very controversial or explosive. However, in the thirteenth century, the Cathari or Albigensian heretics of southern France, who might have learned this important secret, and in the fourteenth century, the Knights Templar, were destroyed by the Catholic Church with the aid of the French monarchy.

However, write Baigent, Leigh, and Lincoln, the Prieure de Sion survived to continue its support of the Merovingian line in its attempt to regain its heritage in Europe. This support came in the form of dynastic intermarriages and a clandestine attack on the Roman Church through Hermetic and esoteric thought, Rosicrucian manifestos and similar writings and Freemasonry; but it also came in the form of political intrigue and direct seizure of power, as by the Guise and Lorraine families of France in the sixteenth century and by the architects of the French Fronde (civil war) in the seventeenth century. According to many of Prieure de Sion's cryptic documents, it is waiting for the right conditions and moment to establish a united European theocracy under a member of the Merovingian line, who will rule as a symbolic priest-king but not actually govern because presumably the Prieure de Sion will do so. There are today at least a dozen families in Europe of the Merovingian line, including the Hapsburg-Lorraine, Luxemburg, Montpezat, and Montesquiou of France, the Sinclair, Stuart and Devonshire of Britain and many others. The authors include among the former alleged Grand Masters of the Prieure de Sion, Leonardo Da Vinci, Robert Boyle, Isaak Newton, Victor Hugo, and Claude Debussy. But, as the authors admit, theirs is only an hypothesis and is filled with speculations, most of which are farfetched and difficult to accept because they are based on flimsy evidence. Although this work holds one's attention as a good detective story, hard evidence is hardly there. The authors did not find Jesus' body at Rennes-le-Chateau, or for that matter any remains of Jesus' family members. They did not find any writings concerning Jesus' Messianic aims and the fact that he might have survived the cross. They do not know which of Jesus' heirs, if there were any, married Merovingians, and they did not find the mysterious treasure of the Prieure de Sion. All they have to support their hypothesis are the cryptic Prieure documents, difficult to decipher and subject to interpretations; and in any case, these documents might not be official but mere fiction.[29]

5. The Shroud of Turin, the Holy Light of Jerusalem, Rozabal, and the Need for Scientific Investigation

The Ahmadis and the Shroud of Turin

The Ahmadis and their supporters have referred to the now famous Shroud of Turin as proof that Jesus did not die on the cross. The Shroud of Turin was first revealed in the West in 1357, when it was exhibited in the French town of Lirey in a small collegiate church founded by Geoffrey de Charny. Because Charny was killed the year before at the battle of Poitiers during the Hundred Years' War between England and France, his destitute widow, Jeanne de Vergy, revealed Jesus' burial sheet, hoping to escape from poverty by collecting the monetary offerings of pilgrims. The Shroud of Turin has been controversial ever since its appearance. Two Catholic bishops quickly denounced it as a painted forgery, and historians and scientists have been quarreling over it ever since. On October 13, 1988, the shroud's custodian at Turin, Italy, Anastasio Cardinal Ballestero announced that carbon 14 tests independently conducted that year in three different laboratories concluded that the Shroud's cloth originated between 1260 and 1380 A.D. Although Cardinal Ballestero had permitted a series of scientific tests on the Shroud in 1978, he would not permit a carbon 14 test until it was improved so that only postage-size samples of the cloth would be needed instead of handkerchief-sizes. The British Museum in London coordinated the testing and sent four unmarked samples of the Shroud about the size of postage stamps with three control pieces, one of which dated from the first century, to the University of Arizona, Britain's Oxford University, and Switzerland's Federal Institute of Technology in Zurich. Only the British Museum knew which samples were which. The collective data has produced a 95% probability that the origin of the Shroud's cloth lies between 1260 and 1380, and near absolute certainty that its existence dates no earlier than 1200 A.D.[1]

The Shroud of Turin, however, appears to be still mysterious and will probably remain quite controversial. Some Catholics still hold out the slim hope that somehow a scientific error occurred that might mean a re-dating of the Shroud in the future. (Certain Columbia University scientists are already expressing doubts concerning the accuracy of the carbon 14 test [*N.Y. Times*, May 31, 1990]). Even though the dating dispute appears to be settled, the Shroud contains an uncannily accurate, detailed, and inexplicable life-size image of a crucified man. Historical evidence of the Shroud's presence before 1200; the depiction of accurate and detailed gruesome results of the torture and crucifixion that the deceased suffered, not revealed, it seems, in any other painting; professional pollen analysis, which confirms its authenticity; and the verification by a majority of western scientists that the image (which looks just like a three-dimensional photographic negative) was not painted and cannot be reproduced by modern means, indicate that the image is still mysterious and that it still might be an accurate revelation of Jesus entombed.

The Shroud of Turin, which is 14′ 3″ (436 centimeters) long and 3′ 7″ (110 centimeters) wide, contains the image of a naked male Caucasian 5′ 11″ tall, 30 to 35 years of age, and weighing about 178 pounds, who underwent a very similar if not identical ordeal to that suffered by Jesus during his passion and crucifixion. The image is very faint, and unless one views it from a distance of about fifteen to twenty feet, its details are difficult to see. Its color is of a pure sepia monochrome, and the closer one tries to examine the image, the more it fades away. As the image reveals, the Shroud was dropped over the dead naked man's head, covering both the front and the back of his body from head to toes. He was laid on his back with his arms over his body and with his left hand over his right wrist.[2]

The Shroud's origin is rather obscure. The gospels are not clear as to whether Jesus' corpse was covered with a single piece of linen (sindoni in Greek) or wrapped in strips (othonia). Luke (24:12) and John (19:40) indicate that more than one strip of linen was used, but Luke contradicted himself because, in an earlier passage (23:53), he wrote of one linen sheet being used. Luke's first passage appears to be correct since the version of 24:12 was a later insertion and not Luke's. Both Mark (15:46) and Matthew (27:59) refer to a singular cloth covering Jesus, but early Christians evidently made references to Jesus' burial cloth both in the singular and plural forms, as Luke did, without any concern for the discrepancy. In any case, there was confusion, because apparently a napkin, strips of linen, and a main sheet were all used to cover the dead Jesus.

The details in the Shroud's image of the dead man's manner of burial are astounding. It appears that he was wrapped in strips around the head, wrists, and feet in exact agreement with John's account of Lazarus (11:44), who also had a napkin tied around his face. John also writes (20:57) that a napkin had been over Jesus' head. Jewish laws, the Mishnah and the "laws of Mourning," instruct that the chin of the deceased be tied or bound before burial. The Soudarion, a small piece of cloth or a napkin, was used for that purpose. It was twisted and placed around the chin and tied over the head to keep the mouth closed before rigormortis set in. No book of the New Testament describes a wrapping of the corpse Egyptian mummy style, the method some individuals have maintained was used. Lazarus came out of the tomb of his own volition, but he was impaired and had to be untied because his hands and feet were bound. He was not, however, completely wrapped up. When the Essenic community graves at Qumran were opened, they revealed that the dead were buried in the same position as the man in the Shroud, with elbows extended. Jewish laws for mourning dictated that an executed man should be buried in a single sheet and his body not be washed. The Shroud depicts an unwashed body, and the gospels hint that Jesus' burial was incomplete because of lack of time, since the Sabbath was quickly approaching (Luke 23:54). A large quantity of spices was probably packed around Jesus' body during the burial (John 19:39-40) to arrest decomposition until the women could return to wash and anoint it with spices and aromatic oils (Luke 24:1-4; Mark 16:1-3). Evidently, the Shroud image compares well with the gospels' testimony and reveals that the method of its occupant's burial agrees with scriptural accounts as well as with Jewish customs of the first century.[3]

Some evidence exists that the Shroud of Turin (or a Shroud image of Jesus) existed long before the fourteenth century. Its past is not easy to trace, however, because of relatively few references. Two of the earliest accounts concerning the Shroud are the testimonies of St. Braulio, who in 631 wrote that the Shroud was then a known relic, and of Arculph, who claimed to have kissed the "Lord's winding sheet" in Jerusalem around 640. At the end of the tenth century, John Geometer, a priest in Constantinople, the capital of the Byzantine Empire, wrote explicitly of the image of Christ on a shroud, after that references to an imprinted shroud became rather frequent in Constantinople. In 1171, William of Tyre, who accompanied the king of Jerusalem to the Byzantine capital, wrote that, while visiting the imperial palace, he saw a shroud with body impressions alleged to be those of Christ. While in 1203, Robert de Clari, a participant in the fourth crusade, which ended with the conquest of Constantinople in 1204, was the last person to see the shroud of Constantinople before it disappeared. He wrote that in the Byzantine capital, there was the church of "St. Mary of Blachernae where was kept the *sydoine* [linen] in which our Lord had been wrapped, which stood up straight every Friday, so that the features of Our Lord could be plainly seen there. And no one, either Greek or French, ever knew what became of this *sydoine* after the city was taken."[4]

It appears that, around the sixth century, shrouds of Jesus were being discovered throughout the Middle East. None of these shrouds, however, bore an image, but their discoveries reveal a widespread belief in the existence of such a relic. Shrouds have been found in Egyptian tombs dating long before the time of Jesus, and a few Christian shrouds have also been found, including shrouds of known martyrs, some of which contained imprints; but none of these contain a photographic-like image as on the Shroud of Turin. A seventh-century Mozarabic (Muslim-dominated Spanish period) liturgical rite presents the first documentary evidence that at least one shroud contained images on it. The rite expresses "traces on the linen of the dead and risen man," but scholars cannot agree as to what exactly the word "traces" denotes. In any case, during the Middle Ages, there existed at least forty shrouds of Jesus, some of which were copies of the Shroud of Turin. Thus, forgeries of the Shroud were not uncommon.[5]

Art History and the Holy Mandylion (Handkerchief)

Art history has also been used to trace the history of the Shroud of Turin. It too confirms that the Shroud's image of Jesus entombed existed long before the fourteenth century. The image of the man in the Shroud has influenced the way many artists have painted Jesus in the past several hundreds of years. Art historians, including British historian Ian Wilson, have extensively compared the face on the Shroud with those in medieval paintings, especially Byzantine icons, and have speculated that the Shroud was known to artists as early as the sixth century and had influenced them to produce a conventional likeness of Christ. Although earlier portraits depicted Jesus as a beardless, short-haired youth, beginning in the sixth century, Jesus' appearance changed drastically. He was then depicted as a long-haired, fork-bearded man having facial characteristics similar to those of the Shroud's image, including a right or left raised eyebrow, a streak across the forehead and a "V" feature at the end of the nose. The high frequency of similarities in Byzantine frescos, mosaics and canvas paintings, at least in fifteen of them that are very close to the Shroud's facial image, suggests a strong relationship between the Shroud image and Byzantine art.[6]

This change in sixth-century art occurred because of the Holy Mandylion (Handkerchief) or the Image of Edessa (or the Edessan Image), a painting that depicted Jesus' face with streaks of blood on it. Confusion has existed in the past concerning the Holy Mandylion's existence and whether it was actually the Shroud image itself, but new evidence by Ian Wilson and others reveals that the Mandylion and Shroud image were the same. The Mandylion was a cloth facial image of Jesus discovered in 525 A.D. in a niche or crevice above the west gate of the wall of Edessa (Urfa) in southern Turkey. As mentioned earlier, Edessa's ruler or toparch, Uchomo Abgar V, asked Jesus to come to Edessa to cure him. Jesus did not go but wrote him a letter promising to send him a disciple. Eventually, the Apostle Thomas sent Thaddeus, who brought with him the Holy Mandylion cloth containing Jesus' image. The sight of this Holy Mandylion healed the Abgar (ruler), who allowed the establishment of Christianity in his city. Although Eusebius' *History of the Church* does not mention the reason for the establishment of Christianity in Edessa but merely indicates that Thaddeus himself healed the grateful Abgar, an early Edessan tradition maintained that the Lord's holy image was responsible for Edessa's acceptance of Christ. The Holy Mandylion, however, disappeared early. Abgar V's son, who succeeded him, did not attack Christianity, but Ma'nu VI, another son, who took over in 57, became a pagan and persecuted the Christians. The Mandylion suddenly vanished and did not reappear until 525. Even though Christianity was reestablished in Edessa about the end of the second century, those who hid the Mandylion or knew of its hiding spot in the niche of Edessa's west gate were probably killed or had died. Only the memory of the Holy Mandylion remained, until it was accidentally rediscovered when the walls were being repaired. The niche in the wall was high and dark and protected this cloth image from the elements, especially from the severe floods of Edessa.[7]

Eventually, the Holy Mandylion was moved to the Byzantine capital, Constantinople. With its reappearance at Edessa, the Mandylion image was again venerated, and it began to have an influence on art. The sixth-century emperor Justinian the Great built a cathedral at

Edessa to house the Holy Mandylion, but in the same century a riot against religious paintings or icons took place, during which rioting soldiers threw stones even at this miraculous image of Jesus. Such attacks against religious art as idolatrous and pagan had not been uncommon since early Christian times. The Holy Mandylion also survived the Byzantine Empire's iconoclasm in the eighth and ninth centuries, when many icons and statues were destroyed in an effort to purify the Church from idolatry. By the eighth century, Edessa fell to the Muslims, and eventually the Christians became a minority. In order to remove the Mandylion from Muslim territory to Constantinople and thus to have its divine protection, in 944 the Byzantine emperor Romanos I Lecapinos had his most able general, John Carcuas, besiege Edessa and using threats make a deal with its Muslim ruler for the holy image. In spite of the protests of the Edessan Christians and their two attempts to fool the Byzantines with forgeries (evidently not close enough to the real), the true holy cloth was turned over to Carcuas, who brought it to Constantinople with great pomp. (Fortunately, the Byzantines had brought with them to Edessa, Abraham, bishop of Samosata, who had seen and remembered the true Mandylion's appearance and was not fooled by the forgeries.) The Mandylion was placed in the Pharos Chapel of the Great Palace, which contained such other holy relics as two large pieces of the true cross, two of the nails used in the Lord's crucifixion, the Roman lance used to pierce Jesus' side, and the crown of thorns thrust on Jesus' head. The holy cloth, which was now called by the Greeks the Mandylion, was revered and guarded as one of the holiest of relics.[8]

According to Ian Wilson and others, the Mandylion and the Shroud might have been the same. Interestingly, neither the Mandylion nor the Shroud image is mentioned in the New Testament, or in any early Christian writings. Wilson speculates that for early Christians and Jews, a shroud was unclean, religious images were forbidden, and a naked Jesus might have been an embarrassment. Therefore, it was hidden and kept secret. But evidently, once the Shroud was brought to Edessa from Jerusalem, probably for reasons of security, Aggai, Thaddeus' aid and successor, a skilled worker in silks and gold, folded the Shroud in a double-in-four manner that exposed only the face of the dead man's image and covered the Shroud with a gold trelliswork typical of the headresses and costumes that he made for monarchs and worthy Parthians. It was probably in this fashion that the Shroud was presented to King Abgar V, thus becoming the famous Mandylion. Byzantine copies of the Mandylion reveal traces of trelliswork decoration, and the recent Shroud of Turin Research Project found in a new series of photographs of the Shroud a visible eight-fold pattern of folds, the product of a double-in-four folding. Also, a scientist of the research project discovered that doubling the cloth in four exposed only the image's face area. The image area was no more discolored than the rest of the protected cloth, says Ian Wilson, probably because the Shroud had remained mainly in the dark and protected from the elements. (However, the lack of discoloration might also be taken as an indication that the cloth was a fourteenth-century forgery and not in any way the Mandylion.) In describing the Mandylion image, a Byzantine author of the tenth century writes that it was of "a moist secretion without coloring or painter's art," and this also can be said of the Shroud's image. In addition, the sons of the Emperor Lecapenus, who observed the Mandylion, were disappointed because they were not able to see Christ's facial features. Such is also the case with the Shroud image, the features of which are faint and must be observed from a distance of three feet. Therefore, the Mandylion and the Shroud could be one and the same.[9]

The Mandylion's appearance at Edessa gave rise to stories about its miraculous origin and powers. One of these stories asserted that Jesus once washed his face with water, and after he wiped himself with his towel or the Mandylion, the moisture miraculously left an impression of his holy face on it. He then gave it to Ananias to take to his master, Abgar, who had requested Jesus' portrait. Another story maintained that, while anticipating his crucifixion in agony and praying to God in the Garden of Gethsemane, Jesus used the Mandylion to wipe his face, all covered with sweat like drops of blood. This produced the Mandylion image, which Jesus ordered sent to King Abgar. The Mandylion cured not only this ruler of chronic arthritis and leprosy, but many others who had been afflicted as well. In the West, there appeared the story of Veronica's Veil. Veronica, a pious woman of Jerusalem, offered Jesus her veil to wipe his sweat and blood-soaked face while he was being led to his crucifixion. After he wiped the blood and sweat from his face and returned the veil to her, Veronica discovered that it contained an image of the Lord's holy face. Although these stories are fables, they do indicate the existence of such an image-bearing cloth and of a general belief that this image had not been painted on the cloth.[10]

Sometime after its arrival in Constantinople, in the eleventh century, someone must have removed the trelliswork from the Mandylion. Thus, the Byzantines discovered that the Mandylion was the Shroud, and observed for the first time since the days of the Apostles the naked body of Jesus entombed. In the eleventh century, the old mummy-style entombment scene gave way to the Lamentation or Threnos scene, whereby Christ was depicted, in both eastern and western paintings, at the foot of the cross (following his crucifixion), dead and naked with his hands crossed over his loins; also shown in these paintings was a full size linen reminiscent of the Shroud. Paintings of Jesus' entombment in this style were being produced on into the twelfth century. Certain western works, "Ecclesiastical History" by Ordericus Vitalis (in Migne, PL, 188.690) and Vatican Library Codex 5696 (fol. 35), dated around 1130, refer to the Shroud sent to Abgar as containing the full image of Jesus, not only his face but his body as well. In the 1190's, Pope Celestine III received from the Byzantine capital an umbella (ornamental tapestry canopy) that contained as its center a representation of Jesus entombed in exactly the same manner as depicted by the Shroud image. In Russia and in the Eastern Orthodox world in general, there appeared, evidently in the twelfth century the "epitaphios," a ceremonial cloth depicting Jesus of the Shroud with his hands crossed over the loins. This cloth was and is still placed in a symbolic bier during the Holy Friday service. Paintings or icons also began to appear of the Mandylion and with it the wound-bearing Christ of Pity figure. The Grail stories about the legendary King Arthur were being circulated with stories containing a vision of Christ wounded, which their several authors attributed (interestingly) to an inspiration from Constantinople. In 1201, the keeper of the relic collection in the Pharos Chapel, Nicholas Mesarites, while defending this chapel against a mob, mentioned the sindoni or shroud which "is of linen, of cheap and easily obtainable material . . . defying decay because it wrapped the mysterious naked dead body after the Passion."[11]

However, the Byzantines also perpetuated the Mandylion tradition by producing on a tile, it seems, a painting of the Mandylion as it had been in its original form; and they retained this tile copy, now often referred to as the Keramion (Tile), along with the full Shroud and its image. It is for this reason that an unknown English pilgrim wrote in 1150 that the relic collection of Constantinople contained the sudarium or shroud that was over Christ's head. In 1157, an Icelandic abbot, Nicholas Soemundarson, who listed the relics of Constantinople but relied on hearsay alone, wrote of both "linen bands with the sveitaduk" (sweat cloth) and of a "maetull," which according to some scholars denotes the Mandylion. Robert of Clari, the French crusader and, in 1204, an eyewitness to Constantinople's relic collection, told a story of how the image of Jesus face got on the tile from a cloth image (the Mandylion) and clarified how both the Mandylion tile copy (the Keramion) and the Shroud were preserved in "two rich vessels of gold hanging in the midst of the chapel by two heavy silver chains." And, evidently, the Keramion image was venerated as miraculous just as was that on the Shroud, thus perpetuating the Mandylion image on into World War I, when Russian troops entered Thessaloniki, Greece, carrying on their banner the Mandylion icon, which looked almost the same as that on Ivan the Terrible's imperial standard in 1532 (when the Russians fought the Tartars at Kazan).[12]

With the conquest and plunder of Constantinople in 1204, both the Shroud and the Mandylion (Keramion) disappeared. However, and this is most curious, the Pharos Chapel, which should have sheltered both relics, was not plundered. Yet Granier de Trainel, bishop of Troyes, who listed in writing all the sacred objects that he found in this chapel after the plunder, did not mention the Shroud. Relics were brought to the West from Constantinople after 1204, large sums were paid for many of them, and their whereabouts were often advertised, but no one revealed the Mandylion or Shroud. It might be, as Robert de Clari suggested, that the Shroud was kept at the Blachernae district in the church of St. Mary, which was most likely one of the first to be overrun and plundered by the crusaders, who probably stole the Holy Shroud. There is, however, uncertainty concerning the date of the Shroud's disappearance. Although Ian Wilson indicates that it must have disappeared in 1204, Kurt Berna writes that, according to Nicholas Idruntino of Tarant, who made a list in 1207 of the relics in the Great Palace, the Holy Linen or Shroud was still in Constantinople, while Nicholas Mesarites confirmed that in that same year (1207), the grave clothes and the sweat cloth were in Constantinople. As Kurt Berna indicates, it might be that the Shroud was moved from the East to the West sometime between 1248 and 1262 A.D.[13]

Many speculations exist concerning the disappearance of the Shroud or Sindoni. But the most probable explanation is that between 1204 and 1357, the Shroud might have been protected and used by the wealthiest and most powerful order of medieval warrior-monks, the Knights Templar. It appears that the members of this order (which was created for the defense of Jerusalem and Palestine but which eventually moved its headquarters to Paris) worshipped a mysterious head at night during their secret ritual. When in 1307, King Philip IV of France, who coveted this organization's wealth and feared its power, destroyed the order and interrogated some of its leaders, it was discovered that its members venerated a painting of a human head "very pale and discolored, with a grizzled beard like a Templar's." Evidently, just as the Byzantines in the sixth century had produced copies of the Mandylion and generally placed painted versions of it in contact with something that had in turn been in contact with the original, the Templars produced copies of this head for all their quarters from the original, which they held in Paris. Four such copies were to be found in England alone, and, according to Ian Wilson, they did resemble to some degree the Mandylion image or Jesus' face on the Shroud. While the Templar members were being interrogated under torture and executed, the Shroud might have been turned over to Geoffrey de Charny, who was related to one of the Templar leaders, and whose widow revealed it in 1357 in the church of Lirey to pay off her debts. Eventually, the Shroud found its way to Turin, Italy, in the Cathedral of St. John the Baptist as the property of Italy's ex-royal house of Savoy. During a fire in this cathedral on December 4, 1532, the Shroud was damaged by a piece of molten silver that fell on the folded cloth and burned it through in three places, but the image survived virtually untouched with very little damage to it. As a matter of fact, the scorched cloth provided recent scientists with the opportunity to better examine the origin of the Shroud's image. Today, the Shroud belongs to the Pope of Rome.[14]

Could it be that the Shroud of Turin is merely a copy of the original? There would appear to be little doubt that a shroud existed in Constantinople long before the fourteenth century. But since the carbon 14 test with its ninety-five percent accuracy indicated that it is a fourteenth century product, the Shroud of Turin might be merely a French forgery. Ian Wilson's historical evidence seems to reveal that the Shroud of Turin is genuine, and there are also positive scientific data, unanswered scientific questions, and a division of opinion among scientists which indicate that perhaps the Shroud of Turin might be the original Byzantine shroud with its miraculous image, unless of course the Byzantine original did not have an image (contrary to evidence) or its image was also man-made.

The Shroud of Turin was denounced as a reproduction just as soon as it made its appearance in France. In 1389, Jean de Vergny and her son, Geofrey de Charny, bypassed their diocesan bishop, Henry, Pierre

D'Arcis of Troyes, by obtaining permission directly from Peter of Thury, the cardinal legate visiting the area at that time, to exhibit the Shroud a second time. Bishop D'Arcis became extremely angry, and in his letter to Pope Clement VII, known as the D'Arcis Memorandum, indicated that the Shroud had been known to be a forgery since its first exhibition in 1357. His predecessor, Bishop Henry of Poitiers, after being urged on by many theologians and others, found and questioned the artist responsible for producing the Shroud. As a matter of fact, according to Bishop Pierre D'Arcis, after the artist admitted that he had produced the image on the cloth, Bishop Henry of Poitiers terminated this first exhibition of 1357 and denounced the Shroud as the "work of human skill and not miraculously wrought or bestowed." However, Pope Clement VII, who was the uncle of Jean de Vergny's second husband, without making an investigation of the Shroud, silenced Bishop D'Arcis by going as far as to threaten him with excommunication. Nevertheless, the Pope also did ratify an earlier decision that the Charnys should describe their relic only as a "likeness" or "representation" of the Shroud. No evidence exists, however, besides the D'Arcis Memorandum, that the bishop of Poitiers ever conducted an investigation concerning the Shroud's authenticity, and Bishop D'Arcis did not say when such an investigation had taken place, who conducted it, what the name of the artist who forged the image was, and how he painted it (or perhaps copied it, because the language is not clear in the Memorandum). Neither did the Charnys ever explain how the cloth came into their possession, which gives credence to the charge that they were guilty of fraud. In 1902, after the publication of the 1898 photographs of the Shroud by the Italian photographer Secondo Pia, the learned English Jesuit Herbert Thurston, in an article in the *Catholic Encyclopedia*, declared the Shroud to be a forgery, as did the French medievalist Ulysse Chevalier. But both these men based their conclusions primarily on the D'Arcis Memorandum. The suggestion has been made that Bishop Pierre D'Arcis might have been referring to a copy of the de Charny Shroud. Thus, D'Arcis complained to the pope that unscrupulous men had tricked him into approving the exposition of a fraudulent relic. Historians claim that more than forty "true shrouds" existed during the Middle Ages, and those that still survive are merely painted copies of the Shroud of Turin. Evidently, none of them are of the same quality as the Shroud, and therefore, none of them have been so sensational.[15]

Recent scientific studies of the Shroud of Turin, prior to the carbon 14 test, confirmed the evidence of pro-Shroud historians. In 1973, Max Frei, a Swiss criminologist and botanist, after meticulously studying and identifying the pollen spores of forty-nine different plants that had collected on the Shroud cloth, concluded that the Shroud must have been present in the past in Palestine, the southern steppe of Turkey (where Edessa or Urfa is located), Constantinople, and France. He also decided that the time overlay of the pollen grains that have evolved since is convincing but not absolute proof that the Shroud originated in the first century after Christ. Textile analysis based on threads removed from the Shroud by scientists revealed that the Shroud linen weave, so the experts thought, was a type common in the Middle East during the first century. The threads also contained traces of cotton among the linen fibers, indicating that it might have been woven on a loom also used for cotton, which is grown in the Middle East and not in Europe. In addition, certain scientists thought they had discovered in 1976 that coins had been placed over the eyes of the Shroud's occupant. These two coins were leptons issued by Pontius Pilate between 29 and 32 A.D., which underlines a first-century origin for the Shroud cloth. Indeed, studies of first-century Jewish cemeteries have revealed that the Jews did place such coins over the eyes of their deceased.[16]

After a thorough examination of the Shroud in 1978 by all modern technological and scientific means, the majority of scientists of the U.S. Shroud of Turin Research Project (STURP) concluded that the Shroud is chronologically and topographically genuine and that its image is definitely not a forgery. Since its image is non-directional, revealing no brush-strokes, it was not painted or stained. Nor was it caused by a body contact print from fluids or other elements, such as body vapors, uric acid, and burial unguents, all of which had been proposed in the past. No traces of aloe, myrrh, or of any other spice were found on the Shroud cloth, nor oils, which might have oxidized. The oxidation and dehydration process found in the Shroud image reveal that the fibers were heated. Therefore, the Shroud image was caused by a heat or light scorch. In addition, bloodstains on the Shroud were proven to be genuine blood and not painted. The majority of the American scientists of the Shroud of Turin Research Project thought that, evidently, a cold dead body had produced some kind of heat in order to scorch the linen's fabrils only at the surface and to produce a negative three-dimensional image, which was discovered only after 1898 because of the development of photography and the VP-8 image analyzer, able to produce 3-D images of objects with depth. The image, concluded the American scientists, was projected onto the linen from a distance of up to four centimeters, but in a gentle, light fashion that caused distortion only in areas where there was direct contact between corpse and linen. But how could a cold corpse in the tomb produce heat enough to scorch the cloth from within in such controlled manner that it dissolved and diffused blood flows onto the linen and burned only the topmost surface of the fibers in order to create a detailed three-dimensional human image encoded in the number of fibrils? No other artist or forger has ever created an image in the past that is three-dimensional, superficial, and non-directional. John H. Heller, a member of the Shroud of Turin research team and a biophysicist, aided by Alan Adler, a physical chemist, wrote that the image was formed by a dehydrative acid oxidation of the linen with the formation of yellow carbonyl chromophore. However, Heller conceded that the method by which such a selective dehydrative acid oxidizing agent produced the image on the cloth is unknown, and he concluded that the image might be the product of some form of molecular transport, not understood at present. Efforts to reproduce the image on a cloth with all the modern means available failed, which convinced most of these STURP scientists that they really had no idea as to how the image was formed on the cloth.[17]

However, a minority of scientists, including Walter McCrone, a member of the Shroud of Turin Research Project and a famous microscopist, thought of the Shroud as a forgery. The recent carbon-14 test finding, of course, has revealed that this minority of scientists might have been correct. McCrone, who examined sticky tape samples taken from the Shroud's image, maintains that the image consists of yellowed fibers evidently colored by a cellulose degradation or dehydration process, which was caused by red ochre, an artist's pigment, also called Venetian Red. Venetian Red contains iron oxide particles identical to those that McCrone detected on the Shroud image, and it could have been rubbed on to the cloth in powdered form to produce only a superficial penetration of the fibers as on the Shroud. The STURP's contention that the blood areas on the Shroud are indeed blood and only blood is not established, says physicist Marvin A. Mueller, because as much as fifty per cent of the bloodstain color could be due to iron oxide and vermilion, an often-used pigment during the Middle Ages containing mercury and sulfur, which McCrone detected on the Shroud image. (Heller indicates—*Report*, 193-197—that he and Adler could not find any red ochre and not enough iron oxide or vermilion to account for one painted drop of blood. In addition, he found no contaminants as one would have found if red ochre had been used.) In any case, Mueller writes, old blood always turns brown or black, and the Shroud's bloodstain areas appear much too red to be just blood. The presence of vermilion in the bloodstain areas strongly indicates that the image was at least partly produced by an artist. Joe Nickell, a former professional magician, private investigator, and opponent of the miraculous theory, was able partially to demonstrate how an artist might have produced such a work. Using a bas-relief sculpture of former singer Bing Crosby's face, Nickell was able to produce a negative image on a cloth. He first molded the cloth while wet to the bas-relief. When the cloth dried, he gently rubbed on it a powdered pigment of myrrh and aloes, producing an image. He eventually also created negative images (not photographic) of Jesus' face on cloths by rubbing iron oxide pigment on them. However, certain scientists rejected Nickell's bas-relief effort as directional and not three-dimensional. In addition, there was no such fourteenth-century French tradition nor any record of artists using sculpture to produce such clear anatomical realism. Although Nickell indicates that the production of negative images was known to medieval artists, he has not been able to produce or point to any other painted shroud that contains such detailed realism with all the characteristics of the Shroud image.[18]

Joe Nickell also rejects Ian Wilson's contention that the Shroud image can be traced in the past through iconography or religious art. First of all, Nickell correctly indicates that the gospels and the entire New Testament do not mention any such image, and the image tradition itself is of a later development. Although from the third and fourth centuries Christ was depicted without a beard, as Wilson says, he was also being painted in icons with a beard and long, flowing hair, and with large eyes and a prominent nose. Gradually, the Semitic bearded image of Christ became popular and prevailed both in the Byzantine Empire and in western Europe. In the beginning, the artists were supposedly depicting Jesus according to a traditional secret portrait of Jesus produced by St. Luke himself. But as early as the sixth century, a new tradition was begun, whereby images of Jesus appeared miraculously, not made with man's hands. Many legends arose to account for these images, among them the legend of the Image of Edessa, while another legend dealt with the image of Veronica's Veil. Neither the Mandylion

nor the Veronica icons, says Nickell, ever depicted Christ's face with
the crown of thorns and blood as does the Shroud of Turin; therefore,
these icons cannot have been influenced by the Shroud's image as
Ian Wilson claims. The famous Byzantine historian, Steven Runciman,
refused to identify the Mandylion with the Shroud, indicating that the
Mandylion probably perished during the French Revolution, when the
ship carrying it with other booty sank at sea. As far as Nickell is
concerned, it was the traditional artists' vision of Jesus' appearance that
served as a model for icons, including the fourteenth-century Shroud
image, and not the other way around. This artistic vision gradually
evolved from depictions of Christ's face alone to representations of
Christ's whole body. In any case, Nickell maintains that, until the
twelfth century, shrouds of Jesus did not bear images, not even the
burial clothes or linen of Christ in Constantinople, which Patriarch
Nicholas Mesarites indicated "have defied decay because they enveloped
the ineffable, naked, myrrh-covered corpse after the Passion." The same
applies to Robert de Clari, who wrote of the shroud that was shown
every Friday in the church of St. Mary of Blachernae in Constantinople.
Since Robert arrived in Constantinople with the crusaders, says Nickell,
he probably never saw the shroud (sindoni) that he bemoans was lost.
He had only heard about it. (Whether he saw it or not, a shroud did exist
in that city.) Anyway, says Nickell, both the Byzantine shroud and the
Mandylion were in the church of the Blessed Virgin in the Great Palace
and not in the Palace of Blachernae. (But it could have been exhibited
elsewhere in Constantinople.)[19]

Nickell also refutes the idea that the Shroud cloth was a Palestinian
product. Palestinian linen was plain weave, while the Shroud's weave
is "a three-to-one twill, stripped in the herringbone pattern." No such
weave pattern was to be found among Palestinian linen of Jesus' time,
and interestingly the weave patterns in the image areas are what cause
one to see what he wants to see. Cotton cloth was manufactured in
France, says Nickell, including in the area where the Shroud first made
its appearance. In any case, in spite of its age and even though very few
examples of Palestinian cloth survive because of the climate's excessive
humidity, the Shroud is amazingly well preserved. In addition, writes
Nickell, the Shroud is too large to have survived intact for so many
centuries. Nothing quite as large as the Shroud, which is fourteen feet
in length, has been wholly preserved since ancient times, except for
Egyptian mummy wrappings found in tombs; and if we add to nature's
destruction, man-made destruction or past attacks on religious images,

including those of Christ, it is incredible that Jesus' shroud could still be with us.[20]

Shrouds and miraculous images were popular during the Middle Ages as relics that brought churches fame, prestige, and money from pilgrims. Churches claimed to have not only the bones and garments of the Apostles, saints, and martyrs, thousands of pieces of the true cross (sufficient in quantity to build one or two ships), and nails and Roman lances used during the crucifixion, but also relics of Joseph and Mary, including Mary's hair and shirt and vials of her breast milk—not to mention baby Jesus' swaddling clothes, his foreskin (preserved in six churches) and navel, hair, pap-spoon and dish, gifts from the Wise Men, and baby teeth. Neither were the Old Testament prophets neglected. Moses' rod was present in Europe as well as in Kashmir, and a cathedral in England even had a branch of the burning bush that God used to speak to Moses in the desert. Many of the faithful, of course, accepted these as genuine and as possessing miraculous powers, which only undermines the claims concerning the Shroud image.

However, the Shroud of Turin has amazed even many of our present-day scientists because they cannot produce or explain such a detailed and anatomically realistic image of the front and back of a man (quite possibly Jesus) who had been tortured, crucified, and entombed. It is difficult, of course, for scientists to accept any miraculous and supernatural act in the production of such an image. After all, the scientific method seeks solely naturalistic explanations for observable or sensorily perceived phenomena. However, being unable to explain the Shroud image and finding the explanations of descending scientists insufficient, some of the STURP scientists have been hinting at a supernatural cause. The recent finding of the carbon-14 test that the Shroud cloth is a fourteenth-century product, has given great support to those who have thought of it as a forgery. But there is still a five per cent chance that both the carbon-14 test and descending scientists might be wrong, that the Shroud image might be genuine and, therefore, that it might realistically depict none other than Jesus Christ himself.

Certain pathologists who have studied the Shroud image hold that it accurately depicts in detail an actual human corpse that had undergone the same ordeal as Jesus Christ, as described in the gospels. This is revealed in both the front and back images of the Shroud. Dr. Robert Bucklin, coroner and forensic pathologist of Los Angeles County, and Dr. Joseph Gambescia, a pathologist in Philadelphia, Pennsylvania agree that the Shroud's images, front and back, are anatomically correct, and that the pathology and physiology depicted of a tortured and crucified man, although obvious to pathologists today, represent medical knowledge unknown 150 years ago. This, of course, indicates that the Shroud's image could not have been painted. They also agree that the man was Caucasian, 5' 11" in height and weighing about 178 pounds. In agreement with the previous findings of Dr. Pierre Barbet, a French Catholic, and Yves Delage, professor of comparative anatomy at the Sorbonne in Paris, they indicate that he had been bleeding from several punctured wounds on the top and on the front and back of his head. He had been beaten on the face, which left him with a swollen cheek and also undoubtedly a black eye. He must have fallen because his nose tip is abraded, and the nasal cartilage may have separated from the bone. The wound in the left wrist (the right one is covered by the left hand) is a typical lesion of a crucifixion. A crucifixion with nails through the palms, as portrayed in art and legend, cannot hold up a man of this weight without tearing the bones, muscles, and ligaments in his hands. In addition, pathologists recently discovered that, when a nail goes through the space of Destot in the wrists, it severs or damages the median nerve, causing the thumbs to draw tightly to the hands, as computer-enhanced photographs of the image have revealed—the thumbs are not visible on the Shroud image. One has to assume that a fourteenth century artist would have had to know all this, in order to produce such an accurately detailed image. The streams of blood go down the arms in response to gravity from angles that can occur from the only two positions a body can take during crucifixion. Lesions on the back and front, which appear to be scourge marks, could have been made by the Roman whip, called the *flagrum*, which had two or three thongs with pieces of metal at the end like small dumbbells to gouge out flesh. The Shroud's victim was whipped from both sides by two men, and the angle of the thongs indicate that one man was taller than the other. Swelling with abrasions on both shoulders indicates that the victim had carried something rough and heavy across his shoulders, just hours before his death, while his right side reveals that it had been pierced by a long, narrow blade in an upward direction. Bucklin and Gambescia found no evidence that the victim's legs were fractured, but one of his knees had an abrasion (as on his nose), the result of a fall, and a spike had been driven through both feet.[21]

Almost all the modern pathological findings confirm the gospels' accounts of Christ's passion. Pilate had Jesus flogged before he was crucified (John 19:1; Matthew 27:26; Mark 15:15). The cloth images reveal about 120 lacerations and wounds, a flogging that some pathologists suspect was severe enough to have killed him. According to the gospels (Mark 15:19; Matthew 27:29; John 19:2), the Roman soldiers also hit his head with a cane, spat on him, and mocked him, just as the Shroud reveals in the man's swollen face and broken nose; they also placed a crown of thorns on his head. Jesus bore his own cross on the way to Golgotha (John 19:17), but since he was too weak to carry the cross on his shoulders, the Roman soldiers forced Simon of Cyrene to carry the cross behind Jesus (Luke 23:26; Matthew 27:32; Mark 15:21). The Shroud image reveals that Jesus must have had a bad fall, hurting especially his left knee which disabled him. Jesus was finally nailed to the cross and lanced on his side, leaving him with wounds which were later visible (Luke 24:39; John 20:25). Recent findings have revealed that the Romans crucified individuals through the wrists and feet with their legs propped up somewhat toward their chest.

There are, of course, some scientists who disagree and refuse to accept that the back and front images depict an actual traumatized corpse. They indicate that the images were not produced by a body in actual contact with the cloth. If they had been, the images would have been distorted in some places where the cloth did not touch the corpse. They, of course, exclude any unnatural or supernatural process that might have caused the Shroud image. Dr. Michael M. Baden, deputy chief medical examiner of Suffolk County, New York, rejects the Shroud's anatomical authenticity. According to Baden, scourge marks would not have left any imprint on the Shroud, not even the *flagrum* markings, and the blood markings around the head are even more difficult to accept because, when the blood flows from the head, it mats on the hair and does not flow in rivulets as in the Shroud image. Baden even noticed that some of the scalp's puncture wounds seem actually to lie outside of its outline. Dr. Anthony Sava, a member of the Executive Council of the Holy Shroud Guild, indicates that the Shroud's victim was not crucified through the wrists but just above the line of the wrist joint in the space between the lower ends of the radius and the ulna bones. The right radius of John (Yehohanan in Hebrew), the first century crucifixion victim unearthed in Jerusalem in 1968, appears to have a scratch perhaps made by a nail, which seems to confirm Sava's contention. In any case, says Joe Nickell, art depicting Jesus crucified through the wrists was not absent in the past. Several symbolic crucifixes, dating from the Middle Ages and found in churches in Europe, depict Jesus distinctly crucified through the wrists and not the palms. The verification by a computer-enhanced photograph of a faint thumb imprint in the Shroud image is proof that the thumb did not contract toward the palm (the hands, as Heller maintains), as it would have done if the nail had penetrated the wrist's Destot space. As for the lance wound on the right side, Baden says that he did not see any concrete injury to the chest, only a darkened area. How the Shroud's victim was crucified through the feet is not clear and thus open to argument. John (Yehohanan) was crucified through the heel bones with a seven-inch long nail. Numerous anatomical anomalies have also been observed, primarily by the Shroud's opponents: for instance, the right arm is longer than the left, measurements for the lower portion of the front part of the legs are excessive, the head appears to be detached from the rest of the body because of the apparent absence of shoulders, and the fingers are excessively long. For Baden and the opponents, such anatomical inaccuracies, along with the fact that the Shroud image is undistorted, cannot but lead one to conclude that the image is the product of a clever artist. Baden denies the idea that the Shroud image is an impression made by the corpse itself. He indicates from examples of wounded bodies in a morgue that no dry blood from a corpse could stick on a cloth like the Shroud. Dead bodies, he says, "don't produce this kind of pattern."[22]

It appears that the majority of pathologists believe that the Shroud image is authentic, but controversy does exist. One might speculate that since the carbon 14 test has revealed with ninety-five per cent accuracy that the Shroud cloth is a fourteenth-century product, it is merely a copy, perhaps, of an original. But if that is the case, what has happened to the original, and as Ian Wilson asked, how could a medieval artist have produced "something so different from anything produced at that time" (*N.Y. Times*, June 11, 1989)? No one since, not even our modern scientists and artists with all modern technology available to them can reproduce it.

The Shroud of Turin as Ahmadi Proof that Jesus Did Not Die

Some Ahmadis accept the Shroud of Turin as the true shroud of Jesus, primarily because they are convinced that it offers proof that Jesus survived the cross and was brought down from it unconscious but alive. They believe that the Shroud image must have been made by the spices, the myrrh, and aloe that had been placed on the body of Jesus. They rely, however, only on western publications for proof that Jesus was still alive while in the Shroud. Quoting from John Reban's *Inquest on Jesus Christ*, Muhammad Zafrulla Khan indicates that according to Theodore Hirt, a German, Jesus was still alive when he was brought down from the cross and wrapped in the Shroud. His heart evidently was still beating because the Roman soldier's lance that pierced his side did not harm it. Jesus suffocated and stopped breathing, Khan explains, because of the vapors of the vinegar that was raised up to him, but his heart continued to beat. Giving up the ghost (pnevma in Greek) merely meant the cessation of one's breathing, not of the heart or blood circulation, whose function was entirely unknown. The heart, says Khan, was simply not recognized as a decisive factor in life. A person was considered to be dead when he stopped breathing, and not according to modern medical standards, which take other factors into consideration including the heart's beating. Aziz Kashmiri accepts that Jesus was alive because the lance did not penetrate the heart to kill him, and as the Shroud image reveals, his blood did not coagulate and become dry because his heart was still active. Had it dried, it would not have soaked into the cloth as it did.[23]

In support of Ahmadi claims, Andreas Faber-Kaiser points out that according to Kurt Berna, secretary of the German Institute of Investigations of the Holy Shroud at Stuttgart and a Catholic, who in 1957 published *Jesus night am Kreuz gestorben* (Jesus Did Not Die on the Cross), Jesus was still alive in the grave. The Shroud image reveals that his heart was still beating. The trace of blood fluid on it and the fluid's position and nature give positive scientific proof that the so-called execution had not been legally completed. Berna, who based his investigation on 1931 photographs of the Shroud, maintains that Jesus' head wounds caused by the crown of thorns were still bleeding while he was in the Shroud as was the nail wound on the hand the blood having flowed down the arm when the hand was unnailed. If the heart had stopped, the blood would have ceased to circulate and would have begun to retract in the veins. The capillary blood vessels below the skin surface would have drained and the pallor of death would have appeared on the body. Because he had stopped breathing, Jesus appeared to be dead, but it is possible in such a case, in which the heart is still beating, to revive the person with intensive medical treatment. (This, of course, would not have been done to Jesus during his time because a person who had stopped breathing was considered to be dead.) Berna was certain that the Roman soldiers' lance did not penetrate the heart and that the flow of blood and water mentioned in John (19:34) could not have come from the heart. Jesus' heart was still faintly beating and he was still alive. Therefore, in his letter of February 26, 1959, to Pope John XXIII, Berna indicated that the Shroud of Turin depicts a man who was not dead and asks the Pope to allow a scientific investigation of the Shroud using modern techniques, including a carbon 14 test to determine the precise date of the Shroud's origin. Berna's request was refused, but in 1969, the Pope set up a committee that investigated the Shroud and reached the same conclusion as Berna that the man depicted in the Shroud of Turin was still alive because his heart had been beating.[24]

Many scientists however, disagree with those who claim that the Shroud image reveals a person who was still alive. More recent investigations by European and American doctors and anatomists contradict the thesis entirely and unequivocally. Dr. Pierre Barbet, a reputable surgeon at Joseph's hospital in Paris, Judica-Cordiglia, professor of forensic medicine at the University of Milan and a member of the 1969 Commission on the Shroud, and English physician David Willis agree that the Shroud's victim was dead, that a lance or a long narrow blade entered the man's right side and passed through the pericardium and the heart. Forensic pathologist Robert Bucklin, previously mentioned, who was also STURP's leading pathologist for the post-1978 Shroud research, after examining recent photographs of the Shroud, reported that some kind of narrow blade pierced the Shroud victim's right side, entered the diaphragm, and penetrated into the thoracic cavity through the lung into the heart. However, says Bucklin, separate components of red blood cells and clear serum that oozed from the right lesion verify that the blade wound was a post-mortem incident. The victim was already dead when he was pierced with the lance. Bucklin maintains that the victim was dead before he was brought down from the cross for burial. Rigormortis froze his body, which appears stiff and rigid. When Jesus died, his body was leaning away from the cross and his head was bent forward. A three-dimensional image analysis of the Shroud image by STURP scientists confirmed this, lending support to John's gospel (19:30) that Jesus bowed his head forward when he gave up his spirit. The Shroud image also reveals that, while on the cross, Jesus' left leg was drawn back up when rigormortis set in. The blood that flowed from the left side of the wound did not spurt out, as it would have if the heart had been beating, but slowly drained because of the pull of gravity. Bucklin diagnosed the cause of death as cardio-pulmonary failure, which is typical in cases of crucifixion.[25]

Kenneth E. Stevenson and Gary R. Habermas, scientists and members of STURP, are convinced that the Shroud image verifies not only the gospel story of Jesus' torture and death but also that of his resurrection. They indicate that the victim's body was not decomposed, nor was it removed from the Shroud once it was placed in it. Scientific tests of 1978 revealed no evidence of decomposition. The body was there in a state of rigormortis, but it could not have been there for very long. Severe bodily decomposition can take place even within a few days. The Shroud also indicates, say these two scientists, that the corpse was not removed from it by human hands. The blood clots are not smeared or broken. They are intact, and each bloodstain reveals anatomical correctness including precisely outlined borders. If the Shroud had been removed from the corpse, the blood clots that were in contact with the cloth would have been removed and the edges of the bloodstains would have been disturbed. Obviously, Stevenson and Habermas conclude, the undisturbed bloodstains indicate that the body did not leave the Shroud cloth by any known physical means.[26]

Rozabal (the tomb of Yuz Asaf) and the Shroud of Turin offer us interesting possibilities. If by some five per cent chance the Shroud image could still be authenticated as the miraculous image of Jesus, this might mean that Jesus was resurrected by some supernatural process and was able to reveal himself to his disciples, but that his physiognomy had somewhat changed. As previously mentioned, according to the gospels, Jesus' disciples had difficulty in recognizing their master after his resurrection because he had changed in appearance, but he was there with them physically. It is also possible that, though the resurrection took place, the ascension did not. After all, as previously discussed, only Mark records it (16:20), stating that "he was taken up to heaven," and this is a later addition. If the ascension did not occur, Jesus might have gone to the East in search of the lost tribes of Israel only to die there eventually of natural causes. It would be interesting, therefore, to discover whether there are any remains in the tomb of Yuz Asaf in Srinagar and if they resemble in any way the physical characteristics of the man in the Shroud. A thorough scientific investigation of Rozabal is needed to determine the age of the grave and of its remains, if any. Should grave and remains date from the first century and should the skeletal finding resemble that of the image of the Shroud of Turin, it might mean that the Shroud image was that of Jesus, who by an unknown process was resurrected and who ended his life in Kashmir. How much research, if any, the archaeological department of the government of India has conducted on Yuz Asaf's grave is not known. It has indicated that "from the Archeological [sic.] point of view and in absence of such physical evidence, they cannot confirm that this is the grave of Jesus." It is rather doubtful that any archaeologists and anthropologists were ever allowed to investigate thoroughly Yuz Asaf's grave and its remains. In any case, the Ahmadi thesis appears to be doubtful, not only because of their weak evidence, but also because there is an event that takes place in Jerusalem every year that confirms Jesus' resurrection along with the authenticity of his tomb which is found in this holy city.[27]

The Annual Eastern Miracle of the Holy Light in Jerusalem

The Eastern or Greek Orthodox Church and generally all Christians maintain that there was only one tomb for Jesus, from which he was resurrected in order to ascend to heaven forty days later. This was the tomb of Joseph of Arimathaea below Golgotha, in which Jesus was entombed for three days and which today is preserved in the Church of the Resurrection, as the Greeks call it, or of the Holy Sepulchral in Jerusalem. The truth concerning Christ's resurrection is proclaimed and verified by the miracle of the Holy Light of the Greek Orthodox Church of Jerusalem, which takes place in this city every year on Holy Saturday at twelve o'clock noon. It is the greatest, most famous, and most consistent miracle of the Greek Orthodox Church, a miracle that not only annually validates Christ's resurrection, but also denotes the Greek Orthodox Church's supremacy.

The miracle of the Holy Light takes place in the famous and historic Church of the Resurrection or of the Holy Sepulchral. This Church was first erected as a basilica between 326-335 A.D. by order of Emperor Constantine the Great and through the efforts of his mother, Helen. It was built near Mount Golgotha and houses Jesus' cross and tomb. However, when in 614 the Persians under Chosroes captured Jerusalem and took the cross of Jesus to their capital, Ctesiphon, they also destroyed the Church of the Resurrection. After the Byzantine Emperor Herakleios defeated the Persians and recovered the cross of Jesus, the Church was rebuilt in 629 as it had been originally. When it was almost completely destroyed again in 1009 by the fanatic Caliph El Hakim of the Fatimid dynasty, it was again rebuilt in 1048 but on a much smaller scale by the Byzantine Emperor Constantine IX Monamachos. The original basilica style was abandoned and only the rotunda was retained along with the open courtyard. The western crusaders who conquered Jerusalem in 1099 erected a Romanesque-style church on the site of the original. The rotunda with the tomb of Jesus was retained and the site of Golgotha, which up till then was on the outside, was brought into the main body of the Church as a raised side chapel. The famous Church of the Resurrection or of the Holy Sepulchral, the most famous shrine in Christendom, was damaged in 1808 by fire and again in 1927 by an earthquake. But in 1959, the major Christian denominations in Jerusalem, Greek, Latin, and Armenian, which have several chapels and sacred spots within this church, agreed to repair these damages and have since done so. There are six Christian denominations in Jerusalem that claim sacred places within this large Church.

There have been speculations in the past concerning the authenticity of the tomb of Jesus and even the site of Golgotha. After all, Jerusalem's buildings were leveled by the Romans during the Zealot rebellion (66-70 A.D.). The English general Charles Gordon, made famous by his nineteenth-century Egyptian campaigns, found in 1882 the "garden tomb," which he claimed was the original tomb of Jesus. Gordon questioned the authenticity of the tomb in the Church of the Resurrection because it was within the city, and he correctly assumed that graves, which were considered to be unclean by the Jews, had to be located outside their cities. However, he failed to consider that the "garden tomb" was Jerusalem's north side, beyond a sixteenth-century Ottoman wall located further to the north than the second wall of Jerusalem that existed during Jesus' time. This second wall undoubtedly ran south and east of Golgotha, and therefore, Jesus' place of crucifixion and entombment was beyond or outside this second wall but within the Ottoman wall.

Other evidence supports the holy tomb's authenticity, much of it can be drawn from an historical tradition going back to early Christianity. The early Christians knew exactly where Jesus had been crucified and buried. There is no interruption in the list of the bishops of Jerusalem during this period, and the site of Christ's death was well known even several years later. The veneration of the holy places in Jerusalem had become so widespread by the second century that the Roman Emperor Hadrian (117-138) decided to raze Jerusalem to the ground, as mentioned previously, destroy its Christian churches and Jewish synagogues, and build a new city without Christians and Jews, who were not permitted to enter. However, even though in 130 the Romans erected a new temple to Venus at the site of the tomb of Jesus and a statue of Jupiter at Golgotha, the Christians maintained a knowledge of these places. Thus, Bishop Makarios of Jerusalem was able to direct the Empress Helen, Constantine's mother, on her visit in 326 to the sacred sites of Jesus' tomb and of Golgotha and to the nearby subterranean Roman cistern where, according to tradition, Helen miraculously discovered the genuine cross of Jesus.[28]

As mentioned earlier, the miracle of the Holy Light takes place on Holy Saturday. Between ten and eleven o'clock in the morning, the chapel containing the tomb of Jesus, called the Chapel of the Holy Sepulchral, located within the Church of the Resurrection, is thoroughly inspected by the local authorities, who are in turn closely watched by the Armenian Christians and others. They all want to ascertain that nothing is available that the Greek Orthodox Patriarch can use, like matches or a lighter, to ignite and light a candle or a vigil lamp. The competition among the different Christian denominations for control of the holy places within this Church of the Resurrection has been very keen, and the representatives of these denominations are not particularly pleased that only the Greek Orthodox Patriarch of Jerusalem can cause the miracle of the Holy Light. After the Holy Tomb has been inspected two more times to make certain that all is dark, that no lighted candles or vigil lamps are present, at eleven o'clock the Chapel of the Holy Sepulchral is sealed at its entrance with two big white ribbons. Thus, the tomb of Jesus is made ready for the ceremony that is to follow. Around twelve o'clock noon of this same day, Holy Saturday, the Greek Orthodox Patriarch of Jerusalem, or if necessary, his representative, with an entourage of bishops and faithful, arrive in a solemn procession at the Church of the Resurrection. Upon entering the Church, led by the Patriarch, they proceed to the Chapel of the Holy Sepulchral, located at the center of the Church; and while going around this Chapel three times, they sing both in Greek and in Arabic the famous Greek Orthodox hymn of the resurrection: "Your resurrection Christ our Lord is praised by angels in heaven. . . ." Then, after the Patriarch stops in front of the Chapel's entrance, they chant one of the oldest and most beautiful of hymns in Christendom, "Fos Ilaron Ayias Thoxis" (Resplended Light of Holy Glory).

The moment has arrived for the Patriarch to enter the most holy place for all Christians. After the white ribbon is cut, unsealing the Chapel, two Muslim authorities, in the presence of all the people, Christians and non-Christians, search the Patriarch for matches or for anything that is combustible. Wearing only a simple white garment and carrying four bundles of candles, each bundle containing thirty-three candles, representative of Christ's years on earth, the Patriarch enters the two-chamber Chapel of the Holy Sepulchral. In order to make sure that the Orthodox Patriarch will not employ any physical means to perform the miracle of the Holy Light, an Armenian representative follows him into the Chapel. After going past the front chamber within the Chapel of the Holy Sepulchral (the Chapel of the Holy Stone or of the Angel), which contains at its center the stone which once sealed Jesus' tomb, the Patriarch bows and alone enters through a low door the second chamber, which is the Chapel of the Holy Sepulchral proper, containing Jesus' holy tomb. The Armenian representative observes the Patriarch from the Chapel of the Holy Angel, but only two steps away from the Patriarch's side. The tomb of Jesus is located on the right hand side, just past the low entrance, and it is hewn in a rock just as the scripture tells us (Matthew 27:59; Mark 15:47; Luke 23:53). Forty-three unlighted vigil lamps are hanging over the Lord's tomb. On the top of the marble slab covering the tomb itself is an unlighted vigil lamp with a gold encasement, ready to be lighted, and also a special prayer book held partly opened by a thick candle to the page to be read. To these items, the Patriarch adds his four bundles of thirty-three candles each, which he places on the top of the marble slab.[29]

The solemn moment for the great miracle has arrived. On his knees before the Holy Sepulchral, the Patriarch reads the special prayer from the text on the marble slab before him, and he beseeches Christ to show the Light that sanctifies, loosens sins, heals sickness, and blesses and makes holy those who with devoutness witness it. He also asks Christ to allow the faithful to walk in the light of His commands as children of light. While the Patriarch is praying, the Holy Light appears and lights up the vigil lamp over the tomb and the candles. Ioannas P. Tsekoura's work, *To Ayion Fos Sta Ierosolima* (The Holy Light in Jerusalem), which meets the approval of the Greek Orthodox Patriarchate of Jerusalem, states that a former Greek Orthodox patriarch of Jerusalem once said that, when he read the prayer in peace and with devotion without being disturbed by worldly cares, he would feel an indescribable happiness, and when he raised the bundles of candles, they would light up by themselves along with the vigil lamp over the Holy Tomb. However, if his soul was not at peace, he would not feel this sublime happiness, but the vigil lamp over the Holy Tomb would light up by itself anyway.[30]

Certain devout individuals who have been allowed to enter the chapel of the Holy Tomb with the Patriarch have been astounded by the Holy Light, which they witnessed with their own eyes. In 1926, one of the guards of the Holy Sepulchral was permitted to witness the miracle of the Holy Light. He said that when the Patriarch stooped to enter the chamber of the Holy Tomb, he heard a soft sound as if caused by the wind, and then saw a blue light that filled the entire chamber but turned for a while like a powerful tornado before becoming motionless. The Patriarch, he said, who was all covered by this Holy Light, began to read the prayers in the prayer book, aided by an illumination coming from this strange Light, which had begun to turn again and suddenly burst into a brilliant white glow. The Patriarch then lifted the four bundles, each with thirty-three candles, and they were automatically lighted up along with the vigil lamp on the Tomb. An Ethiopian monk who saw the Holy Light in the chamber of the Holy Sepulchral in 1960 reported that he saw the Patriarch engulfed by fire, and while the Patriarch prayed, the monk saw fire coming out of the Patriarch's mouth. The Holy Sepulchral itself was also engulfed by this Holy Fire, and the monk felt that, if he had died at that moment, he would have died in a sea of heavenly happiness and holy grace. However, it appears that not everyone is able to see the Holy Light. Some have served in the Church of the Resurrection without ever seeing this miracle. The Holy Light, it seems, can be seen only by those chosen by God to see it. However, one thing remains certain. The vigil lamp on the Lord's Tomb never fails to light up on Holy Saturday noon while the Patriarch recites the special prayer.[31]

The Holy Light appears also to some of the thousands of worshippers outside the two-chamber Chapel of the Holy Sepulchral but within the Church of the Resurrection who are anxiously and quietly waiting to receive the Holy Light from the Patriarch. They are each holding in their hands a bundle of thirty-three candles to be lighted up to exalt Christ's triumphant resurrection. According to Tsekoura, suddenly, while the Patriarch is praying inside the Holy Sepulchral, the Holy Light appears also to this crowd in blue and white colors, moving about rapidly from left to right and up and down. It bathes the faces of many of the faithful, filling them with wonder and joy. It also illuminates the holy icons and lights up vigil lamps and even the bundles of thirty-three candles of some of the faithful, from which others light up their own candles; and all this occurs before the Patriarch has come forth from the Chapel of the Holy Sepulchral to offer the Holy Light to the waiting crowd. The Holy Light, says Tsekoura, is not static but moves through the air and occupies a certain space in a moment of time. It may light up the face of one person or of a group of faithful but leave others untouched. It may appear to individuals as a flash or glow of lightning, a shiny line, a radiant cloud, a lighted disk, a radiant garment, lit up balls, fire or fires, a shiny crown, or a heavenly light. Tsekoura cites examples of such manifestations that have occurred between 1984 and 1987, mostly inside the Church, but some even outside; and he indicates that, although the Holy Light manifests itself primarily on Holy Saturday, it has revealed itself to a few individuals on other days of the Holy Week as well. This author also writes that he himself saw the Holy Light as a radiant cloud on Holy Saturday of 1985 as he stood outside but near the two-chamber Chapel of the Holy Sepulchral. He says that he saw descending from the dome of the Church of the Resurrection a cloud of magnificent blue color and that it stopped in front of the Chapel of the Sepulchral but high above the heads of the faithful standing below. Then it began to move toward the vigil lamps located toward the front of the Church, which it suddenly lit up.[32]

The Patriarch eventually brings the Holy Light with his bundles of candles from the Tomb directly to the people, but not immediately. Once the Patriarch's four bundles of candles are miraculously lit up, he returns to the chamber of the Holy Stone. There, he gives the Holy Light first to the Armenian representative. Then, from an opening in the Holy Stone, he gives one of the lighted bundles to an Arabian Orthodox priest who gives the Light to the people waiting outside the two-chamber chapel of the Holy Sepulchral. From another opening in the Holy Stone, the Patriarch hands out a second bundle of candles to an Armenian, who takes it to the Armenian Patriarch. Then two representatives from the Coptic and Syrian churches enter the Chapel of the Holy Stone and receive the Light from the Patriarch. Afterwards, the Armenian representative and the Patriarch come out of the Chapel with the two remaining lighted bundles of thirty-three candles each, and the Patriarch gives the Holy Light to everyone, with the exception of those who, as mentioned earlier, have already miraculously received the Holy Light and have their candles lit. In any case, according to Tsekoura, even after the Patriarch has come out of the two-chamber Chapel, the Holy Light continues to manifest itself within the great center hall of the Church of the Resurrection.[33]

Attempts have been made by others of different Christian denominations to bring forth the Holy Light, but they have failed.

In 1101, after Jerusalem had been taken over by the western crusaders, the Roman Catholics attempted in the Church of the Resurrection to bring forth the Holy Light throughout Holy Saturday and on into the next morning of Easter Sunday, but without any success. After the Catholics left, the Greek Orthodox faithful, who had remained inside the Church, went ahead with their traditional ritual and, according to Tsekoura, the Holy Light appeared in such abundance that it filled the entire Church. In 1579, the Armenians were able to obtain from the Turkish authorities the ownership of the Church of the Resurrection, which belonged to the Greek Orthodox. On Holy Saturday, while the Armenian Patriarch recited a prayer inside the Holy Sepulchral of Christ to bring forth the Holy Light, the Greek Orthodox Patriarch and his faithful were forced to remain and pray outside the Church in front of its main door. The Holy Light, however, according to Tsekoura, did not appear to the Armenians inside the Church, but to the Greek Orthodox who were praying on the outside. As they were praying, suddenly the wind picked up and a deafening thunder was heard as lightning struck the center column of the left side of the main door, charring it and allowing the faithful to light their candles. All those who witnessed this miracle were astounded, including the Muslim muezzin, Emar Dounam, who became so excited that he loudly declared his belief in Christ and fell from the minaret twenty feet below without being harmed. However, because he continued to declare his belief in Christ while on the ground, the Muslims rushed upon him and beheaded him on the spot. Today, one can still see the charred central column of the main door's left side, which was also cut in half by the Holy Light, and which the Greek Orthodox offer as proof of the validity and supremacy of their faith.[34]

There is, however, a certain curious anomaly concerning the miracle of the Holy Light. A rumor persists to the effect that after the Greek Orthodox Patriarch bows before the Holy Sepulchral and recites the special prayer on Holy Saturday noon, a mist forms within the Sepulchral and dew collects on its walls. With a piece of cotton, the Patriarch wipes the moisture from the walls of the Holy Sepulchral and it catches on fire, but for a few minutes does not burn. An eyewitness from Mount Athos, a monk, who was allowed to enter with the Patriarch the second chamber containing the tomb of Jesus, verified the phenomenon to this author and indicated also that when the faithful first receive the Holy Light with their candles from the Patriarch, they put it in their hair, beards and clothes, but for a few minutes do not get burned. A Muslim student who witnessed the ritual on Holy Saturday informed this writer that it is true that some people do not get burned, but others do, and one hears them cry out in pain. Both the monk from Mount Athos and the Muslim student were not aware of Tsekoura's description of the appearance of the Holy Light within the Holy Sepulchral and in the main center of the Church of the Resurrection. When the author in a letter described to the Greek Orthodox Patriarch what he knew about the miracle of the Holy Light through the monk from Mount Athos and asked him to verify this information or deny it or correct it, the Patriarch responded through his secretary by confirming the miracle's existence and generously sending a copy of Tsekoura's work (see Appendix B). As mentioned, Tsekoura indicates that only a few among the faithful see the Holy Light and in different ways, but the vigil lamp over the tomb of Jesus always lights up with the Holy Saturday's ritual, and sometimes other vigil lamps and candles light up also, even those outside the Chapel of the Holy Sepulchral.

A great need exists to reveal this annual miracle of the Holy Light to people throughout the world. With the exception of a few Greek works, very little has been published on this event in other languages and in other countries, especially in the United States. No one has produced a documentary on this ritual and nothing has been shown on television. In addition, no scientific study has ever been made of this great miracle of the Holy Light in order to verify its authenticity, which could only lend support to Jesus' resurrection. The lighting of vigil lamps and candles is not merely a psychological or spiritual phenomenon but a physical manifestation that can be scientifically examined. The Greek Orthodox Church should be glad to have its miracle authenticated and revealed to all the peoples of all religions throughout the world. After all, the Christian faith is based on the belief that Jesus Christ was God on earth, "light of light, true God of true God, consubstantial with the father," and this belief is credited and upheld by Christ's resurrection. As St. Paul himself proclaimed, without the resurrection Christ cannot be divine, he cannot be God.

There is, however, one more interesting and curious matter. The tomb of Jesus in the Church of the Resurrection seems to confirm that the Shroud of Turin which depicts Jesus as 5′ 11″ in height cannot possibly be valid. The tomb itself is only 5′ long, 2′ wide, and 3′ high, revealing that Jesus must have been a much shorter man. A controversy has existed over the fact that the Shroud image reveals an unusually tall man for a Palestinian.[35] Further scientific research on this subject might confirm where authenticity lies, whether with the tomb in the Church of the Resurrection or with the Shroud of Turin. In addition, of course, there is the need to satisfy one's curiosity over Rozabal, the tomb of Yuz Asaf. No one has revealed the measurements of the hidden grave (the true grave of Yuz Asaf or supposedly of Jesus) in the lower level of this tomb. It would be interesting to discover how the measurements would compare with those of Jerusalem and of the Shroud image.

Conclusion

An urgent need exists to obtain the facts concerning the Ahmadi tomb of Jesus and the light of the Holy Light of the resurrection. As the scriptures tell us, God is truth. He wants us to know the truth; therefore, we must not hesitate to acquire the facts and learn the truth. The person of Christ has remained throughout the past and into the present quite mysterious, perhaps just as mysterious as when he walked on this earth. The entire history of Christianity reveals disbelief concerning Christ's mission and divinity as manifested by his resurrection, and as already indicated, scholars and theologians, Christians and non-Christians are still debating and expressing doubts concerning his messianic role and nature. Some simply cannot accept the miracle of his resurrection (much less of his ascension) and suspect that it was all a plot by Jesus and others to save him from death and to show him to his disciples. The books of the New Testament, which were written by several individuals at different periods of time and from different locations, have caused problems for scholars. Certain scholars have themselves caused problems merely selecting suitable passages from the New Testament books and discarding others in order to develop and defend a particular thesis concerning Jesus. The belief that the apparent resurrection was merely a deception might be interesting, along with its defense, but it still remains only a hypothesis. Discrepancies certainly exist in the gospels, but only in some of the details. Although the ascension story appears to be a later addition, this does not discredit the possibility that a divine being such as Jesus could have ascended to heaven, even though his disciples, perhaps, were not witnesses to this event. What is most amazing is that, in spite of the Gnostic exaggerations and their numerous sects and belief to which we may add those of the Essenes, there is a general agreement in the New Testament books concerning Jesus' messianic mission and divinity. The New Testament writers, it seems, sought to refute exaggerated claims and superstitions concerning Jesus and to present his mission and person with guarded zeal. Not even the early Christians of Jerusalem led by James the Just denied Jesus' Messianic mission. For the most part, there is amazingly indeed a general agreement about Christ found in these books rather than disagreement or discrepancies.

The authenticity of the tombs of Jesus in Srinagar and Jerusalem has been held to suspicion. Although the Ahmadis claim to have the tomb of Jesus in Srinagar, India, no historical evidence has been offered to confirm its authenticity except for questionable works based on oral legends. In addition, the Ahmadis have failed to produce any archaeological or anthropological evidence that the grave of Yuz Asaf might be that of Jesus. Therefore, the Ahmadi thesis is based only on the revelation of Hazrat Mirza Ghulam Ahmad, the founder of the Ahmadiya movement. The fact that many peoples throughout the world, including the American Indians and the Japanese, have had legends concerning visits by Jesus, makes the Ahmadi contention concerning Yuz Asaf and his tomb in Kashmir even more questionable. After all, even some Japanese are claiming that they have the tomb of Jesus, and their script validating their thesis appears to be more convincing historically than any of the eastern works the Ahmadis have produced, with the exception of the inscriptions in the Temple of Solomon containing a year but no era. However, very little can be said about the hidden tomb of Yuz Asaf in Srinagar unless permission is granted by the owners for the collection of archaeological and anthropological data on the actual tomb, which is apparently located at a level below the one that is being exhibited.

There is also a need to examine the tomb of Jesus in Jerusalem and the miracle of the Holy Light. With the exception of its measurements, one does not find any archaeological data on the tomb of Jesus. Permission for the study of holy relics has been difficult to obtain. It took scientists many years to receive permission to examine the Shroud of Turin. However, scientific research of these relics must be allowed to discover the facts. Thus far, the Christians have been able to reveal an empty tomb of Jesus authenticated by the miracle of the Holy Light. Christianity has accepted throughout its history that God performs miracles for his people, and miracles he does perform in His own mysterious ways. It is difficult to deny these miracles altogether because the bodies of certain saints are still well preserved without any natural explanations, and icons have been seen to bleed and to cry. Crying icons of the Madonna have been recently examined by scientists in New York and Chicago. The author personally finds it difficult to reject all miracles because he did witness, along with many others, while in Sofades (Thessaly), Greece, in 1946, the icon of Saint Barbara whose pupils were slowly moving up and down. Although he examined the icon with skepticism and suspicion, he found nothing that could have been causing its pupils to move. It seemed as though some mysterious and over-powering force was inducing this writer to see the pupils move. Philosophers have been debating since ancient times whether the world is physical and real or mental and spiritual and to an extent illusory, a fantasy. Personal experiences indicate that it is a combination of all these. Although most scientists and scholars reject the supernatural, and rightly so, because examination of the facts requires doubt and a natural or factual explanation of events, nevertheless, we must not set aside or disregard unusual and mysterious events and declare them nonexistent simply because they cannot be explained. They must be investigated and, if possible, brought into the light of reason. After all, miracles observed must be of a physical nature; otherwise, they could not have been perceived. Even though we may not have at present the means to explain these events, the time will come when science will know enough about man and the universe and will have developed the proper electro-psychic means to understand the operations of the mind and its relationship to the time-space continuum and the eternal.

Notes

Chapter 1

1. Hugh J. Schonfield, *Those Incredible Christians* (New York, 1969), 2-30.

2. Ibid., 38-39.

3. Theodore Gaster, ed., *The Dead Sea Scriptures* (Garden City, 1956), 4-5, 22-23, 39-85, 281-306.

4. Ibid., 18, 39-60. See also A. Powell Davies, *The Meaning of the Dead Sea Scrolls* (New York, 1961), 63-67; and Michael Baigent, Richard Leigh, and Henry Lincoln, *The Messianic Legacy* (New York, 1987), 53-55.

5. Charles Francis Potter, *The Lost Years of Jesus Revealed* (Greenwich, Connecticut, 1962), 44-46. See also Davies, *Dead Sea Scrolls*, 102, 104-105, 145; and Baigent, Leigh nd Lincoln, *Messianic Legacy*, 53.

6. Gaester, *Dead Sea Scriptures*, 20-24.

7. Baigent, Leigh and Lincoln, *Messianic Legacy*, 23, 55-61. See also S. G. F. Brandon, *Jesus and the Zealots* (New York, 1967), 26-63; Hyam Macoby, *Revolution in Judaea* (New York, 1980), 75; A. Powell Davies, *The First Christian* (New York, 1959), 126; and R. H. Eisenman, *Maccabees, Zadokites, Christians and Qumran* (Leiden, 1983), passim.

8. Richard A. Horseley and John S. Hanson, *Bandits, Prophets and Messiahs: Popular Movements at the Time of Jesus* (San Francisco, 1985), 110-131. See also Davies, *First Christian*, 94-95.

9. Constantine Cavarnos, "Greek Philosophy and Orthodoxy," *The Hellenic Chronicle* (Boston), in fourteen issues, April 1-25, 1980.

10. John Herman Randall, Jr., *Hellenistic Ways of Deliverance and the Making of the Christian Synthesis* (New York, 1970), 37-55. See also Moses Hadas, *Essential Works of Stoicism* (New York, 1961), vii-xvii, 40-47.

11. Cavarnos, *Hellenic Chronicle*, issues X and XI. See also Randall, Jr., *Hellenistic Ways*, 162; and Davies, *First Christian*, 98.

12. Gilbert Murray, *Five Stages of Greek Religion* (Garden City, 1951), 158-159.

13. Ibid., 139-154. See also Herbert J. Muller, *The Uses of the Past* (Oxford, 1952), 162-167.

14. Davies, *Dead Sea Scrolls*, 90-91. See also Davies, *First Christian*, 122-125; and Baigent, Leigh and Lincoln, *Legacy*, 36-37.

15. Hugh J. Schonfield, *The Passover Plot* (New York, 1965), 74-75, 78, 207-213. See also Eusebius, *The History of the Church from Christ to Constantine* (Baltimore, 1965), 99-103; and Matthew Black, *The Scrolls and Christian Origins* (London, 1961), 83.

16. James Kallas, *Jesus and the Power of Satan* (Philadelphia, 1968), 18-21. See also Davies, *First Christian*, 63.

17. Davies, *First Christian*, 60-62. See also Augustine Cardinal Bea, *The Study of the Synoptic Gospels* (New York, 1965), 36; and Robert M. Grant, *The Secret Sayings of Jesus* (Garden City, 1960), 22.

18. Elaine Pagels, *The Gnostic Gospels* (New York, 1979), 119-151. See also James Robinson, ed., *The Nag Hammadi Library* (San Francisco, 1981), 1-25; Grant, *Secret Sayings of Jesus*, 38-64, 72-79; Alfred Firmin Loisy, *The Birth of the Christian Religion and the Origins of the New Testament* (New York, 1962), 295-324; J. G. Davies, *The Early Christian Church* (New York, 1965), 72-75; and Jack Finegan, *Hidden Records of the Life of Jesus* (Philadelphia, 1969), passim.

19. Robinson, *Nag Hammadi Library*, 8-10. See also Davies, *First Christian*, 125-126; and Murray, *Five Stages*, 144-146.

20. E. J. Tinsley, *The Gospel According to Luke* (Cambridge, 1965), 18-19.

21. Grant, *Secret Sayings*, 20-22. See also Bea, *Synoptic Gospels*, 40-41; and John Meyendorff, *The Orthodox Church* (Crestwood, New York, 1981), 4, 6.

22. Grant, *Secret Sayings*, 26. See also Bea, *Synoptic Gospels*, 37-42; and Kallas, *Satan*, 35-36.

23. Schonfield, *Christians*, 144-145. See also Albert Schweitzer, *The Quest of the Historical Jesus* (New York, 1955), 281, 277-286; Davies, *First Christian*, 64; Kallas, *Satan*, 194-196; S. G. F. Brandon, *The Fall of Jerusalem and the Christian Church* (London, 1951), Chapter 10; and Willi Marxsen, *Mark the Evangelist* (Nashville, 1969), passim.

24. Schonfield, *Christians*, 123-124. See also Joseph Klausner, *Jesus of Nazareth* (New York, 1957), 320; Nikolaos Kokkinos, *To Ainigma tou Iisou tis Galileas* (Athens, 1980), 51-53; Grant, *Secret Sayings*, 24; Tinsley, *Luke*, 21-22; Raymond E. Brown, *The Birth of the Messiah* (Garden City, 1977), 64-85; Eusebius, *History of the Church*, 53-56; and Bea, *Synoptic Gospels*, 46-47.

25. Davies, *First Christian*, 69, 72-73. See also Tinsley, *Luke*, 11-12.

26. Grant, *Secret Sayings*, 24-25.

27. R. P. C. Hanson, *The Acts* (Oxford, 1967), 113-114, 216, 238. See also Davies, *First Christian*, 33-34, 77-78.

28. Victor Paul Furnish, *Theology and Ethics in Paul* (Nashville, 1968), 162-194. See also Davies, *First Christian*, 139-148; Kallas, *Satan*, 24-25; and Robert C. Tannehill, *Dying and Rising with Christ. A Study in Pauline Theology* (Berlin, 1967), passim.

29. Schonfield, *Christians*, 124-130, 162-163; and Davies, *First Christian*, 160-161. See also Eusebias, *History of the Church*, 11, 142-144; Floy Vivian Filson, *A New Testament History. The Story of the Emerging Church* (Philadelphia, 1964), 216-221, 301-303; Finegan, *Hidden Records*, 165-173; and Walter Schmithalls, *Paul and James* (Naperville, Illinois, 1965), passim.

Chapter 2

1. See Albert Schweitzer, *The Quest of the Historical Jesus* (New York, 1955), passim.

2. Albert Schweitzer, *The Mystery of the Kingdom of God* (New York, 1970), 180-273.

3. Joseph Klausner, *Jesus of Nazareth* (New York, 1957), 330-331, 324-325, 336.

4. Ibid., 340-348.

5. Ibid., 340-348, 353-354.

6. Ibid., 354-355, 357, 359.

7. S. G. F. Brandon, *Jesus and the Zealots* (New York, 1967), 332-342, 350-351. See also S. G. F. Brandon, *The Trial of Jesus of Nazareth* (New York, 1968), 101-104.

8. Brandon, *Zealots*, 198-205, 322-327, 243-245, 255-262, 302-310; and Brandon, *Trial*, 105-116.

9. Hugh Schonfield, *The Passover Plot* (New York, 1965), 104-111, 119, 138-139.

10. Ibid., 135-140.

11. Ibid., 137, 143-153.

12. *Time*, December 10, 1965, 97.

13. Schonfield, *Passover Plot*, 162-168.

14. Ibid., 170-181.

15. Richard A. Horseley, *Jesus and the Spiral of Violence* (San Francisco, 1987), 318-326.

16. A. Powell Davies, *The First Christian* (New York, 1959), 70-71.

17. Charles Foster Kent, *The Historical Bible* (New York, 1908-1916), V, 304-305.

18. Alfred Firman Loisy, *The Birth of the Christian Religion and the Origins of the New Testament* (New York, 1962), 68-99; Rudolph Karl Bultmann, *The History of the Synoptic Gospels* (Oxford, 1963), 371; and Marcus J. Borg, *Jesus: A New Vision* (San Francisco, 1987), 184-185.

19. Rudolf Schnackenburg, *The Gospel According to St. John* (New York, 1982), III, 342-350. See also Charles H. Dodd, *The Interpretation of the Fourth Gospel* (Cambridge, 1968), 441-442.

20. Floy Vivian Filson, *A New Testament History. The Story of the Emerging Church* (Philadelphia, 1964), 147-149, 307-310.

21. Kent, *Historical Bible*, 306-307.

22. Hans Kung, *On Being a Christian* (New York, 1976), 349-359, 426, 444-450. See also *Time*, February 27, 1978, 44-45.

23. *Time*, February 27, 1978, 44-45.

24. *Time*, February 27, 1978, 44-45.

25. *Time*, August 15, 1977, 45.

26. *Time*, February 27, 1978, 44-45.

27. Idem. Also, *Time*, April 8, 1966, 82-87.

28. *Time*, August 15, 1977, 45.

29. *Time*, February 10, 1975, 47.

30. *Time*, October 29, 1965, 80, 82.

31. *Time*, April 8, 1966, 82-87.

32. See *Time*, July 25, 73, and August 15, 1988, 34-36.

33. *Time*, April 8, 1966, 85.

Chapter 3

1. Caesar Farah, *Islam* (Woodbury, New York, 1970), 78-83, 87-92; and Arthur Jeffery, *The Koran* (New York, 1958), 13. See also Alfred Guillaume, *Islam* (Baltimore, 1956), 59.

2. Guillaume, *Islam*, 30, 61-62. See also Farah, *Islam*, 86-87, 92-95.

3. Ibid., 61-62, 195. See also Farah, *Islam*, 96-99; and Jeffery, *The Koran*, 9-16.

4. Geoffrey Parrinder, *Jesus in the Qur'an* (London, 1970), 16, 18-20, 30-32, 60-74, 174. See also Al-Haj Kwaja Nazir Ahmad, *Jesus in Heaven on Earth* (Lahore, 1956), 41, 43, 50, 59, 143-144; Seyed Ameer Ali, *The Spirit of Islam* (London, 1967), 142-143; Abdullah Yusuf Ali, *The Meaning of the Glorious Qur'an* (Cairo, 1938), I, 134-138, 266-267, 771-775, 827; and Guillaume, *Islam*, 63-64, 194-196.

5. Parrinder, *Jesus*, 105-106.

6. Ibid., 108. See also Jeffery, *Koran*, 198-199; Guillaum, *Islam*, 196; and Ali, *Glorious Qur'an*, I, 229-231.

7. Ibid., 109-111. See also Arthur Jeffery, *A Reader on Islam* (New York, 1980), 592; William Goldsack, *Christ in Islam* (1905), 40; and Jean Doresee, *The Secret Books of the Egyptian Gnostics* (Rochester, Vermont, 1986), 22.

8. Muhammad Kemal Hussein, *City of Wrong* (New York, 1966), 222. See also Parrinder, *Jesus*, 111-112, 115, 119, 121; and Ali, *Glorious Qur'an*, I, 230-231.

9. Guillaume, *Islam*, 143-154, 118-119. See also Farah, *Islam*, 208-220; and Ali, *Spirit of Islam*, 141.

10. Ibid., 111-125. See also Ali, *Spirit of Islam*, 122-127, 344-347; and Farah, *Islam*, 174-184, 243-248.

11. Hazrat Mirza Ghulam Ahmad, *Jesus in India* (Rabwa, Pakistan, 1899), 17-18, 43. See also Muhammad Zafrulla Khan, *Deliverance from the Cross* (London, 1978), 75-77.

12. Khan, *Deliverance*, 79-86.

13. Farah, *Islam*, 242-243; and Guillaume, *Islam*, 125-126.

14. Hazrat Ghulam Ahmad, *Jesus in India*, passim. See also Khan, *Deliverance*, 88-89; and Mohammad Yasin, *Rauzabal and Other Mysteries of Kashmir* (Srinagar, 1972), ii-iv.

15. Ibid., 21-22. See also Khan, *Deliverance*, 24-25; Al-Haj Nazir Ahmad, *Jesus in Heaven*, 183-190; and J. D. Shams, *Where Did Jesus Die?* (Lahore, Pakistan, ca. 1960), 9-10.

16. Al-Haj Nazir Ahmad, *Jesus in Heaven*, 188-193. See also Ghulam Ahmad, *Jesus in India*, 27-38; and Shams, *Where Did Jesus Die?*, 21-22.

17. Ibid., 186-191, 196-199. See also Khan, *Deliverance*, 28-41; Yasin, *Rauzabal*, 1-3; and Sufi Mutiur Rahman Bengalee, *The Tomb of Jesus* (London, 1946), 12-21. On the western sources used primarily by Al-Haj Nazir Ahmad, see Ernest Renan, *The Life of Jesus* (New York, 1931), 371; William Stroud, *On the Physical Death of the Christ* (London, 1905), 55; William Hanna, *The Life of Christ* (New York, 1928), III, 325-329; and F. W. Farrar, *The Life of Christ* (London, 1874), 423-424.

18. Ibid., 196-228. See also Hazrat Ghulam Ahmad, *Jesus in India*, 56-58; Khan, *Deliverance*, 59-60; Shams, *Where Did Jesus Die?*, 39-40; J. R. Dummellow, *Commentary on the Holy Bible* (London, 1917), 808; William Milligan, *The Resurrection of Our Lord* (London, 1905), 76-77; and H. Spencer Lewis, *The Mystical Life of Jesus* (San Jose, California, 1982), 270-271.

19. Ibid., 231-236. See also Shams, *Where Did Jesus Die?*, 63.

20. Ibid., 281-282. See also Andreas Faber-Kaiser, *Jesus Died in Kashmir* (London, 1977), 54-55. The two books of Esdra were rejected by the Roman Catholic Council of Trent in 1546 as uninspired.

21. Hazrat Ghulam Ahmad, *Jesus in India*, 101-115. See also Al-Haj Nazir Ahmad, *Jesus in Heaven*, 282-337; Khan, *Deliverance*, 100-102; Shams, *Where Did Jesus Die?*, 93-104; and Bengalee, *Tomb of Jesus*, 32-34.

22. Robert M. Grant, *The Secret Sayings of Jesus. The Gnostic Gospel of Thomas* (Garden City, 1960), 65. See also Al-Haj Nazir Ahmad, *Jesus in Heaven*, 346-347.

23. See Chapter 4, 194-196 and Chapter 5, 239-240, 242.

24. Al-Haj Nazir Ahmad, *Jesus in Heaven*, 357-359; and Hazrat Ghulam Ahmad, *Jesus in India*, 75-79. See also Faber-Kaiser, *Jesus Died in Kashmir*, 76-79; and Bengalee, *The Tomb of Jesus*, 36.

25. Al-Haj Nazir Ahmad, *Jesus in Heaven*, 352. See also William Cureton, *Ancient Syriac Documents* (London, 1864), XXII, 141; and F. C. Burkit, *Early Christians Outside the Roman Empire* (Cambridge, 1899), 155.

26. Ibid., 359-360. See also Faber-Kaiser, *Jesus Died in Kashmir*, 79-80.

27. Ibid., 360.

28. Ibid., 352.

29. Ibid., 360-361. See also Faber-Kaiser, *Jesus Died in Kashmir*, 82-83. On the Kushans, see Vincent A. Smith, *The Early History of India* (Oxford, 1904), 263-267.

30. Ibid., 361-364, 376. See also Faber-Kaiser, *Jesus Died in Kashmir*, 84.

31. Ibid., 368-369. See also Faber-Kaiser, *Jesus Died in Kashmir*, 86. H. H. Cole writes in his Illustrations of Ancient Buildings in Kashmir (London, 1869), 8, that there are two mutilated inscriptions in Persian on each side of the two flank walls encasing the stairs of this temple.

32. Ibid., 369; and Faber-Kaiser, *Jesus Died in Kashmir*, 88-89. See also Aziz Kashmiri, *Christ in Kashmir* (Srinagar, 1984), 52-53.

33. Al-Haj Nazir Ahmad, *Jesus in Heaven*, 365-366.

34. Ibid., 346-354.

35. Ibid., 349-350.

36. Ibid., 350-351. See also Faber-Kaiser, *Jesus Died in Kashmir*, 106-107; Fr. Wrede, *An Account of the St. Thomas Christians on the Coast of Malabar* (London, 1803), 363; and George Milne Rae, *The Syrian Church in India* (London, 1892), 112.

37. Bengalee, *The Tomb of Jesus*, 43. See also E. J. Eitel, *Three Lectures on Buddhism* (London, 1873), 13-14.

38. Ibid., 42-43. See also Rudolf Seydel, *Das Evangelium von Jesus in Seinen Verhaltnissen zu Buddha-Sage und Buddha-Lehre* (Leipzig, 1880), passim.

39. Dwight Goddard, *Was Jesus Influenced by Buddhism?* (White River Junction, Vermont, 1927), 176-183, 244-248. See also Bengalee, *The Tomb of Jesus*, 43-45.

40. Goddard, *Was Jesus Influenced?*, 85-115, 221-249.

41. Nicolas Notovich, *The Unknown Life of Jesus Christ* (Chicago, 1894), 90-96. See also Al-Haj Nazir Ahmad, *Jesus in Heaven*, 339-340; Holger Kersten, *Jesus Lived in India* (Dorset, 1986), 32-38; and Elizabeth Clare Prophet, *The Lost Years of Jesus* (Livingston, Montana, 1987), 3-73.

42. Notovich, *The Unknown Life*, 105-123.

43. Al-Haj Nazir Ahmad, *Jesus in Heaven*, 365; Notovich, *The Unknown Life*, 150-151; and Prophet, *Lost Years*, 295-309.

44. Hazrat Ghulam Ahmad, *Jesus in India*, 81-89.

45. Bengalee, *The Tomb of Jesus*, 37, 45-51; and Ghulam Ahmad, *Jesus in India*, 89-96. See also T. W. Rhys Davids. *Lecture on the Origin and Growth of Religion as Illustrated by Some Points in the History of Buddhism* (London, 1891), 151, 180. H. Oldenburg, *Buddha. His Life, His Doctrine, His Order* (London, 1883), 78; James B. Pratt. *The Pilgrimage of Buddhism and a Buddhist Pilgrimage* (New York, 1928), 2; Henry Thoby Prinsep, *Tibet, Tartary and*

Mongolia (London, 1852), 171; John Mavrogordato, "Byzantine Literature," in *Byzantium* ed. Norman H. Baynes and H. St. L. B. Moses (Oxford, 1961), 238; and Kersten, *Jesus*, 203-206.

46. Al-Haj Nazir Ahmad, *Jesus in Heaven*, 363, 365, 367-368.

47. Ibid., 375; also in Faber-Kaiser, *Jesus Died in Kashmir*, 104-105.

48. Faber-Kaiser, *Jesus Died in Kashmir*, 98-103; Al-Haj Nazir Ahmad, *Jesus in Heaven*, 374-375; and Kersten, *Jesus*, 206.

49. Faber-Kaiser, *Jesus Died in Kashmir*, 90-94.

Chapter 4

1. Hazrat Mirza Ghulam Ahmad, *Jesus in India* (Rabwa, Pakistan, 1899), 77.

2. P. Thomas, *Epics, Myths and Legends of India* (Bombay, 1973), passim. See also Louis Herbert Gray, ed., *The Mythology of all Races* (Boston, 1917), IV, passim.

3. William Wright, ed., *Apocryphal Acts of the Apostles* (Amsterdam, 1968), 155-156.

4. Ibid., 146-298. See also A. E. Medlycott, *India and the Apostle Thomas* (London, 1905), 248-272; and George Milne Rae, *The Syrian Church in India* (London, 1892), 41-61.

5. E. J. Rapson, *Ancient India from the Earliest Times to the First Century A.D.* (Cambridge, 1961), 145-146. See also Sunil Chandra Ray, *Early History and Culture of Kashmir* (New Delhi, 1970), 40; George M. Rae, *Syrian Church*, 51-55; and Medlycott, *India*, 3-17.

6. George M. Rae, *Syrian Church*, 17-18.

7. Medlycott, *India*, 20-33, 102-116. See also J. N. Furquhar, *The Apostle Thomas in Southern India* (Manchester, 1927), 21; and F. C. Burkit, *The Earliest Sources of the Life of Jesus* (London, 1910), 30.

8. Ibid., 42-68, 71-84, 120. See also Vincent A. Smith, *The Early History of India* (Oxford, 1904), 247, 261.

9. Ibid., 135, 188-202. See also George M. Rae, *Syrian Church*, 105-118.

10. George M. Rae, *Syrian Church*, 32-37. See also Eusebius, *The History of the Church* (Baltimore, 1965), 65-70, 72-73; Medlycott, *India*, 36-37; and Smith, *Early India*, 249-250.

11. Medlycott, *India*, 33-37, 145-148, 249-253. See also Eusebius, *History*, 107.

12. George M. Rae, *Syrian Church*, 65-100. See also Medlycott, *India*, 171-202.

13. Al-Haj Kwaja Nazir Ahmad, *Jesus in Heaven on Earth* (Lahore, 1956), 263-268. See also Aziz Kashmiri, *Christ in Kashmir* (Srinagar, 1984), 15-18; Mohammad Yasin, *Rauzabal and Other Mysteries of Kashmir* (Srinagar, 1972), 17-22; and Andreas Faber-Kaiser, *Jesus Died in Kashmir* (London, 1977), 120-122.

14. Al-Haj Nazir Ahmad, *Jesus in Heaven*, 271-275. See also Yasin, *Rauzabal*, 15-24; and Kashmiri, *Christ*, 15-18, 67-68.

15. Ibid., 268, 330-332. See also Kashmiri, *Christ*, 82.

16. J. D. Shams, *Where Did Jesus Die? (Lahore, ca. 1960)*, 90.

17. *Al-Haj Nazir Ahmad, Jesus in Heaven*, 373.

18. Ibid., 374.

19. Ibid., 371-374.

20. Ibid., 381-383. See also Faber-Kaiser, *Jesus Died in Kashmir*, 114-116.

21. Faber-Kaiser, *Jesus Died in Kashmir*, 116-117. See also Al-Haj Nazir Ahmad, *Jesus in Heaven*, 383, 378-379; Kashmiri, *Christ*, 51-52; Prithivi Nath Kaul Bamzai, *A History of Kashmir* (Delhi, 1962), 33, 35; Sunil Chandra Ray, *History and Culture of Kashmir*, 40, 42-43; and Ram Chandra Kak, *Ancient Monuments of Kashmir* (New Delhi, 1971), 12-13, 17.

22. Al-Haj Nazir Ahmad, *Jesus in Heaven*, 380.

23. Ibid., 379-380, 383-385.

24. On Gondophares and Kadephsis I, see also Smith, *Early India*, 244-245. It appears, however, that both Ahmad and Smith may be wrong because according to Bamzai's *History of Kashmir*, pp. 68-69, it was Kadphises (Kadephsis) II, who in 45 A.D. succeeded Kadphises I, the conqueror of Afghanistan, that conquered north-western India to Banaras; and Kanishka succeeded him in 78 A.D., extending the Kushan empire to the borders of Bengal.

25. Al-Haj Nazir Ahmad, *Jesus in Heaven*, 381-382.

26. Alfred Firmin Loisy, *The Birth of the Christian Religion and the Origins of the New Testament* (New York, 1962), 296-300. See also J. G. Davies, *The Early Christian Church* (New York, 1965), 72-73; Hugh J. Schonfield, *The Passover Plot* (New York, 1965), 50-57, 252; and Kashmiri, *Christ*, 15-16.

27. L. Taylor Hansen, *He Walked the Americas* (Amherst, Wisconsin, 1963), passim.

28. See also ibid., 205, 208.

29. Michael Baigent, Richard Leigh, and Henry Lincoln, *Holy Blood, Holy Grail* (New York, 1985), passim.

Chapter 5

1. *Time*, October 24, 1988, 81; and *New York Times*, October 14, 1988.

2. Ian Wilson, *The Shroud of Turin* (Garden City, 1979), 21. See also John Heller, *Report on the Shroud of Turin* (Boston, 1983), 2; and Kenneth E. Stevenson and Gary R. Habermas, *Verdict on the Shroud* (Wayne, Pennsylvania, 1981), 42, 98.

3. Stevenson and Habermas, *Verdict*, 53-68, 258-261.

4. Robert of Clari, *The Conquest of Constantinople* (New York, 1966), 112. See also "How in Fact Was Jesus Christ Laid in His Tomb?" *National Review* (July 20, 1973), 785; Bob Wilcox, "The Shroud of Turin," *Charleston* (W. Va.) *Gazette*, December 19, 1972, no. 2 of 6 articles published on December 18-23, 1972.

5. Wilson, *Shroud*, 250. See also Wilcox, "Shroud," *Charleston* (W. Va.) *Gazette*, December 19, 1972.

6. Ibid., 104-105.

7. Ibid., 126-132, 135. See also Stevenson and Habermas, *Verdict*, 15-22.

8. Ibid., 147-156. See also A. A. Vasiliev, *History of the Byzantine Empire* (Madison, Wisconsin, 1961), I, 254-256, 363.

9. Ibid., 120, 134, 273; and Stevenson and Habermas, *Verdict*, 31-32.

10. Wilson, *Shroud*, 276-277. See also Stevenson and Habermas, *Verdict*, 32.

11. Ibid., 157-163.

12. Ibid., 157-163, 166-169, 174. See also Robert of Clari, *Conquest*, 104.

13. Ibid., 176-177; and Kurt Berna, *Christ Did Not Perish on the Cross* (Zurich, 1975), 140. See also Geoffrey de Villenharouin, *Conquest of Constantinople* in *Chronicles of the Crusades* (Baltimore, 1967), 91-95.

14. Wilson, *Shroud*, 176-198. See also Michael Baigent, Richard Leigh, and Henry Lincoln, *Holy Blood, Holy Grail* (New York, 1985), 74-76, 82-83.

15. Ibid., 86-88, 266-272; and Stevenson and Habermas, *Verdict*, 37, 129-134.

16. Stevenson and Habermas, *Verdict*, 33-36; and Wilson, *Shroud*, 68-72, 77-81, 229-231.

17. Heller, *Report*, 38-39, 193-217, 220; Wilson, *Shroud*, 248-249; Stevenson and Habermas, *Verdict*, 135-143, 230.

18. Marvin M. Mueller, "The Shroud of Turin: A Critical Appraisal," in *Science Confronts the Paranormal*, ed. Kendrick Frazier (Buffalo, 1986), 324-343. See also Joe Nickell, *Inquest on the Shroud of Turin, New Updated Edition* (Buffalo, 1987), 95-106, 119-140; and Stevenson and Habermas, *Verdict*, 135-143.

19. Nickell, *Inquest*, 41-48, 53-54.

20. Ibid., 31-39.

21. Heller, *Report*, 2-4; and Stevenson and Habermas, *Verdict*, 42-50. See also Nickell, *Inquest*, 57-71.

22. Nickell, *Inquest*, 57-75. See also *Time*, January 18, 1971, 64-65.

23. Muhammad Zafrulla Khan, *Deliverance from the Cross* (London, 1978), 42-58; and Aziz Kashmiri, *Christ in Kashmir* (Srinagar, 1984), 40-42.

24. Andreas Faber-Kaiser, *Jesus Died in Kashmir* (London, 1977), 29-35. See also Berna, *Christ Did Not Perish*, passim.

25. Heller, *Report*, 3-4. See also Stevenson and Habermas, *Verdict*, 174-177.

26. Stevenson and Habermas, *Verdict*, 203-205.

27. Director of Tourism to Paul C. Pappas, June 4 and November 4, 1988. See Appendix A.

28. *Baedeker's Israel* (Englewood Cliffs, New Jersey, ca. 1970), 148-174. See also Jerome Murphy O'Connor, *The Holy Land, An Archaeological Guide from earliest Times to 1700* (Oxford, 1980), 36-43; and I. G. Hatzi, *O Panayios Tafos: Vasilefs ton Proskineimaton* (Athens, 1963), 23-27.

29. Ioannas P. Tsekoura, *To Ayion Fos Sta Ierosolima* (Lamia, Greece), 37-45. Tsekoura's work was generously sent to the author by the Greek Orthodox Patriarchate of Jerusalem and meets its approval. See also Hatzi, *Tafos*, 48-52; *Baedeker's Israel*, 149; *Nea Eliniki Enkiklopedia* (Athens, ca. 1960), I, 526; and *Thriskeftiki kai Ethniki Enkiklopedia* (Athens, 1963), II, 560-561.

30. Ibid., 45-46.

31. Ibid., 47-51.

32. Ibid., 51-66.

33. Ibid., 54-56.

34. Ibid., 89-94. See also Hatzi, *Tafos*, 49-51.

35. Emmanuel Dehan, *Our Visit to Israel* (Tel-Aviv, 1982), 24. See also Nickell, *Inquest*, 71-74; and Stevenson and Habermas, *Verdict*, 42-44.

Bibliography

Works on the Tomb of Yuz Asaf

Ahmad, Al-Haj Khwaja Nazir. *Jesus in Heaven on Earth.* Lahore, Muslim Mission and Literary Trust, 1956.

Ahmad, Hazrat Mirza Ghulam. *Jesus in India.* Rabwa, Pakistan, The Ahmadiyya Muslim Foreign Missions Department, 1899.

Bengalee, Sufi Mutiur Rahman. *The Tomb of Jesus.* London, The Moslem Sunrise Press, 1946.

Faber-Kaiser, Andreas. *Jesus Died in Kashmir.* Translated from the French by Gordon Cremonesi. London, Gordon and Cremonesi, 1977.

Kashmiri, Aziz. *Christ in Kashmir.* Srinagar, Roshni Publications, 1984. 3rd edition.

Kersten, Holger. *Jesus Lived in India.* Translated from the German. Dorset, England, Element Book Ltd., 1986.

Khan, Muhammad Zafrulla. *Deliverance from the Cross.* London, The London Mosque, 1978.

Shams, J. D. *Where Did Jesus Die?* Lahore, Ripon Printing Press, ca. 1960.

Yasin, Mohammad. *Rauzabal and Other Mysteries of Kashmir.* Srinigar, Kesar Publishers, 1972.

Works on Islam, Buddhism, Christianity, and the Far East

Ali, Abdullah Yusuf. *The Meaning of the Glorious Qur'an.* Cairo, Das Al-Kitab Al-Masri Publishers, 1938.

Ali, Seyed Ameer. *The Spirit of Islam.* London, University Press, 1967.

Bamzai, Prithivi Nath Kaul. *A History of Kashmir.* Delhi, Metropolitan Book Co., 1962.

Davids, T. W. Rhys. *Lectures on the Origin and Growth of Religion as Illustrated by some Points in the History of Indian Buddhism.* London, William and Norgate, 1891.

Eitel, E. J. *Three Lectures on Buddhism.* London, Trubner, 1873.

Farah, Caesar. *Islam.* Woodbury, New York, Barron's Educational Series, Inc., 1970.

Goddard, Dwight. *Was Jesus Influenced by Buddhism?* White River Junction, Vermont, Charles H. Cummins, 1927.

Goldsack, William. *Christ in Islam.* New York (?), Christian Literature Society, 1905.

Gray, Louis Herbert, ed. *The Mythology of All Races.* 13 vols. Boston, Marshall Jones Company, 1917.

Guillaume, Alfred. *Islam.* Baltimore, Penguin Books Inc., 1956.

Hussein, Muhammad Kamel. *City of Wrong.* Translated from the Arabic by Keneth Cragg. New York, Seabury Press, 1966.

Jeffery, Arthur. *A Reader on Islam.* New York, Books for Libraries, 1980.

————. *The Koran.* New York, The Heritage Press, 1958.

Kak, Ram Chandra. *Ancient Monuments of Kashmir.* New Delhi, Sagar Publications, 1971.

Medlycott, A. D. *India and the Apostle Thomas. An Inquiry With a Critical Analysis of the Acta Thomae.* London, David Nutt, 1905.

Notovich, Nicolas. *The Unknown Life of Jesus Christ.* Translated from the French by Alexina Lorager. Chicago, Rand, McNally and Company, 1894.

Oldenberg, H. *Buddha. His Life, His Doctrine, His Order.* Translated from the German by William Hoye. London, Edinburgh, Williams and Norgate, 1883.

Parrinder, Geoffrey. *Jesus in the Qur'an.* London, Faber and Faber, 1970.

Pratt, James B. *The Pilgrimage of Buddhism and a Buddhist Pilgrimage.* New York, Macmillan and Company, 1928.

Prinsep, Henry Thoby. *Tibet, Tartary and Mongolia.* London, W. H. Allen, 1852.

Prophet, Elizabeth Clare. *The Lost Years of Jesus.* Livingston, Montana, Summit University Press, 1987.

Rapson, E. J. *Ancient India from the Earliest Times to the First Century A.D.* Cambridge, University Press, 1916.

Rae, George Milne. *The Syrian Church in India.* London, William Blackwood and Sons, 1892.

Ray, Sunil Chandra. *Early History and Culture of Kashmir.* New Delhi, Munshiram Manoharlal, 1970.

Randal, Jr., John Herman. *Hellenistic Ways of Deliverance and the Making of the Christian Synthesis.* New York, Columbia University Press, 1970.

Seydel, Rudolf. *Das Evangelium von Jesu in Seinen Verhaltnissen zu Buddha-Sage und Buddha-Lehre.* Leipzig, Breitkopf und Hartel, 1880.

Smith, Vincent A. *The Early History of India.* Oxford, Clarendon Press, 1904.

Thomas, P. *Epics, Myths and Legends of India.* Bombay, D. P. Taraporevala Sons and Company, LTD., 1973.

Wrede, F. *An Account of the St. Thomas Christians on the Coast of Malabar.* London, Veender and Hood, 1803.

Wright, William. *Apocryphal Acts of the Apostles.* Amsterdam, Philo Press, 1968.

Works on Judaeo-Christian Subjects

Baedeker's Israel. Englewood Cliffs, New Jersey, Prentice Hall, Inc., ca. 1970.

Baigent, Michael, Richard Leigh, and Henry Lincoln. *Holy Blood, Holy Grail.* New York, Dell Publishing Co., Inc., 1985.

————. *The Messianic Legacy.* New York, Henry Holt and Company, 1987.

Bea, Augustine Cardinal. *The Study of the Synoptic Gospels.* New York, Harper and Row, 1965.

Berna, Kurt. *Christ Did Not Perish on the Cross.* Zurich, International Foundation for the Holy Shroud, 1975.

Black, Matthew. *The Scrolls and Christian Origins.* London, Thomas Nelson & Sons, Ltd., 1961.

Borg, Marcus J. *Jesus: A New Vision.* San Francisco, Harper and Row, Publishers, 1987.

Brandon, S. G. F., *The Fall of Jerusalem and the Christian Church.* London, S. P. C. K., 1951.

———. *Jesus and the Zealots.* New York, Charles Scribner's Sons, 1967.

———. *The Trial of Jesus of Nazareth.* New York, Stein and Day, 1968.

Brown, Raymond E. *The Birth of the Messiah.* Garden City, New York, Double Day & Company, 1977.

Bultmann, Rudoph Karl. *The History of the Synoptic Gospels.* Translated by John Marsh. Oxford, Basil Blackwell, 1963.

Burkit, F. C. *Early Christianity Outside of the Roman Empire.* Cambridge, University Press, 1899.

———. *The Earliest Sources of the Life of Jesus.* London, Archibald Constable, 1910.

Cavarnos, Constantine. "Greek Philosophy and Orthodoxy." *The Hellenic Chronicle* (Boston), in fourteen issues, April 1-25, 1980.

Clari, Robert of. *The Conquest of Constantinople.* Translated from the old French by Edgar Holmes McNeal. New York, Octagon Books, Inc., 1966.

Cox, Harvey. *The Secular City.* New York, Macmillan Company, 1966.

Cureton, William. *Ancient Syriac Documents. Relative to the Establishment of Christianity in Edessa and the Neighboring Countries.* London, Williams and Norgate, 1864.

Davies, A. Powell. *The First Christian.* New York, Mentor Books, 1959.

———. *The Meaning of the Dead Sea Scrolls.* New York, Mentor Books, 1961.

Davies, J. G. *The Early Christian Church* in *History of Religion Series,* ed. E. O. James. New York, Holt, Rinehart and Winston, 1965.

Dehan, Emmanuel. *Our Visit to Israel.* Tel-Aviv, Emmanuel Dehan, 1982.

Dodd, Charles H. *The Interpretation of the Fourth Gospel.* Cambridge, University Press, 1968.

Doresse, Jean. *The Secret Books of the Egyptian Gnostics.* Rochester, Vermont, Inner Traditions International, 1986.

Dubisch, Jill. "Golden Oranges and Silver Ships: An Interpretive Approach to a Greek Holy Shrine." *Journal of Modern Greek Studies,* VI (May 1988), 117-134.

Dummellow, J. R. *Commentary on the Holy Bible.* London, Macmillan and Company, 1917.

Eisenman, R. H. *Meccabees, Zadokites Christians and Qumran.* Leiden, 1983.

Eusebius. *The History of the Church from Christ to Constantine.* Translated by G. A. Williamson. Baltimore, Penguin Books, 1965.

Farquhar, J. N. *The Apostle Thomas in South India.* Manchester, University Press, 1927.

Farrar, F. W. *The Life of Christ.* London, Cassell, Peter and Galgin, 1874.

Filson, Floy Vivian. *A New Testament History. The Story of the Emerging Church.* Philadelphia, The Westminster Press, 1964.

Finegan, Jack. *Hidden Records of the Life of Jesus.* Philadelphia, Pilgrim Press, 1969.

Furnish, Victor Paul. *Theology and Ethics in Paul.* Nashville, Abingdon Press, 1968.

Gaster, Theodore, ed. *The Dead Sea Scriptures.* Garden City, New York, Doubleday & Company, 1956.

Grant, Robert M. *The Secret Sayings of Jesus. The Gnostic Gospel of Thomas.* Garden City, New York, Doubleday and Company, Inc., 1960.

Hadas, Moses, ed. *Essential Works of Stoicism.* New York, Bantam Books, 1961.

Hanna, William. *The Life of Christ.* New York, The American Tract Society, 1928.

Hansen, L. Taylor. *He Walked the Americas.* Amherst, Wisconsin, Amherst Press, 1963.

Hanson, R. P. C. *The Acts.* Oxford, Clarendon Press, 1967.

Hatzi, I. G. *O Panayios Tafos: Vasilefs ton Proskineimaton.* Athens, 1963.

Heller, John H. *Report on the Shroud of Turin.* Boston, Houghton Mifflin Company, 1983.

Horsley, Richard A. *Jesus and the Spiral of Violence.* San Francisco, Harper and Row, Publishers, 1987.

———and John S. Hanson. *Bandits, Prophets and Messiahs: Popular Movements at the Time of Jesus.* San Francisco, Harper and Row, Publishers, 1985.

Kallas, James. *Jesus and the Power of Satan.* Philadelphia, The Westminster Press, 1968.

Kent, Charles Foster. *The Historical Bible.* 6 vols. New York, Charles Scribners, 1908-16.

Klausner, Joseph. *Jesus of Nazareth.* Translated from the Hebrew by Herbert Danby. New York, The Macmillan Company, 1957.

———. *From Jesus to Paul.* Translated from the German by W. F. Stinespring. New York, The Macmillan Company, 1943.

Kokkinos, Nikolaos. *To Ainigma tou Iisou tis Galileas.* Athens, Hrisi Tomi, 1980.

Kung, Hans. *On Being A Christian.* Translated from the German by Edward Quinn. Garden City (N.Y.), Doubleday & Company, Inc., 1976.

Lewis, H. Spencer. *The Mystical Life of Jesus.* San Jose, California, [Rosicrucian Library] Supreme Grand Lodge of AMORC, 1982.

Loisy, Alfred Firmin. *The Birth of the Christian Religion and the Origins of the New Testament.* New York, University Books, 1962.

Maccoby, Hyam. *Revolution in Judaea. Jesus and the Jewish Resistance.* New York, Taplinger Publishing Co., 1980.

Marxsen, Willi. *Mark the Evangelist.* Translated from the German. Nashville, The Abington, Press, 1969.

Mavrogordato, John. "Byzantine Literature" in *Byzantium,* ed. by Norman H. Baynes and H. St. L. B. Moss. Oxford, Clarendon Press, 1961.

Meyendorf, John. *The Orthodox Church.* Crestwood, New York, St. Vladimir's Seminary Press, 1981.

Milligan, William. *The Resurrection of Our Lord.* London, Macmillan and Company, 1905.

Mueller, Marvin M. "The Shroud of Turin: A Critical Appraisal" in *Science Confronts the Paranormal,* ed. Kendrick Frazier. Buffalo, Prometheus Books, 1986.

Muller, Herbert J. *The Uses of the Past.* Oxford, Oxford University Press, Inc., 1952.

Murphy-O'Connor, Jerome. *The Holy Land. An Archaeological Guide from Earliest Times to 1700.* Oxford, University Press, 1980.

Murray, Gilbert. *Five Stages of Greek Religion.* Garden City, New York, Doubleday and Company, Inc., 1951.

Nickell, Joe. *Inquest on the Shroud of Turin, New Updated Edition.* Buffalo, Prometheus Books, 1987.

Pagels, Elaine. *The Gnostic Gospels.* New York, Random House, 1979.

Potter, Charles Francis. *The Lost Years of Jesus Revealed.* Greenwich, Connecticut, Fawcet Publications, Inc., 1962.

Randall, Jr., John Herman. *Hellenistic Ways of Deliverance and the Making of the Christian Synthesis.* New York, Columbia University Press, 1970.

Renan, Ernest. *The Life of Jesus.* Translated by J. K. Allen. New York, Modern Library, 1898.

Robinson, James M. ed. *The Nag Hammadi Library.* San Francisco, Harper and Row, 1981.

Robinson, (Bishop) John A. T. *Honest to God.* London, SCM, 1984.

Schmithalls, Walter. *Paul and James.* Translated from the German by Dorothea M. Barton. Naperville, Illinois, Alec R. Allenson, Inc., 1965.

Schnackenburg, Rudolf. *The Gospel According to St. John.* Translated from the German by David Smith and G. A. Kon. 3 vols. New York, The Crossroads Publishing Company, 1982.

Schonfield, Hugh J. *The Passover Plot.* New York, Random House, 1965.

————. *Those Incredible Christians*. New York, Bantam Books, Inc., 1969.

Schweitzer, Albert. *The Mystery of the Kingdom of God*. New York, Schoken Books, 1970.

————. *The Quest of the Historical Jesus*. New York, The Macmillan Company, 1955.

Stevenson, Kenneth E. and Gary R. Habermas. *Verdict on the Shroud*. Wayne, Pennsylvania, Banbury Books, Inc., 1981.

Stroud, William. *The Physical Cause of the Death of Christ and its Relation to the Principles and Practice of Christianity*. New York, D. Appleton and Co., 1871.

Sullivan, Barbara M. "How in Fact Was Jesus Christ Laid in His Tomb?" *National Review* (July 20, 1973), 785-789.

Tannehill, Robert C. *Dying and Rising with Christ. A Study in Pauline Theology*. Berlin, A. Topelmann, 1967.

Tillich, Paul. *Systematic Theology*. 3 vols. Chicago, University of Chicago Press, 1951-63.

Tinsley, E. J. *The Gospel According to Luke*. Cambridge, University Press, 1965.

Tsekoura, Ioannas P. *To Ayion Fos Sta Ierosolima*. Lamia, Greece, 1988.

Tuchman, Barbara W. *Bible and Sword*. New York, Ballantine Books, 1984.

Vasiliev, A. A. *History of the Byzantine Empire*. 2 vols. Madison, The University of Wisconsin Press, 1961.

Villehardouin, Geoffroy de. *The Conquest of Constantinople* in *Chronicles of the Crusades*. Baltimore, Penguin Books, Inc., 1967.

Vahanian, Gabriel. *The Death of God*. New York, G. Brazziler, 1966.

Wilcox, Bob. "The Shroud of Turin." *The Charleston* (W. Va.) *Gazette*. Presented in a Seven Part Series, Dec. 18-24, 1972.

Wilson, Ian. *The Shroud of Turin*. Garden City, New York, Image Books, 1979.

Appendix A

907 Laurel Rd.
Charleston, W. Va.
USA   25314
May 16, 1988

Director of Tourism
Srinagar, Kahmir
India

To whom it may concern:

    We are a group of curious individuals who have heard of
Rozabal Khanyar and would like to have more information
concerning this tomb before we decide, perhaps, to visit your
city. If it is possible, please send to us all available
information including, perhaps, photographs of this
particular tomb and /or who to contact for further inquiry.

    Thank you very much.

                              Sincerely yours,

                              Paul C. Pappas

                              Paul C. Pappas
                              Chairman
                              Curious Seekers
                              Anonymous (CSA)

J&K TOURISM

No:- Ɛ]7236-37/T
Dated:- 4-6-88

Mr. Paul C. Pappas,
Chairman,
Curious Seekers Anonymous (CSA)
907 Laurel Rd.
Charleston, WV
USA 25314.

Dear Sir,

　　　　　Please refer your letter dated
16th May, 1988.

　　　　　We are forwarding a copy of your
letter to Superintendant Arcological Department,
Govt. of India, Srinagar for furnishing you
details about Tomb at Rozbal Khanyar.

　　　　　　　　　Yours faithfully,

　　　　　　　　　Dy. Director Tourism
　　　　　　　　　Reservations.

Director

J&K TOURISM

No.E/ 14729 /T·D
Dated. 4-11-88

Shri Paul C. Pappes,
Chairman, Curious Seekers
Anonymous (CSA)907 Laural Rd,
Charlesten,WV USA 25314.

Dear Sir,

      In continuation to this office
letter No. E/7236-37/TD dated 4.6.1988 enclosed
please find a copy of brief discussion on
Rezabal temb at Khanyar for your reference.

      Yours faithfully,

      Dy.Director Tourism
      Reservation.

BRIEF DESCRIPTION ON ROZABAL TOMB AT KHANYAR IN
DISTRICT SRINAGAR, (POPULARLY KNOWN ROZABAL MOSQUE)

——————

Rozabal tomb is situated at a distance of
about $3\frac{1}{2}$ Km from Srinagar City. The famous ancient
places near the tomb are Ziarat of Dastgeer Sahib,
Roshangarmala mosque, Zamia Masjid and further deep
towards the same direction are Madin Sahib and Adalat
Masjid.

The tomb is rectangular on plan (Approx. 9m x 6m)
having two chambers which are inter-connected. The main
gate to the tomb is on the south side. After entering the
main gate, one has to turn to west and enter the second
bigger chamber which contains the grave. About a decade
ago, the grave was without any wooden enclosure but now
a wooden enclosure has been fixed with glasses by the
Committee which looks after the tomb. The inner grave
chamber is $4\frac{1}{2}$ Mts x $1\frac{1}{2}$ Mts and the size of grave is
3 Mts x 0.80 Mts. The tomb built in brick masonary in
three tiers is with G.I. sheets on the top. The wooden
ornamental design have been provided in both windows
openings (window). The ceiling is also/ornamental wood.
As the structure stands today, it does not seem to be
ancient structure in any way excepting the grave inside.

The local tradition reveals that this tomb is a
Ziarat of Hazrat Youza Asaf. The sign board displayed at
the site reads " Ziarati Hazrati Youza Asouph". Syed
Nasir-udrin "Tariki Azami", and Mullah Nadiri and Mirza Bak-
Gulam Ahmad of Qadian have expressed in some or other
context that the grave therein is of Jesus christ but from
the Archaeological point of view and in absence of such
physical evidence, it can not be confirmed as the grave of
Jesus Christ.

Appendix B

West Virginia Institute of Technology
Montgomery, West Virginia   25136

August 1, 1988

DEPARTMENT OF HISTORY

His Beatitude Diodoros
Patriarch of the Greek Orthodox Church
of Jerusalem
Jerusalem, Israel

Dear Holy Father:

    With all due respect, I would like to have a
confirmation by you, if at all possible, concerning the Holy
Light of the Resurrection of our Lord and Savior Jesus
Christ. I would like to mention this in a chapter that I am
writing on Christian mysteries and miracles which buttress
and rekindle our faith.

    My understanding is that the miracle of the Holy Light
occurs every year on Saturday noon, before Easter Sunday. At
that time, the Holy Patriarch, or his representative
appointed by the Holy Synod, enters the Church of the
Resurrection and, after being inspected by Muslim keepers for
matches, the two chamber Chapel of the Holy Sepulchre. Upon
entering the Chapel with two bundles of thirty-three candles
in each bundle and going through the Chapel of the Angel
which contains in its center the stone that once sealed
Jesus' Tomb, the Holy Father all alone enters through a low
door the second chamber containing the Tomb of our Savior,
which is located on the right. While on his knees, His
Beatitude recites a special prayer calling upon our Lord for
His Holy Light of Salvation to appear, during which time, a
mist appears in the Holy Tomb and dew collects on the walls
of the Holy Sepulchre. The Holy Father with a piece of cotton
wipes the moisture from the Holy Sepulchre's walls and it
catches on fire, which for a few seconds does not burn and
with which he lights the two bundles of candles in order to
distribute the Holy Light of our Lord's Resurrection to the
throng of faithful anxiously waiting with bundles of thirty-
three candles of their own outside of the Chapel of the Holy
Sepulchre.

    If my knowledge of this event is in any way in error, or
if something is missing or needs to be added, please let me
know. I shall be very grateful. Is there any possibility that
your Beatitude would allow scientists to observe or perhaps
examine this miracle in order to advertise it throughout the
world. Very little is known about this great event,
especially in the United States, and there is hardly anything
published on it. If there are any publications on the Holy
Light of our Lord's Resurrection in any language, I shall be
very grateful in being informed of them.

I am a member of the Greek Orthodox Church of America, an author and professor of history. My book, which will deal with the Muslim Ahmadya movement and attack its claim that Jesus did not die on the cross but went and died in Srinigar, India, hopefully will be ready for publication at the end of this year. It is, therefore, urgent that I have a confirmation of this great miracle which I intent to use as evidence of the truth of our Church's belief concerning the death and resurrection of our Lord and Savior.

Should you be kind enough to respond, I shall be ever respectfully grateful.

With high respect and sincerety,

Paul C. Pappas, Ph.D.
Professor of History
West Virginia Institute of
Technology

No: 699   *Tel. 284917*

Paul C. Pappas, Ph.D.   *P. O. B. 19632 - 633*
Professor of History
West Virginia Institute of
Technology
Montgomery, West Virginia 25136
U.S.A.

Dear Dr. Pappas,

     His Beatitude Diodoros I, Patriarch of Jerusalem
received your letter dated August 1, 1988 and expresses
appreciation for your earnest concern about the Orthodox
faith, life and the teachings of the Church.

     Part of this mystical life is the Liturgical and
ceremonial moments in the Church which the faithful witness and participate every year.

     This miraculous ceremony of the Holy Fire rekindles
Our faith and triumphantly proclaims the Glorious
Resurrection of Our Lord Jesus Christ from the Holy Tomb.

     This miracle which occurs every year is described through-
out the Centuries by many historians and pilgrims beginning
from the 4th Century.

     Lately, two books have been published in Greek on this
subject which I am forwarding to you for your information.

     I hope that this informative book will be your guideline
to help you prove the truth of Our Church's belief.

     With best regards,

Jerusalem,
September 28, 1988.

                  Bishop Timothy
                  of Porphyroupolis
                  Chief Secretary of
                  Greek Orthodox Patriarchate

Appendix C

Exterior and interior views of Rozabal, the Tomb of Yuz Asaf (Jesus), in Srinagar, India.

Index